Seven Million

SEVEN MILLION

A Cop, a Priest,
a Soldier for the IRA, and
the Still-Unsolved
Rochester Brink's Heist

GARY CRAIG

ForeEdge

ForeEdge

An imprint of University Press of New England

www.upne.com

© 2017 Gary Craig

All rights reserved

Manufactured in the United States of America

Designed by Mindy Basinger Hill

Typeset in Minion Pro

For permission to reproduce any of the material in this book,
contact Permissions, University Press of New England, One Court Street,
Suite 250, Lebanon NH 03766; or visit www.upne.com

Library of Congress Cataloging-in-Publication Data

Names: Craig, Gary, 1959– author.

Title: Seven million: a cop, a priest, a soldier for the IRA,
and the still-unsolved Rochester Brink's heist / Gary Craig.

Description: Lebanon, NH: ForeEdge, [2017] |
Includes bibliographical references.

Identifiers: LCCN 2016049143 (print) | LCCN 2017007927 (ebook) |
ISBN 9781611688917 (pbk.) | ISBN 9781512600629 (epub, mobi & pdf)

Subjects: LCSH: Brinks, Inc. | Robbery—New York (State)—
Rochester—Case studies.

Classification: LCC HV6661.N72 1993 .C73 2017 (print) |
LCC HV6661.N72 1993 (ebook) | DDC 364.15/520974789—dc23

LC record available at https://lccn.loc.gov/2016049143

5 4 3 2

Dedicated to my wife, Charlotte
Thanks for being you, and for marrying me

CONTENTS

— — —

PART 1

The Heist and the IRA

CHAPTER 1

— — —

Surrounded by millions of dollars—stacks and piles and mounds of green—Milton Diehl could not miss the irony.

He regularly played the New York State lottery, joining the masses who imagined that the six numbers they'd selected were their portal to wealth and all the accoutrements that riches would bring. Whereas many lottery-playing hopefuls chose six numbers of significance to them, perhaps an amalgam of birthdays or anniversaries, Diehl used an entirely different system. He always tried to choose different numbers than he'd selected with his previous play. To Diehl, this made as much sense as any other bit of lottery voodoo employed by would-be millionaires.

And here he was, on a frigid January day in 1993, tallying millions, knowing that in the next twenty-four hours he was likely again to drop a buck on a lottery ticket, hoping to win a few thousand or maybe a few hundred thousand. He was bored with the cash heaped around him. He enjoyed the part of his job as a Brink's Inc. guard based in Rochester, New York, when he drove the truck around the western part of the state, picking up and delivering cash. But the evening count of the money was just plain mind-numbingly dull.

Tuesdays were the worst. Sometimes he and the other Brink's guards would have more than $6 million to account for, most of it trucked in from the Federal Reserve Bank branch in Buffalo. A retired financial official at Xerox Corporation, the sixty-six-year-old Diehl had spent a career processing money. But then he'd largely shuffled papers, watching the dollar signs move across his desk on expense vouchers and project cost estimates. Never before joining Brink's on a part-time basis had he seen cash like this.

A man of lesser moral fiber than Diehl might have considered pocketing some of the cash, then concocting a way to cover up the crime. But not Diehl. He'd simply continue playing the lottery—though, truth be told, he felt pretty comfortable in his postretirement life, even without a major lottery score. Diehl had taken the part-time Brink's gig simply because he liked to stay busy. As he told his family, he could play only so many rounds of golf.

Not that Diehl didn't imagine hitting it big with the lottery. Everybody did. But in the meantime, he'd work another Brink's shift. There, in a cluttered tiny depot, he'd again count millions of dollars with the same lack of interest as someone working on an assembly line.

A small, single-story cinderblock building the color of rich brown soil, the Brink's depot was inconspicuous and unsightly. On the southern edge of downtown Rochester, the depot was in a neighborhood that decades before had been vibrant and alive but was now, in the early 1990s, forlorn and beset by urban blight.

With its paint peeling in flakes, chips, and slivers and a rickety corroding fence lining one side of its property and leaning so far it seemed to defy gravity, the depot appeared to passers-by to be nothing more than another struggling business with one foot in the grave and the other flailing madly to survive.

That was, of course, when its pocked parking lot was empty and the fleet of Brink's armored trucks was on the road, rumbling through the highways and byways, the valleys and wooded stretches of western New York. Then, there was little indication that this squat structure was a perfect portrait of the Rochester paradox—poverty and wealth, urban decay and pricy sylvan subdivisions all coexisting only miles from each other yet separated as if by an apartheid that had not been institutionalized.

Inside the Brink's depot, in a neighborhood whose better days seemed well in the past, Rochester's wealth was regenerated and recycled each day. C-notes, $10 bills, $20s, singles—many crisp with that distinctive feel of new currency—all filtering in and out, en route to the automated teller machines and banks in the surrounding suburbs where cash still flowed abundantly.

Now another struggling industrial city perched on a Great Lake, Rochester was a city with a past of wealth, grandeur, and style fashioned by men who'd left their imprint for generations to come. Here, George Eastman created celluloid film. Here, the Xerox machine was born. Here, it once seemed, each Rochesterian secured a patent before a driver's license.

Rochester's industrial patriarchs, including Kodak's founder, the bespectacled Eastman, had long bestowed philanthropic good will on the city. They'd built museums that would be the envy of many regions. They'd heaped millions of dollars on the city's prestigious universities. They'd left behind a legacy that now, with big business more cutthroat and focused solely on the bottom line, was left unmatched.

But, like its Rust Belt brethren, by the 1990s Rochester had seen its vitality and its very core sapped by generations of suburban flight, the demise of blue-collar and white-collar manufacturing jobs, and the corporate hemorrhaging of tens of thousands of workers.

Left behind was a city that reeked of contradictions. Its white-collar saviors—the Kodaks, Xeroxes, and Bausch and Lombs—were leaner but still spewed out goods and gadgetry sought by everyone from the Defense Department to the kid longing for the hippest shades his $45 could buy. Millionaires still made their homes in Rochester, most of them in manicured suburban havens, and their wealth caused the decennial census figures for median incomes to leap to surprising heights. Men—and, at last, women—could still get rich in Rochester. And many still did.

The powers that be often overlooked the other half of the contradiction: the urban underbelly of narrow littered streets where kids hawked crack cocaine, where the child poverty rate skyrocketed, and where each summer—a season of true brevity—a new batch of fatal shootings erupted. An active hooker trade thrived in some neighborhoods, despite repeated police attempts to squash it. A ballyhooed school reform program, expected to prove that urban schools could be an educational beacon, had failed miserably. Those who had the wealth to live in Rochester's crusty upper echelons had always thought their city immune to the atrophy that similar cities had suffered. With each passing year, they realized how wrong they were.

Brink's had maintained an operation in Rochester since 1920, when the city's prominent clothing manufacturers went searching for outside professionals to handle their payrolls. The company's depot bounced to different locations across the then-booming city. By 1993 it had landed in a building that, before the neighborhood began its downward slide, had housed one of Rochester's most popular veterinarian clinics.

Brink's had longer relationships with only two other cities: Cleveland and Chicago, where, in 1859, it all started when Perry Brink hitched a horse to a newly purchased wagon, painted the name Brink's City Express on the side, and started ferrying the luggage of the hordes of visitors to the Windy City. Only a year into his new business, he was shuttling the suitcases and hand-stitched bags of delegates to the Republican convention in Chicago, where a tall fellow named Abraham Lincoln was, despite being a significant underdog, nominated the party's candidate for president.

Even in those days, during the start of a business that would later ship billions of dollars in currency, precious jewels, and gold, the danger was the same as it would be later. Some bandit, armed and ready, might see a Brink's wagon as an easy target. In those early years, Perry Brink hired beefy muscular men, their heft in and of itself intimidating. Many of them were single for the simple reason that Brink didn't want his men returning home for early suppers when the wives summoned them.

The generations that passed brought more security to Brink's, with the evolution from wagon to fully armored truck. But the hazards never changed. Somewhere out there, there was always some pistol-wielding crook, full of ideas about how easy it would be to knock off a Brink's truck, grab a million or two, take the money, and run. In 1917, two Brink's guards were murdered—the head of one rocked by the buckshot of a shotgun, the body of the other riddled by a revolver's bullets—during the robbery of a $9,100 payroll delivery to a Chicago iron and brass manufacturer. The company's history included very few tragic incidents of that sort, but there were enough to make some guards wary. A guard was fatally shot during a 1981 armored-car robbery by the Black Liberation Army in Nyack, in downstate New York. Though more than a decade had passed, many guards still knew that tale well.

Nevertheless, the sheer monotony of the job as a Brink's guard—the routine of moving and handling money day in and day out, the protective firearm holstered at the side—could breed a false sense of invulnerability. Stultifying torpor could set in.

And it had in Rochester.

In winter the drab weather and the seeming weight of the slate-gray skies added to the tedium. For Rochesterians, 1993 had opened with sunshine and temperatures slipping into the 60s, a rare reprieve from the season's bite. But it was short-lived. Mother Nature was playful, teasing. By Tuesday, January 5, she'd pulled the plug on the extended New Year's celebration and turned moody, spitting out a wintry venom. Frigid winds whipped and swirled across the water of Lake Ontario, colliding with the lake's moisture to manufacture a bone-chilling concoction of drizzle laced with light snow.

This wasn't unusual—just a standard Rochester winter. Despite its predictability, the city's electronic media trumpeted each minor shift of the weather as an event worthy of blanket coverage. The newspapers also got in on the game, offering seasonal advice about how to endure the chill. "Wear layers," readers were told—sage advice, to be sure.

For Diehl and his colleagues at Brink's, the weather simply added to the tiresome evening task of counting cash. Who knew that millions of dollars could be so damned dull?

Puzzled cops would later consider the job's boring nature as a partial explanation for what happened on January 5, 1993. On that night, Rochester cops, agents of the Federal Bureau of Investigation (FBI), and officers of the New York State Police Department would all find themselves dismayed that someone had had the *cojones* to hold up a Brink's facility, making away with more than $7 million—the fifth largest amount ever stolen from a US armored car company. The magnitude of the heist was startling, and the apparent ease with which it had been pulled off was unfathomable.

Some things just shouldn't be so easy.

CHAPTER 2

— — —

A week before the robbery, as 1992 wound to a close, a vice president of a Rochester bank ordered millions of dollars with a few simple touches of his fingertips. First, he telephoned the Federal Reserve branch in Buffalo and dialed into a phone menu. He then punched in the numerical code signifying that his order originated from the First Federal Savings and Loan in Rochester. The terse beeps were almost melodic as he followed the usual weekly process.

The telephone menu provided further instructions, directing him to designate how much money would be needed for the coming week. The banks relied on an equation combining gut experience and assumptions for the answer. There were more than a dozen bank branches with automated teller machines, most of them in the growing suburbs stretching outward from Rochester's urban core. People would need cash. Christmas had passed, but post-holiday sales and New Year's Eve parties ensured more consumer spending. Factor that in with the typical cash demands of the bank branches. The answer from the bank vice president: $3.5 million.

The phone menu questions didn't stop there. Banks could choose some "fit" money—new, unsullied bills—and the remainder in "circulated" currency. "Circulated" bills had passed through many hands. The bank official chose at least $60,000 in new money, preferably $40,000 in $20 bills and another $20,000 in $10s.

Six days later a Brink's truck, carrying the First Federal order and similar orders from other banks, pulled out of the Buffalo Federal Reserve's garage, heading to the New York State Thruway for the seventy-mile trek to Rochester. The truck, like the rest of those in the Brink's 1,200-vehicle fleet, was constructed to appear intimidating. There were no rounded soft edges on the truck, only hard angles from front to back and from top to bottom. The truck resembled a prehistoric creature, its compact and sturdy build too formidable to attack.

Banks commonly received more new money than they'd ordered, and this shipment was no different. First Federal would get the $10 and $20 bills it had requested. But the Federal Reserve branch had been steadily ridding itself of a stash of new $100 bills it had kept on site for more than two years. The bills had been created at the new US Treasury engraving plant, a sparkling high-tech facility in Fort Worth, Texas, that spat out almost four billion separate bills a year. The $100 bills had been shipped to Buffalo in the fall of 1991 for circulation across upstate New York. The Brink's cargo en route to Rochester included $250,000 in mint $100 bills. It also included a detailed accounting of the serial numbers—a combination of ten digits and letters—for each of the new bills. These numbers were like fingerprints, not replicated on any other currency.

Serial numbers were not maintained for the older bills; this recirculated cash had often traveled far and wide by the time it made its way back to a Federal Reserve branch, where it waited to be redistributed again. It had passed through banks and grocers and ATMs; the Federal Reserve did not record the serial numbers when the currency returned to a branch.

"As you can see," the Federal Reserve says in a video about the life cycle of our money, "the currency and coins that we receive from our local bank, store, or restaurant have traveled many miles to reach our wallets."

— — —

At the Brink's depot in Rochester, Dick Popowych was ready to call it a day.

Work at the depot had seemed a perfect part-time job for the fifty-two-year-old Popowych. As a capital assets manager with the Rochester-based film giant Eastman Kodak, he had established systems to track and protect the company's flow of money. And, as a gun enthusiast for most of his life, he found something else appealing at Brink's—the job not only allowed him to tote a revolver, it required him to. The guards were expected to be armed at all times, whether driving or carrying or counting money. When the armored trucks rolled into the garage of the depot, Brink's workers pulled out their firearms and stood watch. Managers constantly encouraged Popowych to carry the revolver the company provided. But he found the company gun too unwieldy, too much of a hassle to have holstered as you counted up tens of thousands of dollars. Five feet eight inches tall, Popowych struggled to keep the 6-inch barrel comfortably at his side.

Popowych preferred his own snub-nose revolver—compact, comfortable, and nice and light to handle. He didn't mind a bigger gun, like the Colt he kept under his mattress at home, if he didn't have to carry it. But at Brink's, where he had to be armed at all times, he wanted a firearm that was more portable. Instead he was carrying a gun that looked like something from a Western movie. Maybe the Brink's managers considered the gun intimidating; Popowych found it to be a nuisance instead.

Which gun he should carry wasn't the only difference Popowych had with Brink's managers. He'd been hired to set up a better process for tallying the bundles of money at night. Workers were spending hours of overtime, botching money counts, starting over, and botching them again. The process of counting the cash varied, depending on who was working. Because there was no single systemwide process, the money often had to be counted more than once.

Popowych helped settle the crew into a system. He was surprised that Brink's managers were not more thankful, or better able to develop their own processes to be followed. And he had other issues with Brink's.

This was the same company, after all, that had a depot he considered incredibly vulnerable. He'd beefed about the pathetic external mirror that office employees used to catch a glimpse of whoever knocked on the depot's front door. The mirror, positioned outside the depot's office area, was tilted to capture images from the front. But the lighting outside was dim; employees often couldn't distinguish who the visitor was. Then there was the front door itself. It was constructed with an electronic entry system; to unlock the door, someone pushed a button in the depot's main office. But all it took was one good shove on the door to pop it open. Popowych had seen Brink's workers knock it ajar simply by lowering a shoulder against it. There were interior dead bolts on the door, but they were often left unlatched.

Popowych could see that the other precautions, like the interior girded armored door between a narrow hallway and the vault room, wouldn't be much of a barrier. The vault room, where the vault was housed and the money counted at day's end, was the heart of the depot operation. Popowych had been around long enough to see just how slack security had become around the vault. Depot workers, in need of a bathroom break, propped the vault room door open with magazines. One night a delivery man strolled into the vault room with a pizza before anyone realized he'd entered the depot. Another time an employee's girlfriend, coming to pick up her beau's paycheck, sauntered unobserved into the room. For the most part, the workers had grown accustomed to the lapses. Just like they'd grown accustomed to the millions in their hands.

— — —

For Milton Diehl, the workday started before dawn. That now seemed long ago. He and a colleague, Richard Nichols, had loaded a truck around 6:00 a.m. for a run through New York's Southern Tier. There'd been stops at banks in many of the quaint towns and villages in the western part of the state, from Hornell to Canisteo. They'd driven near the Finger Lakes, eleven elongated narrow lakes that resembled the spindly fingers of a witch as they stretched across western and central New York from north to south. At each bank, Diehl and Nichols unloaded bags of currency. By day's end, as they rolled back into Rochester and the depot, they'd put 250 miles on the truck.

Diehl had spent most of this day just wanting to get home. For Christmas, his son had bought him and his wife a golden retriever puppy, a feisty, playful little pet they'd named Holly. With his wife out of the house, this was the first afternoon the dog had been left alone. A pet lover, Diehl didn't want Holly spending too much time by herself.

By the time Diehl and Nichols returned to the depot, the truck carrying the millions from Buffalo's Federal Reserve was already parked inside, being unloaded. The job done, a guard backed the vehicle out of the depot, its throaty cough echoing in the garage as it exited. Nichols slowly maneuvered the armored car into the garage and parked it. It took only ten minutes to unload the remaining money they'd brought back from their run. Nichols backed the truck out and headed home. But Diehl still had hours of work ahead of him, helping tally the Federal Reserve and other money for shipment the next day.

Quickly, Diehl got to work with Popowych and Tom O'Connor, another part-time Brink's guard. O'Connor, fifty-three, was a jovial Irishman, a rarely serious fellow who'd held several security jobs after putting in two decades as a city police officer. O'Connor always seemed to have his mouth curled into a semi-smile, as if aware of something humorous that was apparent to no one but him. His eyebrows angled sharply, giving him an impish look that, coupled with his red hair, gave him the appearance of a man who'd never quite shed the mischievous ways of a young boy. He'd been popular with some police colleagues, an enigma to others. One longtime police commander once commented that he knew something of the home lives of everyone whom he supervised, with the exception of O'Connor. O'Connor could be both jocular and distant, and some who knew him thought he had a "disconnected" personality.

O'Connor also had strange quirks, particularly when it came to money. Rarely did he write checks for anything, except out-of-town bills. He paid local utility and telephone bills with cash. He kept very little money in a checking account, preferring to stash it in odd places. In the past, he'd stored some under a metal floor in a closet at his apartment. Some he kept in a freezer, alongside meat awaiting its preparation for a future meal. When his adult son once complained to him that he was irresponsible, O'Connor tucked some cash away in the trunk of his car, as if that was a more appropriate place for it. His financial methodology was unusual, to be sure, but a time would come when it provided him with an explanation for bundles of cash that he otherwise could not explain.

In a city known for its high-tech industries, the routine at the Brink's depot was remarkable because of its absolute lack of automation. The centerpiece of the depot was the vault, its interior completely encased in armor. The size of a small bedroom, the walk-in vault swallowed up much of the vault room. The vault's interior, like the rest of the depot, was a cluttered mess. Coin boxes, which could hold up to $500 in quarters, were piled high in the vault. Money bags littered the floor and several shelves.

The vault room itself was where the money was counted at makeshift tables at each day's end. There was not a single bright color in the room, adding to the dreariness of the task at hand. Along one wall opposite the vault, cinder blocks were stacked in four columns, each four blocks deep. Scarred boards were laid across the blocks to create tables. The concrete floor was splotched and aged. A set of large double doors led from the vault room to the garage. Five surveillance cameras were wired into the vault room ceiling, some aimed directly at the vault, some at the money-tallying tables. A clipboard, holding a lined register, hung from one exterior side of the vault. "If you come into the vault room, you must sign the vault room register," a sign warned. Sometimes workers did; sometimes they didn't.

The depot's front door fed into a narrow hallway called the "trap." In turn, the trap opened into the vault room. The solid armored door between the trap and the vault room was, if left closed and locked, supposed to be impenetrable. But guards had gotten used to leaving the door open and unsecured.

It was surprising at times how quiet the vault and vault room could be. With dusk enveloping the area, the rumblings of cars on nearby roadways would slow as downtown underwent its metamorphosis from a bustling weekday office complex to near solitude. Even the panhandlers, busy hassling passers-by during the daylight, joined the corporate executives in a mass exodus at nightfall. They, too, knew the pickings were slim once the sun had set.

In the vault room, there was only the quiet shuffling of money and occasional conversation. The Buffalo Bills, within days of their third consecutive Super Bowl loss, dominated the talk in the winter of 1993. O'Connor was a rabid Bills fan; Popowych simply hated the Bills. But more often than not, there was common ground. Popowych considered himself one of conservative radio commentator Rush Limbaugh's cadre of "dittoheads." He was even a member of New York's Conservative Party, which often found itself to the right of the Republicans. O'Connor, though he appeared largely dispassionate about many political issues, held similar beliefs. There was one political issue that was of significant importance to O'Connor, but not one that arose in workplace conversation: a man proud of his Irish roots, O'Connor wanted to see Northern Ireland free of British rule one day. He had many friends around Rochester who shared the same ancestry and desire. Some of them, like O'Connor, were members of the Irish Northern Aid Committee, or NORAID, an American nonprofit that helped the families of imprisoned Irish Republican Army (IRA) soldiers. But at the depot, where O'Connor was the only one who cared even a whit about Northern Ireland, he did not discuss such things. Conversation tended to center on sports and life's mundanities.

On this night, there was little talk; it had been a long day, and the work hours, coupled with Rochester's chill, had sapped the energy from the room and the guards. They just wanted to get the money counted and get the hell home.

The Federal Reserve money was, as always, contained in blue plastic trays, each divided into ten compartments. The trays measured about two feet by one foot. There would be one stack of money—or a "brick," in the argot of Brink's security staff—in each compartment. A single brick, encased in a clear plastic wrap, held ten piles of bills. And each of those piles contained a hundred bills. In a single tray alone, there could be hundreds of thousands of dollars, visible through a cellophane covering. The trays were protected by a heavy-duty plastic strap that workers had to slice away.

A single brick always consisted of bills of the same denomination, but the denominations varied in each tray. Following the system he'd help put in place, Popowych set to work taking money out of the trays and sorting the bricks by their denominations.

Using one of the tables in the vault room, Popowych stacked bricks of $10 bills with other bricks of $10, $20s with other $20s, and $50s with other $50s. When a stack went over a foot in height—the point at which adding another brick could cause them all to topple like a failed Jenga move—he started another pile.

Diehl was armed with the "manifest," the document that specified how much money would be delivered to banks in the Rochester area the following day.

Working from the piles of cash Popowych had heaped on the table, Diehl sorted the money for delivery. He'd add up the money to be delivered to one branch, count it again for accuracy, then place it into canvas bags for transport to area banks. Meanwhile, O'Connor was dealing with cash destined for a series of ATMs around Rochester. This cash was loosely bound, held together only by rubber bands. O'Connor divided the cash for placement in individual machines.

Around 6:25 p.m.—an hour or so into the money count—O'Connor decided they needed more canvas bags to complete the job. They were running low, he said.

"I'm going to the shed," O'Connor told his colleagues. Nobody paid much attention. By this time, Popowych was carrying individual cash-filled sacks into the vault for overnight safekeeping. When the job was complete, he'd make a final check—one last count—to see that the bags contained the proper amount of money.

Diehl didn't see why more bags were needed. There appeared to be plenty to do the job. But he didn't concern himself, except to realize that he had no desire to go into the shed. Far from airtight, the shed absorbed the season's cold temperatures and let winter's frigidness creep in everywhere. The bags sucked it up, becoming chilly to the touch.

At 6:35 p.m. Diehl glanced at his watch. He'd started the day sure he would be back at his suburban home by 6:30 p.m. But there was still more money to be bagged. At best, it would be another half hour now before he made his way home; at worst, an hour or more. O'Connor returned quietly, and laid some more bags at Diehl's feet.

It was only minutes later when Diehl heard a soft voice behind him in the vault room. This wasn't O'Connor's voice. Nor was it Popowych's. Diehl turned, unsure just who else was still at work.

Diehl smiled slightly at first when he saw the gunman—masked and holding a revolver with Diehl in the cross hairs. This had to be a joke, he guessed, some wacky kind of Brink's management scheme to see how the guards would react. Brink's managers could occasionally skew to the weird; this might be the sort of on-the-job training they'd ruthlessly subject workers to.

"Get down on the floor before I blow your fuckin' head off!"

The voice was icy and insistent. Diehl now knew the truth—this was no joke. A marksman who had been involved in the D-Day invasion of Europe in World War II, Diehl knew there were times for heroics.

This was not one of them.

CHAPTER 3

— — —

Not again.

Dick Popowych had already had one standoff with an armed nut case; it seemed unfair that now he'd have another. But here he was again with a pistol aimed smack at his chest. It was hard not to focus on the gun. The vault's light seemed to reflect off of it, illuminating it with an otherworldly gleam. The pistol—Popowych could clearly see it was a .38 caliber—became the focal point of the vault, everything else secondary. The gunman was about five feet ten inches tall, with a muscular stocky build. He wore beige overalls, and a black ski mask—with openings for the eyes and mouth—covered his face. His hands were gloved. The attempts to conceal his identity didn't cloak his unmistakable strength and intimidating seriousness. There was no indication of nervousness. Not a good sign. He seemed intent on completing what he'd started.

It had been almost a quarter-century since Popowych last found himself in such a grim situation. Then he'd been driving a taxi around Rochester. One night, in the late 1960s, a passenger stepped out of the taxi without paying and pulled a gun from his jacket. While the would-be robber talked, demanding money, Popowych kept his thumb on the mike button, relaying the threats and taunts to the cab service's dispatcher.

Calmly, Popowych told the man how stunned he was that he'd given him a ride to a city address—Popowych even repeated the address for the dispatcher to hear—and "you go and pull a gun on me." Popowych kept the microphone low on the seat so it couldn't be seen. It seemed only seconds before the cops arrived and arrested the man without a struggle.

That night Popowych probably couldn't have turned over more than $25 to his would-be robber. This was different. Quite different. Popowych was now several career changes past his years as a taxi driver. He estimated there could be as much as $4 million with him in the depot's vault, and maybe another $4 million out in the vault room. People robbed cabbies on a whim, hoping to grab some extra cash for a cheap drunk or maybe a few ounces of pot. Those robberies often weren't premeditated, just the work of somebody with a loose screw and little opportunity on the horizon.

But a man who walks into a Brink's depot, waving a gun at the money counters—that's a man who means business, a man who's done some planning and who likely doesn't see the need for live witnesses. You don't suck down a pint of Jim Beam on a street corner, bullshit with your friends and fellow drunks, and decide it's a good night to knock over a Brink's depot for a few million.

How'd he get straight into the vault this easy? Popowych asked himself. *Milt, Tom—where are they?*

Popowych had only heard a slight grunt, a noise that sounded ominously out of place in the cluttered vault, before he turned and saw the man. The man had said nothing yet. Popowych might have been able to take him in a fair fight. But with the .38 drawn and ready, the intruder clearly had the advantage. It was an advantage Popowych was willing to concede.

"You better get down," the man said, his voice firm and unfamiliar.

Popowych went down on his stomach, his nose pressed solidly against the armored floor. He placed his hands straight out to his side, a position he would later describe as a "dead man's float." The gunman, holding the pistol steadily between his hands, walked over to Popowych. He reached down, one hand now holding his gun, and used the other to remove Popowych's .38 revolver from his side holster.

Popowych could hear the man's footsteps moving away, then returning. He felt the canvas of the money bags on his face, as the gunman piled five or six of them on his head and neck.

Popowych felt pressure on his wrist, pulling his arm toward him. His wrist was placed behind his back. Popowych complied, silently, and placed the other hand behind his back. He felt his wrists being tightly bound behind him, his shoulders tugged back into an awkward and uncomfortable position. The muscles in his chest strained. The plastic binding—self-locking ties like those electricians used to bundle wire—bit into the flesh of his wrists.

The gunman bound his ankles. Popowych didn't dare move to test the strength of the ties. The vault's floor was ice-cold against his face, but comfort was of little concern. His head swirled with ways to try to ensure he'd live.

Don't react aggressively. Do as they say. Go along, get along, and hope for the best.

— — —

"Get down on the floor before I blow your fuckin' head off," the man said to Diehl.

The deep voice was tinged with an accent, Diehl thought, maybe Asian. Diehl went down on the floor of the vault room. He felt his firearm lifted from his side. So much for getting home to his golden retriever and his wife.

How had this happened? Diehl wondered. *How had somebody breached the security system at a Brink's depot? No noise, no resistance.*

Where's O'Connor?

Diehl remembered that O'Connor had brought bags back from the shed, dropped them in front of him, then disappeared again. The best Diehl could recall, O'Connor had gone into the depot's garage through the double door. There was no sign he was still in the vault room. And Popowych—he was in the vault. What happened to him?

Diehl closed his eyes, as if darkness would provide refuge. Someone draped canvas bags over his head. Diehl knew right away that the bags were from the batch O'Connor had brought in. They were damp and cold, their moistness causing the material to cling to his face.

His wrists and ankles were bound, the plastic from the ties nearly cutting into his skin. He could feel the bags being removed from his face, one after another. A gloved hand was now at his head, the leather light against his right temple. The hand applied a mild pressure, the fingers grasping his forehead, slightly twisting his head to the right. His glasses had shifted when he dropped to the floor, and now they rested askew. His breath grew erratic, unsteady; his pulse quickened as if his heart were prepared to make a run for it. But he knew better than to talk. He felt his glasses being removed, the hand leaving his face. Then a lone bag was pulled over his head, ensuring that he would see nothing.

The only noises in the vault room were the steady patter of footsteps, light rhythmic thumps on the concrete floor. Typically the sounds wouldn't resonate as sinisterly as they now did. Yet when the footsteps halted and silence returned to the vault, there was an even greater sense of foreboding, as if the quiet itself augured a deadly end.

Diehl could feel the circulation to his hands slowing. His fingers began to grow numb; his whole body ached, especially his back.

A voice again, farther away, not the same one who'd first spoken to him. No accent this time. This voice was clearly American.

"There's usually four of the fuckers around here. Make sure there's nobody hiding."

Footsteps again. Thank God for the footsteps. Stay occupied with something else; leave us alone.

— — —

There's more than one person here, Popowych thought. He could hear multiple sets of footsteps, striding in and out of the vault, moving money bags from around him. Someone lifted him under his armpits, pulling his chest slightly off the vault floor.

Popowych had no time to think, to wonder what was about to happen, before he felt himself being dragged from the vault. He slid easily across the vault's floor, though a quick ping of pain jabbed his chest when he was pulled across a small corrugated metal ramp placed at the vault's door. Some of the bags slid from his head; a few stayed in place.

Once out of the vault—Popowych guessed he'd been pulled almost fifteen feet—he was lowered, almost caringly, to the floor. The gentleness was mildly comforting. He could feel the chill of the vault room's concrete floor against his chest. Now the gloved hand was at his head again, lifting it up. The actions were unhurried, methodical, and calm. He felt a canvas bag being pulled across his forehead. The material tugged slightly at his hair as the bag engulfed his head. Slender threads of light seeped in through the bag's tiny pores. The world had closed in, becoming miniaturized, and it now consisted of what little room Popowych had left for breath inside a First Federal money shipment bag. The canvas was restricting, but he could breathe.

The footsteps continued, possibly even three sets of them now. Then there was a slight whirring and grinding sound, the recognizable noise of the depot's garage door opening. The door slid on a curved metal track, just like a residential garage door. The door was controlled by a simple mechanism—an electronic panel with three buttons. The panel was located in a small adjacent room, from which a narrow window allowed Brink's guards to see the movement of the door. One button raised the door, one lowered it, and one could stop it instantly. Clearly, someone was at the control panel.

There was a loud clicking sound. Popowych knew the sound. He never realized before how distinct the noises of the depot routine were. The depot door was now completely open, Popowych knew.

Then he heard the sound of an engine starting and a vehicle pulling into the garage. It didn't have the diesel growl of the Brink's' trucks. Even when idling, the Brink's trucks had an easily identifiable rumble. No, this was something different. A small pick-up truck perhaps. Maybe a van.

The garage door whirred again, being lowered.

With the engine still running, someone opened a door on the vehicle. It was a sliding door, Popowych thought. Diehl recognized the sound as well. He'd driven a van that serviced twenty-five automated cash machines at various Eastman Kodak complexes. Fifty times a day, five days a week, for three years, he had opened and closed that door. He'd heard that sliding door open thousands of times, and this, he was sure, was the same kind of door.

The vehicle's engine went silent, but there were new noises. The Brink's guards used carts, set on wheels, to move the weighty bundles of money around. The carts were nothing more than canvas sacks draped and secured around a metal frame two feet by four feet—similar to what postal workers used to maneuver mail through post offices. The carts were now rolling. The door from the vault room to the garage was surely open. Popowych could make out the shuffling sound of bags, likely being moved from the carts and loaded into the vehicle.

Popowych began to think he'd survive.

If they were going to kill us, they'd have done it. We haven't seen their faces; we've hardly heard their voices.

Yet another set of footsteps, heading toward him. These were different, lighter, maybe sneakers. A woman perhaps. Nearing him. Closing in. Getting too goddamned close.

The footsteps stopped next to him, just inches away. Popowych waited. Seconds morph into millennia when you think someone is standing over you, deciding whether you live or die. Was she armed?

Of course. They had to get all the money and then off us. They'll be long gone before anybody responds to reports of gunfire.

Take the money and go. We don't know who you are. Just go.

Popowych felt a hand at his mouth, a small hand, reaching under the canvas bag. What was she doing? The woman—Popowych grew more sure of the gender—removed her hand.

Popowych heard her footsteps again, heading away, disappearing. Then it became apparent; she was checking to make sure he could breathe. *They have no intention of killing us,* Popowych thought. He was now sure of this.

Just stay still, stay quiet, let them leave with their millions.

The pain set in. With the specter of death hanging around, Popowych hadn't noticed how much his shoulders hurt. But the dull throbbing ache started to grow. He tried to ignore it, because the last thing he wanted to do was howl. His wrists stung from the binding.

"We got your buddy."

Popowych recognized the voice—the calm one, that of the man who'd first taken him down.

Diehl sensed the gunman was next to him, speaking to him directly. His hands were without feeling. He waited, hoping the ordeal was near an end. His breath grew shallow.

"We're going to take him. If you call the police, we'll kill him."

The voice again—composed, almost passive: "Did you hear me?"

Popowych then heard Diehl answer, softly and nervously: "Yes, I heard."

Diehl was still nearby, Popowych realized. *They've got O'Connor.*

Footsteps again, moving away. The van door, sliding shut, a slight thump signaling its closing. Now the garage door, opening. Each sound unique. Popowych and Diehl both focused on the sounds, using each noise as an aural buoy marking events totally out of their control. Even the click of the van's ignition could be heard, its engine sparking to life. There was a momentary squeal from the engine, lasting only a second or two. *Probably a squeaky fan belt,* Popowych thought.

They both heard the vehicle backing up and the garage door sliding down the track again.

Momentary silence. Then footsteps again. Maybe only one person now, walking away. The closing of a door—the heavy armored door into the vault room. Then another—the front door being yanked shut. Then silence. Godly silence. Ecstatic silence.

They were alive.

CHAPTER 4

— — —

Never had the light in the depot's vault room been such a welcome sight. But for Popowych, free from the First Federal bag, the fluorescence was magnificent. He'd managed to slide his head uncomfortably across the concrete floor until the bag slipped off. Liberated, he saw he was only feet from Diehl, who'd also maneuvered out of his canvas sack. Diehl looked like hell, his face ashen. He exhaled in sickly puffs.

"I'm having trouble breathing," Diehl whispered.

Popowych tried to pull his wrists apart, succeeding in part. He pulled harder, bringing his wrists together, then separating them. The ties loosened more. Each movement, no matter how slight, brought a new pain to his back. But finally he felt he had enough room to free himself.

Sliding his hands along his back, Popowych managed to push the loosened ties off his wrists and down his hands. He wiggled his hands free. Nearby lay a pair of pincer-like pliers, used to sever the protective straps on the money trays. Popowych crawled along the floor, like a soldier ducking enemy fire, his ankles still bound, until he reached the pliers. He clipped his ankles free, then released Diehl from the wrist and ankle ties. The vault room was silent, except for the erratic breath of the two men. Too drained to move, Popowych and Diehl lay on the cement floor, exhausted.

"You think the building's clear?" Popowych finally asked, the first words they'd spoken in minutes. Diehl, lightheaded, nodded slightly, his strength still ebbing. Eventually, the two men stood, their legs unsteady beneath them. Popowych called 911 from the office. Diehl found his handgun in the garage. The gun could have done some damage, if he'd only had a chance. But they'd had no chance. None at all.

— — —

The first two Rochester cops to arrive at the Brink's depot were women—an indication of the department's continuing evolution from an all-white men's club. Lisa McKay, who'd spent five years patrolling a peaceful college town just west of Rochester before joining the city force, heard the call come across the scanner at 7:15 p.m. There were reports of a robbery at the Brink's depot at 370 South Avenue, the dispatcher relayed. There were still guards inside, but it appeared that whoever pulled off the heist was long gone. McKay knew that she was close to the depot. She gunned the Crown Victoria patrol car.

At the depot McKay connected with Officer Margaret Perez-Dunham. The parking lot at the depot was dead still and, from the front at least, there were no clues of anything untoward. As the two plotted their next steps—McKay decided to wander around the depot's front, while Perez-Dunham made sure the rear was secure—more officers rolled into the depot lot. Within minutes, police commanders were on hand, the army growing quickly. With winter taking a bite out of crime, there were plenty of cops on patrol with time on their hands, and they all wanted to see just how one pulls off a Brink's heist. Few people, after all, appreciate a well-orchestrated crime better than a cop.

An officer had to knock several times on the front door before Popowych and Diehl opened it. Diehl's fear was apparent: his face was pale and drawn.

Once inside, the police separated Diehl and Popowych. McKay took Popowych aside, and Perez-Dunham handled Diehl. Officers brought in a German shepherd to try to pick up any scent that could lead to the robbers.

In the garage, officers found empty money carts and plastic trays. Somebody had made off with quite a bounty. How much the cops didn't yet know, but it was clearly a hell of a score. One thick block of $10 bills had been left behind on the vault room floor. That lone block of bills totaled $10,000.

— — —

There was little that Roy Irving enjoyed more than watching his ten-year-old son play hockey. This evening he'd hung around at the team's practice, pleased at how well his son had taken to the game, zipping along the ice with speed and fluency. The ritual had become a fine father-son bonding time. Dad watched the practice with pride; son maneuvered on the ice as if it were a second home. The practice typically ended with the two of them driving to a nearby sporting goods store, where they would go in, chat with familiar employees, and have the skates sharpened. But not tonight. Irving, Rochester's police chief, heard something across the scanner as he was about to step out of his car at the sports store. He was sure the dispatcher said something about a Brink's robbery. *This sounds big,* he thought.

"Go on in yourself," he told his son. "And hurry."

He listened to the squawks and shrieks of the scanner traffic. More units were responding. The evidence technicians were on the way. The canine unit was en route. Yes, someone had hit the Brink's depot.

How do you rob a Brink's depot? Irving wondered. *You'd have to be either ballsy, dumb, or lucky.*

Or all three.

— — —

Each crime scene tells a story. But it's a coded and cryptic tale, waiting to be deciphered. Fortunately, the Rochester Police Department (RPD) had some of the best to be found at unraveling the mystery.

Painstakingly, meticulously, they went to work at the depot. This would likely end up a case for the feds, but for now it was the domain of the Rochester cops. All the more reason to do the job right. All a cop wanted to hear was a federal agent in a starched shirt griping later on about how the locals had botched the collection of the evidence. But the FBI had come to expect thorough and reliable legwork from the RPD folks. And if there were ever a time for good cop work, this was it.

It was, so far, a surprisingly bloodless crime. Two witnesses had been left behind. And these two men, based on the stories they would tell police over the next few hours, had shown remarkably good sense. Too often, the men who worked as security guards were what the police liked to call "cowboys." They liked to carry the guns, wear the uniforms, at least feel as if they were living on the edge. Some had been washouts at police training academies; others had the good sense to realize they couldn't cut it as cops. But they were also the sort of men who, when faced with a robber, might foolishly draw a gun. And might end up dead. Popowych and Diehl had shown more smarts than that. These guys clearly took the job as a job—not as a chance to masquerade as policemen.

But where was O'Connor? No one had yet heard from him.

Having dropped his son off at home, Irving arrived at the depot around 7:40 p.m. The police had established a perimeter around the parking lot, marking it with the yellow tape common to crime scenes.

"We've got to work with the FBI," Irving told one of the police officials already at the depot.

"Do we have to?" the official answered. "Can't we handle it ourselves?"

The city police and the FBI had an excellent working relationship, but old resentments often rose to the surface. Some Rochester cops felt that the FBI could barrel roughshod into an investigation and take it over. City cops complained that, too often, the FBI relished getting credit for their successes but disappeared quietly after failures, leaving the locals to field the tough questions. Still, Irving knew the FBI had to be involved.

His officers would do the initial evidence gathering at the depot, the work that could be the most important. It would be, for all practical purposes, a joint investigation.

For the Rochester police, solving crime had become a respite. Since 1990, the department—more than 600 cops strong—had been under siege from the media and public alike. Once known for some of the nation's most innovative law enforcement programs, the city's police department now seemed under permanent taint.

In 1990, Gordon Urlacher, then the city's police chief, was arrested for pocketing money from a fund used to make drug buys and pay off snitches. A gregarious man with a slight beer belly and a permanent smile, Urlacher had simply used the money to do what he liked to do—take cops out for an occasional drink; treat them to a meal; and spend an evening with the boys discussing sports, police work, and his prized baseball card collection. He'd lift some money here, some money there—just enough to make do. But he didn't quite know when to stop. By the time of his arrest in October 1990, the feds figured he'd taken somewhere between $100,000 and $300,000 and had even used the money to help pay for a child's college tuition. In 1992, he was convicted for embezzling public funds and sent away to a low-security federal prison in North Carolina, where he proceeded to trim down and grow a stylish beard.

Then there was the police Highway Interdiction Team, a unit of department vice cops who the FBI claimed took the squad's acronym—HIT—far too seriously. Local civil right activists had long told tales of police abuse by the HIT squad, but generally the activists were shrugged off by the authorities as malcontents seeking the limelight. However, shortly after Urlacher's arrest, one of the squad's members squealed to the feds about what he claimed was his cohorts' overzealousness.

In August 1991 five HIT cops were indicted on federal civil rights abuses. Their methods of intimidation, the indictment alleged, ranged from the brutal to the absurd. One suspect was shoved down stairs; another was threatened with a live electrical wire. The cops, federal prosecutors claimed, cut the dreadlocks off another suspect and inked the words "illegal alien" across the forehead of a juvenile offender.

With Urlacher gone, the department fell into the hands of Irving, one of Urlacher's deputy chiefs. It would be difficult to find a more decent man than Irving, and the city's mayor of two decades, Thomas P. Ryan Jr., recognized that. So he made Irving chief, envisioning him as a stabilizing anchor during the chaotic storm. With his plastic-framed glasses, balding head, and round owlish face, Irving looked more like a college physics professor than a cop. But he'd developed a reputation as a good beat officer, a man of honesty and integrity. Ryan, whom the media nicknamed "Mumbles" for his habit of speaking inaudibly, and Irving shared a certain quality—they were both introverted men who did not like publicity or facing the glare of television cameras and microphones. Yet the public and the media sought constant reassurances that the department had changed course. Irving did bring a level of calm to a police force divided between those who continued to support the former chief and the vice cops and those who didn't. The other half of the equation—having to constantly deal with questions from the public about the department's ethics—remained an annoying link to his predecessor's administration. No matter how much he did to clean up the department, he struggled to convince the public that this was a new and improved Rochester police force.

All in all, the years preceding the Brink's heist had not been good ones for Rochester law enforcement. And the FBI had suffered its own travails. Typically, the FBI would welcome a high-profile case like the Brink's robbery, which would be an investigation to get the juices flowing. But the FBI in Rochester already had its hands full, and its performance of late hadn't been stellar.

In late 1990, two armed men had pulled off the nation's largest armored car robbery, hijacking a truck belong to the Armored Motor Service of America (AMSA) in a Rochester suburb and making off with $10.8 million. Not only had the FBI failed to crack the case, but they had appeared almost comical in their pursuit of their prime suspects, Albert M. Ranieri, the AMSA driver they thought was the inside man, and his father, Albert B. Ranieri Jr., a local mason. These suspects didn't seem to be master criminals by any measure. The feds decided to shadow them and to make the surveillance blatant. The idea was that eventually one of the suspects would crack, turn on the other, or make a slip that the FBI could exploit. It didn't work that way.

In one incident, an FBI agent tailed the younger Ranieri so closely that he rear-ended him. Ranieri got hit with a traffic violation, but he ultimately beat the ticket and two other driving violation charges leveled against him over the next few days as surveillance intensified.

Then there was the reliable tip that the stolen millions were stashed in the masonry shop owned by the older Ranieri. Before searching the shop, the feds arrested the two men on robbery charges. But the search yielded absolutely nothing, and the charges against the pair were dropped. As it turned out, the feds had relied on the word of a jailed con man whose veracity was far from impeccable.

As the calls went out to local FBI agents about the heist at the Brink's depot, some of them wondered when the craziness would stop. Some were preparing to testify about their investigation into the HIT squad tactics and were uneasy at the thought of sending other cops to jail, especially since some police were skeptical of the allegations against their brethren. The HIT squad trial was expected to last one to two months and was to start in a federal courtroom within days. (The trial would ultimately end with the acquittal of the cops—proof, the accused would always maintain, that they'd been wrongly targeted for doing their job and that the drug dealers had lied.)

"It was just one thing after another," an FBI agent said later, remembering how grim the first few years of the 1990s had been.

— — —

Outside the depot, within the area cordoned off by the yellow tape, police used their cars as mobile offices. They placed calls to the State Police and the customs patrol at the Canadian border. The cops could offer little more information than that the get-away vehicle was likely a van. It could be on the New York State Thruway, which stretched east to west across the state, or it could be heading for the Canadian border. Unless the thieves had a local connection to provide a secure hiding place, they would probably try to move the cash out of the area as fast as possible. And according to the Brink's guards, they had O'Connor. Some of the officers who'd responded remembered him from his days as a beat cop and detective. They hoped for the best, for his safe return.

Irving had a different reaction to the news that O'Connor had been kidnapped. When he'd heard O'Connor's name, he looked toward another veteran cop at the depot and the two nodded slightly at each other, as if sharing a secret from the rest of the world. Yes, O'Connor's police career had been unremarkable but unblemished. And, since then, his name seemed to keep coming up at the wrong times.

After his retirement from the force, O'Connor went to work as a security guard at Rochester's Genesee Brewing Company, one of the nation's oldest breweries. A colleague there, Damien McClinton, was fatally shot while on the job. While O'Connor was never publicly identified as a suspect in the killing and the crime was never solved, some homicide investigators thought that he knew more than he was willing to tell. McClinton, after all, was in a serious relationship with a former girlfriend of O'Connor. And O'Connor's alibi, provided by a fellow cop and friend, seemed shaky.

There had also been a homicide in Gates, a Rochester suburb, that O'Connor had been questioned about. Again, he was never identified as a suspect, but again, some police wondered whether he had told all he knew.

About a mile from the depot, at the Public Safety Building—a six-story utilitarian structure that appeared Soviet in design—nearly a dozen cops were meeting to discuss recent parolees who might deserve special attention. Their pagers started beeping one by one, until the noise merged into a single hive-like buzz. One of the cops got word of the depot robbery, and it was clear there was an "all hands on deck" order for the department. Another veteran investigator knew Tom O'Connor worked as a security guard at Brink's.

"If Tom O'Connor isn't dead, he did it," the investigator said.

While cops at the depot and police headquarters recalled their suspicions about O'Connor—some quietly, some vocally—the evidence technicians went to work inside the Brink's facility. Two of Rochester's best techs were on the scene, two men whose skills were admired by the department but whose personalities were polar opposites.

Robert Garland had been collecting evidence—from fingerprints to fibers—for the department for over a quarter-century. Unflappable and quiet, he exuded professionalism. Defense attorneys hated to see him on the witness stand. He couldn't be ruffled, and his work was always cautious, efficient, and thorough. Some defense lawyers long ago gave up trying to rattle him; he often got the better of them with a firm politeness that played well to juries.

The other evidence technician—Greg MacCracken—was, as Irving often called him, the consummate "ball buster," full of high-octane energy and as wired on adrenaline as Garland was infused with steady composure. Irving likened MacCracken to a fine point guard on a basketball court, constantly moving, surveying everything in sight.

MacCracken went to work with a video camera, trying to capture each square inch of the depot on film. One officer demonstrated how unreliable the front door was. With the door locked from the inside, the officer lowered his shoulder and gave the door a hearty shove. It popped open with little resistance. MacCracken caught the moment on film.

Garland used a relatively new piece of law enforcement equipment that was able, through the use of static electricity, to detect footprints or tire tracks on anything from concrete to carpeted floors. The dust on the depot garage floor made the task easy. The van's tracks—and police were growing certain that it was a van, based on what Popowych and Diehl had to say—were the most prominent dusty remnants in the garage. Police checked the measurements. The tires were about five inches across, and there were sixty-six inches from the outside of one rear tire to the outside of the other one.

Garland also picked up footprints on the floor, though their outline wasn't as defined as he would prefer. Still, every tidbit of evidence could be crucial later in the courtroom.

With the tire and shoe prints visible, Garland set up a camera on a tripod to try to capture the images on film. Loyal to Rochester's major employer, Garland loaded the camera with Kodak T-Max black-and-white film. He removed the flash from the camera and laid it on the garage floor so images were bathed in light. The routine was ingrained in him by now—three shots from one position, each with a different f-stop setting and with the flash angled differently. There would always be one good exposure, if not three.

Meanwhile, another technician photographed different areas of the depot. A hasp on the gun locker, located in the trap area, was bent but not broken. Several of the guns appeared to be missing, but the cops couldn't tell how many. They found several revolvers throughout the depot—three in the garage and one on the manager's desk in the office.

The girdered door between the trap and the vault room had been easy to breach. Police found the keys still in the lock. A locked cabinet inside the manager's office protected the videocassette recorder, the machine that police hoped would reveal the images captured by the depot's surveillance cameras. But they found the cabinet open and that key also in the lock. There was no tape in the recorder, and the surveillance cameras had been rendered useless. The robbers clearly knew what they were doing.

— — —

The bar at the Brook House Restaurant, a long-established popular dining spot in the Rochester suburb of Greece, had yet to remove its strands of Christmas lights by January 5. The restaurant was quiet and nearly empty when a frazzled man, his hair mussed and his walk unsteady, stumbled in around 9:15 p.m.

"I think I'm having a heart attack," he muttered to the bartender, Louis Niger. "Could you give me a shot?"

Niger passed along a shot of Southern Comfort and called 911. Niger recognized the man—Tom O'Connor. O'Connor occasionally ate at the restaurant with friends, and Niger knew a little bit, but not much, about him. Retired cop, nice guy, now in some kind of security work—that's about all Niger recalled, except O'Connor usually looked a lot healthier than he did right now. His face was pallid, his forehead sweaty. He did have the tell-tale signs of an impending heart attack.

O'Connor went at the Southern Comfort with a surprising vigor. Niger told him an ambulance was on its way, just hold on.

"What happened? Something happen to you?"

O'Connor nodded, a little life returning to his face as the liquor took hold.

"There was a robbery," he answered.

"Robbery? What was robbed?"

"Brink's. The depot. It was robbed."

Niger knew of Brink's as an armored car company—who didn't—but he knew nothing of the depot. And he knew Greece well enough to know that there wasn't a Brink's depot in the vicinity. There were the car dealerships and a shopping mall and all the fast-food joints within a mile that anyone would ever need or want, but Niger knew nothing of a Brink's facility.

Unsure what to do next, Niger did what any good bartender would do—he gave O'Connor another shot of Southern Comfort. He wondered whether O'Connor was delusional, what with this talk about a robbery, Brink's, and a depot that, as far as Niger knew, didn't even exist.

When the hell will that ambulance get here? he wondered.

— — —

It was after midnight when Popowych sat down at a table in the cramped interview room in Rochester's Public Safety Building, which housed the offices of the brass in the city police and fire departments and the county Sheriff's Office. Two plainclothes officers had driven Popowych the mile from the depot to the cop shop, as police and media alike called it. Popowych had told several cops part of the story of the heist, but not all of it. The cops wanted him to give the detailed version to Leonard Borriello, a major crimes investigator known for his subtle but effective interrogation techniques. They didn't want Popowych worn down before Borriello got a shot at him.

Borriello met Popowych in the interview room. For a moment, the two engaged in small talk. As they chatted, Popowych ran the entire robbery back through his mind, freeze-framing segments, readying himself to provide the best possible descriptions he could of the masked gunman, the steps the thieves had taken, and even the fact that the van probably had a squealing fan belt. He was prepared to tell the story to Borriello from the start. It was up to Borriello to ask the questions, and he'd provide all the answers he could.

But one of first questions from Borriello was not at all what Popowych expected: "Did Tom O'Connor ever talk to you about his interest in the IRA?"

Popowych was speechless. *The Irish Republican Army? What the hell did Tom O'Connor have to do with the IRA?*

CHAPTER 5

— — —

In 1984, while Tom O'Connor was a Rochester police officer, he committed a crime. Over the next two decades, he would be a suspect in other criminal offenses. But his crime in 1984 would be the lone offense to which he would ever admit.

That year, O'Connor did a favor for a friend—a man who'd once been jailed in Northern Ireland for transporting explosives for the IRA. That man, Samuel Ignatius Millar, had served eight years in the notoriously brutal prison Long Kesh, where IRA rebels suffered and died. After being released, he met O'Connor, who was visiting England and Northern Ireland. They became such good friends that, when Millar was harassed by British authorities, O'Connor smuggled Millar into the United States, via Canada, and helped him and his girlfriend hide in Rochester.

Millar was an IRA loyalist, a man whose commitment to a Northern Ireland freed—violently, if necessary—from British control could not be questioned. This explains why O'Connor was so inclined to befriend Millar: O'Connor believed that the IRA was waging a noble fight, and he considered Millar a heroic IRA guerrilla. To help such a hero was pretty cool, and it also elevated O'Connor in the eyes of Rochester's very active Irish American community.

That all had been more than eight years before the Brink's robbery. But FBI Special Agent Bill Dillon, a veteran investigator known for his well-mannered tenaciousness and one of the first agents called to the Brink's building, was very familiar with the history of O'Connor and Millar. In 1985, he'd been tasked with finding Millar, who the FBI believed was then hiding in Rochester.

At the depot, only hours before Leonard Borriello asked Dick Popowych about O'Connor and the IRA, Dillon had mentioned the Millar-O'Connor link, giving rise to investigative questions about the IRA.

Like Police Chief Roy Irving, his longtime friend, Dillon thought the odds were good that O'Connor was the inside man in the Brink's robbery. The early evidence—the robbers' clear knowledge of the security problems at the depot and the missing tape from a surveillance videocassette recorder—pointed to an inside job. If that were the case, O'Connor seemed to Dillon the likeliest culprit.

Dillon knew that O'Connor had been questioned years before about the Damien McClinton homicide. There had been talk of an IRA connection with that killing: both McClinton and O'Connor were sympathetic to Northern Ireland's fight for independence, and both were active in the Rochester chapter of NORAID, which portrayed itself as a humanitarian American-based organization that raised funds for the families of imprisoned IRA fighters. US law enforcement officials—including FBI agents—had long suspected that the millions raised by NORAID were often funneled to the IRA. The feds had never made a solid case, but not for lack of trying.

While hunting for Millar, Dillon became certain that members of Rochester's active NORAID chapter were responsible for sheltering him. Millar was one of Northern Ireland's notorious "blanketmen," IRA prisoners who'd been jailed at Long Kesh and refused to wear traditional inmate clothing because they considered themselves political prisoners. Instead, they cloaked themselves in threadbare blankets, while sometimes plastering their cell walls with their own excrement.

The blanketmen were, to their supporters, exemplars of the IRA cause, men whose strength and unwillingness to bow to the might of British power were emblematic of the struggle of those battling for a free Northern Ireland. To many people, Millar was a hero—and also a likely target for the British authorities once he had been released from prison.

In 1984, within a year after he left Long Kesh, Millar dropped out of sight. The British counterterrorism and security units MI-5 and MI-6 took his disappearance as a bad sign. While his crimes had led to no deaths, the British saw his willingness to move explosives for the IRA as a harbinger of the offenses he might later commit.

The security units started prodding their sources, looking for information on Millar. They learned that he had left the country and had been spirited by someone into the United States.

MI-5 forwarded the fruits of its investigation to the FBI, which through its own legwork developed reliable leads that O'Connor had brought Millar into the country—specifically, to Rochester.

With its NORAID chapter and a bevy of supporters of removing Northern

Ireland from British rule, Rochester seemed as welcoming a place as anywhere in the United States—except perhaps Boston or New York—for Millar. Rochester's Irish population was large and long-established, and some of its ancestors had followed the same route as Millar—from Canada to western New York. With the enclosure movement—a government seizure for agriculture of once-communal land—in the early eighteenth century, many Irish crossed the sea to Canada and then trekked into the United States. Many settled in Rochester, then a thriving commercial hub.

As with most immigrants, the Irish initially confronted bias and bigotry, but as their population grew, they became an essential part of Rochester's community. During the nineteenth and twentieth centuries, Irish Americans dominated much of the political structure of the city of Rochester and its surrounding county, Monroe. Rochester's first elected mayor and many of the city's and county's early elected officials shared Irish roots.

The sizable Irish community in Rochester gave rise not only to an active NO-RAID chapter but also to its precursors. In the early 1980s, Colleen Dunham, a Rochester resident, helped organize regular meetings and coffee klatches around the question, "What about Northern Ireland?" The history of the conflict was explored, as were ways in which US citizens—in particular, those in Rochester who participated in the discussions—could help push Northern Ireland to separation from the United Kingdom. This was a civil group, individuals who wanted a peaceful resolution and were often horrified at the violence—bombings, shootings, and deaths of innocents—committed by both the British and the IRA in the seemingly endless conflict.

Northern Ireland consists of six counties, and its bloody history of civil war never seemed to wane, with a constant struggle over whether Northern Ireland should become one with Ireland or remain part of the United Kingdom. The Unionists who wanted Northern Ireland to remain with the British were mostly Protestant, and most of the people who wanted it to break from British control belonged to Northern Ireland's Catholic minority.

In Rochester, Dunham's group evolved into a chapter of the Irish National Caucus, an American organization that raised funds and lobbied Congress for peaceful intervention in Northern Ireland. Its founder, a Catholic priest named Father Sean McManus, once commented that "Ireland, too, has the right to be one nation under God, indivisible, with liberty and justice for all."

During the 1980s, the caucus's influence in Congress grew, and the organization was credited with a decision by federal lawmakers to suspend the sale of weapons to the British police force—the Royal Ulster Constabulary (RUC)—stationed in Northern Ireland.

At the same time, NORAID, which had grown significantly in the late 1960s, was also expanding across the country. Not long after the Rochester chapter of the caucus was founded, a local attorney, George Conaty Jr., started a chapter of NORAID. As Culver Barr, a law partner of Conaty and a one-time president of the Rochester NORAID chapter would later say, the NORAID members were more militant than the caucus group. NORAID members were not fans of violence, but they understood it—and some endorsed it.

"Were it not for the Irish Republican Army there would be no Ireland at all," Conaty wrote in 1986. "One need not dwell endlessly on the fact that for 800 years every generation of Irish people have risen against British tyranny to free their homeland. What there is today of Irish freedom was untimely ripped from Britain's unwilling womb."

He likened the people living in Northern Ireland to the "Jews, Blacks, Italians, Orientals, Indians, and even Americans [who] gained their rights from British brutality. Did Britain ever go when asked, or by talk, or in peace? Of course not."

Not every dues-paying member of the Rochester NORAID chapter was so fervent about Northern Ireland. Some simply liked the semiannual parties and dinners the chapter threw. In the fall there was typically a fundraising dance, and in the spring a pig roast.

Some people who had no interest in the conflict attended the dinners and dances as guests, and some paid annual dues because a membership in NORAID significantly lowered the entry fees for the events. Once, a federal prosecutor of Italian heritage was preparing a criminal case against two members of NORAID who had been accused of counterfeiting when Barr, who was defending one of the men, reminded the prosecutor that he was on the list of NORAID members because he'd gone to a dinner and opted to pay the yearly dues. The prosecutor recused himself from the case.

NORAID's ostensible mission was to send money to the families of imprisoned IRA fighters. But during the 1980s, US and British authorities saw mounting evidence that some of the money—raised at pubs and dances and dinners like the Rochester gatherings—was being diverted to arms purchases for the IRA.

"At least half of what is raised in America stays in the U.S. for the purchase of weapons," a spokesman for the RUC told the *Christian Science Monitor* in 1985.

Rochester's NORAID chapter did not raise a lot of money compared to the chapters in New York City or Boston. But the commitment of Rochester's NORAID members was unquestioned; a document created when their chapter was founded proclaimed: "This is an authentic committee chartered by the Provisional Irish Republican Army [and the only one] to collect money for their cause. We guarantee that all monies collected will be used for that purpose."

Federal prosecutors used that document in a New York City prosecution in the early 1980s of NORAID officials convicted of illegally transporting firearms to the IRA. The Rochester document, authorities maintained, showed that NORAID was complicit in IRA violence. NORAID officials portrayed the document as a poorly worded record of the chapter's mission to assist families of jailed IRA members.

In the early and mid-1980s, as the Troubles—the name for the increasingly violent Northern Ireland conflict—continued to spread, the membership of the Rochester chapter of NORAID also grew. The chapter attracted national speakers to its dinners, and some of its members joined others in New York City parades honoring the commitment of the men and women fighting for Northern Ireland's independence.

Among those active members was O'Connor, whose genial nature masked his passion for the cause. A retired Rochester policeman, O'Connor might seem to some like the last person willing to commit a crime and bring a once-imprisoned IRA member into the United States illegally.

But Dillon knew better. He knew of O'Connor's connections to Millar and was sure that O'Connor had brought Millar to Rochester. Millar's girlfriend, Bernadette Fennell, had made her way to Rochester on a travel visa, and joined Millar, after which the couple dropped off the radar screen. O'Connor had never been charged with a crime for the simple reason that Millar had not been located.

Once Dillon thought he had Millar nailed. Through sources in Rochester's ample Irish American community, he learned that Millar was living in a city apartment complex. Dillon questioned the complex's manager and found that a couple matching Millar's and Fennell's descriptions was living there. When Dillon got to the apartment, there was tea on the stove but no Millar or Fennell. The couple appeared to have cleared out only minutes before, unbeknown to the manager and the complex's security guard. A month's rent was left unpaid, and the security deposit, apparently loaned to Millar by O'Connor, stayed with the complex.

That was the closest Dillon and his colleagues had gotten to Millar. They did find out that Millar and Fennell had a child while in Rochester—a daughter named Kelly—but they could not track the family down. In 1986, they closed the book on Millar, after growing certain that he was no longer in western New York. They heard rumblings afterward that Millar and his family had slipped off to

New York City, whose sheer magnitude provided people with more opportunities to disappear than Rochester did. FBI agents in the Rochester area tried to stir up interest in Millar among their colleagues in New York City but failed to generate any enthusiasm there for the chase. Wherever Millar and his family were, he was likely safe from the reach of American law enforcement—unless he did something criminal enough or stupid enough to attract attention to himself.

Perhaps, Dillon thought, Millar had finally done just that. He shared the possible lead with investigators—a lead relayed to Borriello before his interview with Popowych, the Brink's guard.

What if the Millar-O'Connor friendship spawned this robbery? Dillon thought. *What if that friendship gave the IRA a way to get its grip on millions of dollars— money that could follow the already established illegal pipeline from the United States to Northern Ireland?*

Money that could buy a lot of weapons.

Dillon knew from his investigation into Millar that British and American law enforcement agencies suspected the existence of a pipeline of money from the United States to fund arms for the IRA—which was also known as the Provisional IRA (PIRA).

"The PIRA . . . was actively and constantly seeking money from American sympathizers to fund their weapons needs, which were significant in that time period," Dillon said.

Throughout the 1980s and early 1990s the IRA was hunting for surface-to-air missiles, weapons whose use would be sure to make the conflict in Northern Ireland even bloodier. As the PBS news show *Frontline* noted in a report on IRA funding, the Northern Ireland guerillas sought both firearms and money from sympathizers in the United States. With enough money, the IRA could also buy weapons from another major arms source, Libya, that it could not get from US sources.

Sympathies for the IRA ran high in many groups of Americans, including members of Congress. And Rochester, with its active NORAID chapter, would be a prime location for millions of dollars to be stolen, channeled through IRA sympathizers posing as NORAID humanitarians, and used to purchase weapons.

More than 3,000 people had died during the Troubles—more than half of them civilians—and while the most violent years had been in the late 1970s and early 1980s, the killing had not stopped. The IRA was still looking for weapons for its continuing war against the British, and civilians were still dying by the dozens each year.

This was the scenario that Dillon imagined: Millar, helped by his buddy O'Connor, hits the Brink's depot for millions and sends the money to the IRA, which uses it to buy more potent and more deadly weapons, including surface-to-air missiles to down British helicopters.

Find Millar, Dillon told the cops at the depot. He and Fennell have a child, Kelly, who may now be school age. And Dillon recalled that information had surfaced after Millar disappeared that Fennell had registered a car in her name. Maybe information on the car or the child—or both—could lead to Millar.

The Millar and IRA connection was just a hunch, but it was one born from Dillon's years of investigative legwork.

As it turned out, it was a pretty good hunch.

— — —

Another bit of policing would later pay dividends.

Knowing that the getaway vehicle was, based on the guards' statements, likely to be a van, Mark Sennett, a veteran Rochester police investigator, had an idea about how to home in on the make and model.

Days after the robbery, Sennett headed for the downtown Civic Center garage, which provided parking for county offices, courthouse officials, Rochester police, sheriff's office deputies, and jail workers. Armed with a tape measure and the estimated width of the tire treads from the depot floor, Sennett walked from van to van in the cavernous parking garage—a shelter for the community's mentally troubled homeless in the winter months.

He found a full-sized Chevrolet van. The tire-to-tire distance was significantly wider than the measurements from the depot. The same was true for a Ford van.

Sennett then tried some minivans—a Chevrolet Lumina, a Dodge Caravan, and a Plymouth Voyager. The distance between the tires matched that of the van at the depot.

He next tested a Jeep Cherokee for comparison. It fell between the minivans and full-size vans.

In an era of leaps and bounds in crime analysis techniques, this was Neanderthal forensics. But Sennett recognized that sometimes the simplest route is the best one to an answer.

"We're probably looking for a minivan," Sennett reported to his investigative colleagues.

— — —

The chatter about the IRA was mostly kept internal, limited to a few cops and FBI agents. Even Dillon, who had raised the prospect of an IRA connection, wasn't sure that the organization—either terrorists or freedom fighters, depending on one's side of the debate—could be behind such a brazen heist. The IRA had deep support among many Irish Americans—including politicians at state and national levels—and rarely would the IRA leaders consider orchestrating a crime in the United States.

And the suspected link was tenuous, Dillon recognized. First, O'Connor would probably have to be involved, though Dillon felt pretty good about those odds. Second, O'Connor's buddy—Millar—would be the likely liaison to the IRA, but he had not been seen in Rochester in eight years.

Nonetheless, there was little else in the way of leads for the police to follow. If nothing else, maybe now American authorities could find Millar and discover just what he was up to.

The police took Dillon's advice and checked Department of Motor Vehicles records for a car belonging to Bernadette Fennell. Sure enough, the records revealed that while in Rochester she'd owned a 1978 Mercury Cougar. The address didn't help, since the car had been registered at the address of Cahal Magee—an active member of NORAID who'd been suspected of helping Millar and Fennell hide in Rochester.

But the records also told investigators something else: Fennell no longer owned the Cougar. Instead she now appeared to be driving something different. The vehicle now registered as hers was a 1984 Plymouth Voyager minivan, much like the one that provided a tire match for Sennett in the Civic Center garage.

This whetted investigators' appetites even more.

Just where was Millar?

CHAPTER 6

———

The troubled Belfast household of young Samuel Ignatius Millar was the perfect petri dish for the breeding of a rebel in the IRA.

His mother, Elizabeth, was a mentally unstable alcoholic who ran an unsuccessful boardinghouse and tried on several occasions to take her own life. His father, "Big Sam," was often away at sea. Meanwhile, the push to free Northern Ireland from British control raged around him. Millar and his friends—many trying to survive in their own difficult homes—would find in the cause a certainty and a passion long denied them elsewhere.

Millar remembered as a young boy visiting his mother in a hospital that reeked of "piss, vomit, disinfectant, and the dry talc smell of death" after one of her suicide attempts. "On the bed, my mother lay motionless, her pallid complexion as one with the linen sheets, making her almost invisible," he wrote in a 2003 memoir. "It wasn't her first attempt at suicide, but it was her most imaginative as well as elaborate. Instead of simply opting for an overdose, she had decided to slash both her wrists. This time she almost made it, having been pronounced DOA [dead on arrival] by the doctor on duty. Her effort was frustrated only by the attentive eyes of my older brother, Danny, who, when upon hearing the doctor's verdict, became maniacal and demanded a medical miracle."

"It worked," Millar wrote. "She would live to die another day."

She abandoned her family when Millar was eight years old. As Millar would say, his mother likely did the family a favor by leaving them; her presence in the home was a constant drunken disruption.

The Millars did not want prying neighbors to know that she had left. "There was such a stigma about your mother leaving home that we'd just say she was sick upstairs," Millar once recalled. "We kept that going for years. The Guinness Book of Records: Sickest Woman in the World."

As a boy and a young teenager, Millar escaped into the fantastical fiction of comic books. Millar's father, a voracious reader, would often bring home comics from his travels at sea, and Millar found the stories of good and evil captivating. He devoured them, developing a taste for the American superheroes. Four decades later, he would fondly recall the first comic book his dad brought back for him. Millar was five when he was handed a copy of the DC comic, *The Flash*, and encountered a thrilling saga in which the speedy protagonist pursued a villain, the Trickster, who—able to walk on air—robbed an airplane in mid-flight.

While sympathetic to the cause of an independent Northern Ireland, Millar's father was not politically active. However, Sam's older brother, Danny, caught the fever, enthused and energized by the activism of some neighbors and friends.

Early one Sunday morning in 1972, Danny awoke his slumbering younger brother and told him that they were going to take a ride in Danny's recently purchased car. A group of protesters was gathering in Derry to march against the British, and Danny wanted to take part.

Sam, then sixteen, squeezed into the cramped car with three of his brother's friends, and they all made the seventy-mile drive to Derry. The scene at first seemed peaceful to Sam—he would later remember the "smell of fish and chips in the air"—but he was youthfully ignorant of the tensions that had been present in Derry in recent weeks, much less the waterfront city's long history as a focal point in the Northern Ireland conflict.

"If the north [of Ireland] was a time bomb, then Derry was its detonator," Gerry Adams, the leader of Northern Ireland's Sinn Fein political party, once said.

Though the city had a Catholic majority, a Protestant-dominated government had maintained control through gerrymandering and other political sleights of hand. Many of the city's Catholic residents saw the blacks in the United States and South Africa—people also denied basic civil rights and electoral representation—as their kindred spirits. In turn, Derry became a hub of the country's growing civil rights movement, much like Mississippi or Johannesburg.

In 1969 a section of Derry known as Bogside erupted in conflict, when young residents rioted in response to a British march commemorating a Protestant victory three centuries earlier. The riots, later dubbed the Battle of the Bogside, raged for three days, with Catholic teenagers tossing petroleum bombs at British police from the Royal Ulster Constabulary (RUC), which was generally unprepared for the uprising. Nearly a thousand people were injured, but no one died. In the end, the British were repelled, their warrior pride stung, and their decisions to avoid the use of deadly force largely questioned. That confrontation helped spark the Troubles.

When Catholics, including Danny Millar, his three friends, and Sam Millar took to the streets in January 1972, the RUC did not intend to have a repeat of the Battle of the Bogside. Violence and bloodshed had become common in the Troubles, especially in Derry. An IRA sniper had killed a twenty-three-year-old British soldier in November 1971, a month after two other British soldiers were killed by bombs tossed into their observation posts.

On Sunday, January 30, 1972, the RUC seemed ready for battle, even if it had to be the party to initiate the conflict. Sent to monitor the march was the army's Parachute Regiment, called "Paras" and known for being brutal.

Marches were prohibited in the city, but that did not stop the protesters. Nor did the barricades set up by the British troops prove to be sufficient impediments. Many marchers tried to push through the barricades, attacking the soldiers with stones and other projectiles. The Paras and other British troops answered with tear gas, water cannons, and then gunfire. Thirteen unarmed marchers died on the day that became known as Bloody Sunday.

"I have no doubt but that the killings were a deliberate military operation designed to strike terror into the hearts of all Irish nationalists living under British rule through the exercise of murderous violence against unarmed civilians," Adams later said.

The Millar brothers and their friends fled to their car and then to their Belfast home. When the brothers reached their house, they found their father in tears, fearful that his sons had been among those killed at Derry.

The killings lit a fire in Danny Millar. "My brother said nothing," Sam Millar later remembered. "His silence said it all: there was no way they would get away with it. The world would make justice prevail."

The seeds of rebellion were also planted that day for Sam Millar. They bloomed shortly thereafter, maturing into a life of crime, revolt, and imprisonment. But Bloody Sunday, perhaps more than any other single day, illuminated for Millar the world of inequity into which he'd been born, and the need for him to fight back.

"You'd have to have lived in Belfast in 1969–70 to understand what it's like to be oppressed," Millar said. "I wasn't brought up to be a slave. There was no sectarianism in my family."

"A lot of it is survivalism," he said.

With an often absent father and no prodding in his home for him to get an education, Millar became consumed by the Northern Ireland cause. By seventeen, he'd joined some of his friends in the swelling ranks of the IRA. Not long after the horrors of Bloody Sunday, Millar was first arrested and charged with "terrorist" crimes—a mix of antigovernment insurgency and teenage hooliganism.

The criminal accusations landed Millar in a historic position: he was the first defendant to appear before what was known as a Diplock Court.

At the time, the British courts were struggling to control the IRA through the traditional judicial apparatus. In a debate that, decades later, would sound much like the issues that confronted the United States after the attacks of 9/11, many British officials contended that the entrenched court system could not contain the revolutionary movement or its adherents.

The accused—men like Millar—needed to be treated more as terrorists than as standard-issue criminals, the officials maintained.

In December 1972, a British commission headed by Lord Kenneth Diplock issued a report known as the Diplock Report. The commission recommended jury-less trials for individuals believed to be part of the IRA or other organizations opposed to British rule.

"The only hope of restoring the efficiency of criminal courts of law in Northern Ireland to deal with terrorist crimes is by using an extra-judicial process to deprive of their ability to operate in Northern Ireland those terrorists whose activities result in intimidation of witnesses," the report said. "The only way of doing this is to put them in detention by an Executive act and to keep them confined until they can be released without danger to the public safety and to the administration of criminal justice."

Samuel Millar was the first test case for a Diplock Court. In February 1973 he was accused of two significantly disparate crimes—the robbery of a candy shop and the hijacking and torching of two public buses.

The police arrested Millar months after both crimes. In the July 1972 armed robbery of £50—about $125—from a Belfast confectionery, Millar and another teenager allegedly rushed into the store, held two female employees at gunpoint, and forced them to turn over cash from the till. The young robbers then sprinted away, after one of the women tried to grab one of them.

While the crime may sound like a boilerplate grab-and-dash robbery, British authorities alleged that Millar and his accomplice were raising funds to pass to the IRA.

The second crime, also in July 1972, was much more radical. According to police, Millar joined a group of youths who hijacked public transit buses on two different days, forced the drivers off, and set the vehicles ablaze.

Available public records, media accounts, and even Millar's memoir provide no insight as to why Millar was not a suspect until seven months after the crimes, but RUC records do describe Millar's February 1973 interviews with police. In his first interrogation, the police asked Millar about various IRA factions in the community where he lived.

Then eighteen, Millar was cooperative—a stance that he would not exhibit in his future meetings with police. "I will help you if I can," Millar told the police, according to court records.

Millar said he was a member of the Provisional IRA Fianna—a youth-oriented arm of the IRA—and he described the group's structure as best he knew it.

"I asked him what function he had performed on behalf of this organization and he told me of a number of incidents—some of which included keeping scout of [British] soldiers," a police detective sergeant wrote of the interview with Millar. "He had on two occasions marched in funerals, one being that of the funeral at the Short Strand of a person killed by a bomb and which he was ordered to attend and marched wearing green coat, green trousers, Sam Browne belt and lanyard and green beret and sun glasses. The second occasion he related to me was on the occasion of the funeral of a youth shot in Ardoyne by troops 'some time ago' at which he wore the same uniform."

Asked why he'd joined the IRA, Millar did not offer an impassioned defense of the organization nor tell of a household that was the launching pad for his rebelliousness. Instead, he simply said that he knew many teenagers like himself who were members. "I was asked to join," he said.

While sounding innocuous, those statements prompted another criminal charge against Millar: "being [a] member of an unlawful association"—namely, the IRA. The RUC investigators alleged that Millar confessed to the three crimes: the robbery, the incendiary attacks on the buses, and membership in the IRA. But when he reached trial in October 1973, Millar instead mounted a defense, contending that he had made no such confession.

On Monday, October 15, 1973, the first cases were called before a Diplock Court in a Belfast courtroom. Millar was the first defendant on the docket; nearly three hundred cases were scheduled for the months ahead.

The new "terrorist" court attracted the Irish media, and the *Irish Times* wrote on October 16, 1973, of "the first case heard under the North's trial without jury system."

Before the trial opened, Millar's attorney, appointed by the court because Millar was indigent, predicted nothing worse than a fine of £30. Then, according to Millar's memoir, the attorney added as a caveat, "Provided of course we don't get Judge Lowry."

However, Robert Lowry was the judge chosen to hear Millar's criminal case. Millar considered Lowry nothing more than a stooge for the British cause, a judge unwilling to give anyone even peripherally associated with the IRA a fair hearing. Lowry's father, Millar wrote, "was a bitter old Ulster Unionist and notorious anti-Catholic." And he continued: "Of course I ended up getting Lowry, and I'll never forget the sight of him that day, sitting there in his red-cushioned bidet with that stupid looking white rag on his skinny dung-beetle head."

The October 15 trial focused solely on the candy store theft and the destruction of the buses. The allegations of IRA membership would be heard at a later date. The focal point of the evidence against Millar was his alleged confessions to the crimes.

An RUC detective testified that Millar admitted that he and another teenage IRA member used a toy gun for the robbery. A female employee handed over cash and then boldly tried to grab the gun. According to the detective, Millar had said that he and his accomplice bolted from the store and later turned over the looted money to the Provisional IRA. Millar also told police that he and other members of the Provisional IRA, known as Provos, destroyed the buses—a successful attempt to provide fiery evidence of the growing ranks of young IRA members.

But the confessions, whether legitimate or fabricated by the police, were not enough to offset the shaky proof against Millar.

The first blow to the prosecution was the wavering testimony of the candy store employees. In court, they could not identify Millar. One testified with certainty that Millar was not one of the two thieves. Lowry found Millar not guilty of that crime.

Similarly, Millar was acquitted of the bus hijackings after the drivers could not identify him as one of the rampaging gang. Lowry's decision, as reported by the media, may have seemed convoluted but was legally rational.

Lowry did not doubt that Millar had confessed to hijacking and setting fire to the buses. But there were other similar incidents in the summer of 1972, so while Millar may have committed similar crimes, Lowry said, the RUC could not prove that he was one of those who committed the specific criminal acts of which he was accused. Yes, Millar might have torched buses, but they might have been different buses.

With the benefit of hindsight and a historical perspective on the controversial Diplock Court, Lowry's rulings do not seem odd, even with Millar's reported confessions to the crimes. Knowing that the media's scrutiny of his rulings would be intense, Lowry may have wanted to demonstrate that the newly created court could be fair, and that evidentiary thresholds still mattered. "I cannot indulge in speculation and I cannot apply a lower standard of proof than I would advise the jury to apply in the conventional way," Lowry said in court.

Unfortunately for Millar, acquittals of the two crimes did not eliminate the evidence of his ties to the IRA. The October 16 article in the *Irish Times* noted succinctly in its final paragraph: "Millar was put back in custody to face additional charges."

Two months later, Lowry convicted Millar of IRA participation. "There is no doubt in my mind that you are a dedicated terrorist," Lowry said, according to Millar's memoir. "I have within the law, the power to sentence you to eight years."

Still, Lowry said, he was mindful of Millar's age and sentenced him to three years. Millar would serve his time in a prison where many of his political brethren were also incarcerated, Long Kesh.

In the history of the Troubles, few places have as controversial a significance as Long Kesh, a former British Royal Air Force base that had been converted into a prison in 1970 to house a growing number of jailed insurgents. As the conflict intensified in 1971, British authorities approved internment without trial for suspected terrorists.

In August 1971, the British military rounded up 342 men suspected of IRA involvement—a military action based on terribly inaccurate intelligence. As the historian Richard English would later report, many of the IRA leaders were not even in the areas that were raided, and "many Republicans had gone on the run, apparently forewarned of the likelihood of internment."

Ultimately, more than a hundred of those arrested were released, while the others were incarcerated—most of them at Long Kesh. The numbers would swell in the following years and would include Millar—twice.

Released from prison in 1975, Millar remained free for only a year. On May 5, 1976, an RUC motorcycle patrol in the New Lodge neighborhood of Belfast, near Millar's home, became suspicious of an orange Volkswagen van that sped past them. Two RUC officers on motorcycles pulled alongside the van and waved for it to stop.

The van pulled over, and the officers asked the driver and the four other men inside to step out.

The driver—later described by an officer as having "short hair with a high forehead"—was clearly the oldest of the group. Once outside the van, as the driver reached for his identification, another member of the group "body-checked" an officer, knocking him to the ground. The five raced off, outrunning the officers.

Summoned to the scene, an RUC evidence team searched the van. Inside, under a wooden lemonade box, the officers found two pistols. Elsewhere, they discovered two more handguns. "Beside these guns were two detonators and some gloves and masks," an officer reported. "At the rear of the van . . . were two packages. One was a white plastic bag and the other a brown parcel. I looked into the bag and assumed there were explosives in it."

By the time the search was complete, the van had yielded a small arsenal: a 9 mm pistol, three .45-caliber pistols, a .38-caliber Smith and Wesson revolver, dozens of rounds of ammunition, and—most ominously—twenty-eight pounds of "nitroglycerine-based high explosive, two detonators and two improvised timer power units."

Later at an RUC station, the officer and a colleague studied photos of IRA members and identified one of the passengers in the van as Millar, and the driver as Lawrence Marley. Marley was proving himself a master escape artist. Like Millar, he'd been imprisoned once at Long Kesh. He and eight others were accused of plotting a 1975 escape from the prison. They were taken to court on the charges and proceeded to escape from the courthouse.

On May 8, 1976, Marley's luck ran out. That afternoon an RUC officer came across Marley and another man working on a stranded motorcycle. This time Marley didn't flee, apparently unwilling to leave the motorcycle. Marley even asked the officer for a ride to the home of someone who could help him with the necessary repair.

"I became suspicious of this pair," the officer later wrote, not knowing who Marley was or that he was being sought by police. "A short time later another police vehicle arrived on the scene."

The officers frisked the two men and found weapons on them. They took the men to a station, where Marley was positively identified as the man who'd escaped from the courthouse in 1975 and who had run away from the weapons-filled van on May 5. He was charged with possession of the weapons and explosives.

Two days later, the police found Millar, who was having his own transportation issues. Shortly after noon, a police patrol group found a red Ford station wagon parked with one front wheel on the sidewalk. They searched the driver, who had nothing on him except the car keys and a pair of black gloves.

His answers to questions about the car were unusual. He told police that he'd borrowed it, planned to have it for only five to ten minutes, and did not have a license or insurance. Taken to the police station for questioning, the man admitted his identity: "All right, my name is Sammy Millar [and] you boys are looking for me for having some guns on the New Lodge."

Questioned about the van, Millar became taciturn.

"You were in the van, isn't that correct?"

"Yes, but I am not telling you the names of the other fellows in the van."

"What happened?"

"I was there, we were stopped by the Army, and when we got out we ran away. That's all I'm telling you."

"The driver of the van has been charged."

"I know. I saw it in the papers but I don't know the names of the others in the van."

"Why were you in the van?"

"I was told to be at a certain place on that Sunday. I can't tell you who told me."

Millar said he knew nothing about the guns or the explosives, and he knew no one in the van other than Marley. Millar was also charged with possession of weapons—designed "to endanger life or cause serious injury," according to the charge.

In January 1977, the two were tried. Marley claimed that he had not been in the van. Millar's admission to police that he'd been one of the five men in the van was the evidence against him. This time he was unsuccessful in denying his previous statements.

A judge convicted the two men and shipped them back to Long Kesh. (Marley would later mastermind another escape from the prison.) At Long Kesh the two would become part of IRA legend—a protest that was the manifestation of the unbending strength and will of the movement.

"Now I was back at my old alma mater, probably for 10 more years," Millar wrote. "A place where men made rules but seldom obeyed them. A place where men sometimes changed the course of history."

CHAPTER 7

— — —

As bad as the beatings were, the baths may have been worse.

The beatings were brutality unleashed and uncurbed. The "screws"—as Long Kesh prisoners called the guards—held nothing back. Whatever anger or frustration they'd carried into the prison, they released tenfold with the beatings.

Day after day, they'd drag Sam Millar and dozens of other IRA inmates across the floors of Long Kesh. They'd pummel the prisoners and kick them in the stomach, chortling as the inmates wailed in agony.

Then there were the baths. The screws submerged the prisoners into baths of ice-cold water, forcing their heads underwater as the inmates imagined their lives ending in a drowning. These baths were rare—ostensibly to clean an inmate before a court appearance—but would forever be scalded into the memory of the IRA prisoners at Long Kesh.

"When they dropped me into the bath of freezing water it took my breath, but that was the least of my worries as my mouth and nostrils began to fill, and fear of drowning raced in my brain," Millar later recalled in his memoir.

Drowning may have been more compassionate than what came next.

The screws would dump a blend of disinfectants and abrasive cleansers into the water and, with a wire brush, scrub inmates with a ferocity that matched the beatings. Repeatedly they pushed the inmate's head underwater as the prisoner gasped for breath, gulping down the searing concoction of cleansing agents.

One of Long Kesh's most notorious prisoners, Bobby Sands, wrote: "Every part of my body stung unmercifully as the heavily disinfected water attacked my naked, raw flesh. I made an immediate and brave attempt to rise out of the freezing, stinging water but the screws held me down while one of them began to scrub my already tattered back with a heavy scrubbing brush.

"I shriveled with the pain and struggled for release but the more I fought the more they strengthened the iron grip. The tears came, flooding to my eyes.

I would have screamed, had I been able to catch my breath. They continued to scrub every part of my tortured body, pouring buckets of ice-cold water and soapy liquid over me. I vaguely remember being lifted out of the cold water—the sadistic screw had grabbed my testicles and scrubbed my private parts. That was the last thing I remembered. I collapsed."

Like Sands and hundreds of others, Millar was one of the blanket protesters—IRA volunteers who refused to wear inmate garb at Long Kesh because they considered themselves political prisoners, not criminals. Their sole makeshift clothing was the prickly blankets that they used to cover themselves in their cells.

Many of the IRA prisoners were young, headstrong, and committed to the cause of a Northern Ireland free from the British. Some had committed acts of violence that they maintained were politically justified; others had been jailed for lesser offenses largely because of their political loyalties.

Many hailed from lower-income Catholic neighborhoods of Northern Ireland, households where they'd seen their parents toil for minimal wages, if they were employed at all. "There was a definite working-class flavor to the Republican movement and its political thought at this time," Richard English, a historian of the IRA, wrote of the era when Millar joined the forces. "That political thought involved a combination of socialist politics and violent aggression."

Situated on 360 acres about ten miles from Belfast, Long Kesh is in its own way as legendary a part of the saga of the Troubles as is Bloody Sunday. The protests at the prison, including a hunger strike that claimed the lives of Sands and nine others, were used as rallying cries by the IRA fighters outside the prison walls. Much as the 1971 riot at the prison in Attica, New York, became a touchstone for prisoner and civil rights in the United States, the IRA protests at Long Kesh—though peaceful, unlike the riot at Attica—energized the faithful.

In January 1975, a British commission produced the Gardiner Report, an analysis of how best to deal with human rights issues with the growing number of paramilitary prisoners and IRA sympathizers. Until then, the prisoners had been granted what was termed Special Category Status, which meant that they were treated as political prisoners and not common criminals. But after the Gardiner Report, anyone convicted of IRA-connected crimes would be treated no differently from any thief or rapist or wife killer jailed at Long Kesh.

Long Kesh was reconfigured to keep IRA prisoners housed together, as recommended in the Gardiner Report. "With this decision Long Kesh divided into what were essentially two separate prisons, surrounded by 17-foot-high, two-mile-long concrete security walls overlooked by a dozen ostrich-like security boxes," David Beresford wrote in *Ten Men Dead*, the definitive story of the prison hunger strikes.

Within the prison were the H-blocks, so-called because eight single-level structures were constructed in the shape of the letter H. Each gray brick building contained four wings—two along each of the sides of the H—with twenty-five cells in each wing.

British authorities hyped the H-blocks as the most progressive prison facilities that could be found. There were horticultural classes, sporting facilities, even lessons in Braille for anyone who wanted to learn. "Imprisonment in the H-Blocks was a status tens of thousands of prisoners around the world would have envied," Beresford writes. "But it was not Special Category Status."

From small moments great protests can be born, and the same holds true for what happened at Long Kesh in the aftermath of the Gardiner Report and the prisoners' loss of Special Category Status.

In 1976 a judge sentenced Kieran Nugent to three years at Long Kesh for the hijacking of a bus. With a full head of reddish hair and a boyishly rounded face, Nugent looked nothing like a man who would ignite a protest that would last years and be an inextinguishable spark for the movement. His first confrontation with the Troubles came in 1973 at age fifteen, when he was shot eight times in the chest and back by British loyalists while he was standing with a friend on a street corner. His friend died in the shooting. Within a year, Nugent was a member of the IRA.

When he was imprisoned in 1976, Nugent was the first Long Kesh inmate to be denied Special Category Status. Prison guards handed him inmate garb for clothing, but he refused to put it on. "A screw said to me 'What size are you in the waist and what size are you for the shoes?'" Nugent later recalled. "I asked him, 'What for?' and he told me 'For a uniform.' I said, 'You have got to be joking.'"

Considering himself a political prisoner, Nugent would not take the clothing. He spent the first night in his cell naked. The next day he was given a blanket.

Other inmates followed his lead, and the "blanket protest" started.

Because they refused to leave their cells clothed, the inmates were locked down twenty-four hours a day. They dumped urine-filled chamber pots out the tiny cell windows or emptied them into cracks along the floor. As the numbers of protesters grew, and the animus from prison officials escalated, the inmates plastered their excrement on the walls.

Thus, the "blanket protest" morphed into the "dirty protest."

The conditions in the cells became horrific, but the inmates refused to concede.

While imprisoned, Sands wrote of a typical day: "Naked, I rose and crossed the cell floor through the shadows to the corner to urinate. It was deadly cold. The stench rose to remind me of my situation and the floor was damp and gooey in places. . . . The stench of urine and excreta was heavy and lingering."

Richard O'Rawe, who was eighteen when jailed at Long Kesh, later said: "You're putting shit on the walls; you're throwing piss out the door; you've got a beard down to your waist. You're not leaving your cell."

O'Rawe would later write two books about his time "on the blanket," the term for the inmates who refused traditional prisoner clothing. While at Long Kesh, he became the inmates' public relations (PR) coordinator, the individual charged with organizing the messages the protestors would send to the outside world when they could.

"It was awful," he later said of Long Kesh. "That's not me being a PR man [for the protesters]. Every day you were on the blanket, it was awful."

The brutality was so incessant and unrelenting that some inmates abandoned the protest. "The beatings were ongoing, day in, day out, year in, year out," O'Rawe said. "Not only were they physically disabling but they were psychologically damaging to the extent that many Republicans quit the protest and conformed to prison rules."

O'Rawe remembers how grimy his lengthy beard would get before the screws took shears—"shears you'd shave sheep with," he said—and cut away the beard and his hair. Typically, they'd keep an odd-shaped patch of hair intact on a prisoner's head. "They'd leave a patch just to make you look ridiculous," he said. He had a small misshapen circle of hair left on the back of his head.

Family and friends visited once a month, and the beatings would usually come afterward, O'Rawe said. By the time a visitor returned, the bruises would have healed.

Millar was one of the first prisoners at Long Kesh to go on the blanket. The protest was only five weeks old, but word of it had already circulated widely. IRA prisoners like Millar knew the drill even before entering Long Kesh.

Like others before him, Millar did not move when placed in his jail and handed the prison clothing. "I had perfected the speech in my head, reiterating it each night on my bunk in Crumlin Road jail. Now that it was time for the main event, my stomach had turned acrid," he wrote in his memoir.

"I refuse to wear the gear," Millar said. He was now a blanketman.

His love for superheroes and comic book characters came in handy for Millar. He imagined how they would respond in his dire situation, and he entertained his fellow inmates with tales of derring-do by the fictional creations who provided some glimmer of hope.

"What we need is someone like the Incredible Hulk to get us out of this bloody mess," Millar once yelled from his cell to others, according to his memoir.

Millar proceeded to tell the stories of other comic creations, and his colleagues in pain found themselves intrigued. Others piped in with memories of the Lone Ranger and other film heroes they loved. For a few minutes, a fictional world where good triumphed became a refuge, and on many days thereafter the prisoners returned to that world with similar conversations.

Millar was in a separate block from Sands and O'Rawe, but they too found ways to escape the reality of beatings and anguish. In the evenings Sands would step to the bars of his cell and regale the other inmates on the block with stories, tales that always focused on a hero fighting forces that seemed invincible. He told the story of Spartacus; he told of the Native American hero Geronimo; and he told the story from Leon Uris's best-selling 1976 novel, *Trinity*, rendering in minute detail the work of historical fiction about oppression in Northern Ireland.

For two to three hours at night Sands's melodic voice soothed the inmates. His stories were enthralling and encouraging, each imbued with the message that the inmates, too, could overcome. Even decades later, O'Rawe remembered those stories and the hopeful visions they provided.

The conditions at Long Kesh were no secret to the outside world. Inmates, when allowed visits, smuggled out notes and other writings through family and friends. Inmates tucked the notes, sometimes scribbled on cigarette papers, in their orifices and discreetly handed them to visitors, who then snuck them out. There were legends about how many tiny notes some inmates slid under their foreskins.

The prisoners did not waver, and, recognizing that the many people outside the walls were aware of and, in some quarters, sickened by their suffering, they presented a list of demands to prison authorities. If their demands were not met, some prisoners said, they would begin a hunger strike.

In a statement released through the IRA, the inmates said that they "were put in the H-blocks and were expected to bow the knee before the British administration and wear their criminal uniform. Attempts to criminalize us were designed to depoliticize the Irish national struggle."

The prisoners demanded that they be treated as political prisoners, be permitted to wear clothes other than the traditional inmate attire, and be allowed to associate with other inmates, including other IRA prisoners in different areas of the H-blocks. Prison authorities refused, and on October 27, 1980, seven prisoners started a hunger strike.

Into the winter, the seven refused to eat. One slipped in and out of a coma. The strike spread. In December, three female IRA inmates at the Armagh Jail joined it, then another two dozen men at Long Kesh.

Recognizing the power of the hunger strike but also fearful that it would end in deaths, IRA leaders advised other inmates to continue with their lives inside Long Kesh as if nothing was out of the ordinary. "Those of us not on hunger strike were impotent in any action, having been ordered to keep a cool head at all costs as any sign of frustration on our side would only be beneficial to the Brits and screws," Millar wrote. "This was probably the hardest of all orders to obey, knowing what our friends and comrades were enduring."

Still, Millar snuck a message scribbled on toilet paper out to the pope, asking for his help. While apologizing for "the paper it is written on," Millar urged the pope to intervene in the hunger strike.

"The Irish people have suffered to[o] long for their political and religious belief," Millar wrote. "Irish history is filled with the blood that Irish men and women have spilled for the nation and the Catholic Church, and now that the Irish nation needs the Church we hear naught but a deadly silence. Why?

"What must the Irish to do get the Church to help? By the time you get this it may be too late to save my comrades. You must speak out now, loudly; behind closed doors is no use. My comrades will die if you don't."

After fifty-three days, the British government relented—or seemed to. A settlement was offered, and the inmates accepted. But there was either a misunderstanding or a purposeful manipulation by the British. The IRA inmates initially thought their demands had been met, but the proposed resolution was instead just a small step in that direction. Even the dispute over clothing—the initial spark of the blanket protest—reignited when prisoners and prison authorities differed over just what types of "civilian" clothes the inmates could wear.

With animosities stirred anew, the prisoners believed that the hunger strike, as dangerous as it could be for them, was an alternative that the British would not ignore. In March 1981 a new hunger strike began, this one including a man who would become the emblem—in life and in death—of the IRA ardor for independence: Bobby Sands.

Sands had been a negotiator in the first strike, and he was angry that the demands, in his opinion, had gone unanswered. He started his hunger strike two weeks before others. He believed that his death, if necessary, might save others.

Gerry Adams, who as president of Sinn Fein would be a key player in the 1980s peace process in Northern Ireland, once described Sands as "a very ordinary man": "If you met Bobby Sands there would be nothing about his demeanor or his appearance that set him apart from the rest of us."

Like Nugent, Sands—with his shaggy mop of brown hair and irrepressible smile—did not look like the stalwart leader of a revolution. Yet his spirit for the fight was unmatched by most. Writing from Long Kesh, Sands likened himself to a lark that stopped singing when caged. The bird's owner, angry over its silence, killed the lark.

"I have been stripped of my clothes and locked in a dirty, empty cell, where I have been starved, beaten, and tortured, and like the lark I fear I may eventually be murdered," Sands wrote. "But, dare I say it, similar to my little friend, I have the spirit of freedom that cannot be quenched by even the most horrendous treatment. Of course I can be murdered, but while I remain alive, I remain what I am, a political prisoner of war and no one can change that."

Days after Sands started his hunger strike, a member of the British House of Commons from Sands's home district suffered a heart attack and died. IRA supporters decided to put Sands's name on the ballot for election to the vacancy.

Sands won, a victory that IRA supporters inside and outside Long Kesh celebrated as an affirmation of their fight. The turnout was remarkably high—more than 85 percent. Millar remembered the joy of the victory, and the efforts—bolstered by a church that he'd grown to detest—to ensure that Sands would not win.

"The Brits tried desperately to have Bobby's name removed from the ballot," Millar wrote. "The Catholic Church, through their slavish priests, informed us that: 'No one would vote for Bobby Sands.' It was truly comforting to know that the British government and the Catholic Church were soiling the same pair of pants."

His electoral victory did not end the hunger strike for the twenty-seven-year-old Sands. But this time the British seemed to have no sense of urgency about bringing the strike to an end. Other inmates at Long Kesh joined.

On St. Patrick's Day of 1981, Sands was seen by a prison physician. His body was thinning, but his spirit remained good. A prison official accompanied him to the visit with the doctor.

"I see you're reading a short book," the man commented to Sands, noticing a thin book the prisoner carried. "It's a good thing it isn't a long one for you won't finish it."

Later that day Sands wrote of how the body suffered without nourishment.

"The body fights back sure enough, but at the end of the day everything returns to the primary consideration, that is, the mind. The mind is the most important.

"If they aren't able to destroy the desire for freedom, they won't break you. They won't break me because the desire for freedom, and the freedom of the Irish people, is in my heart. The day will dawn when all the people of Ireland will have the desire for freedom to show.

"It is then we'll see the rising of the moon."

Seven weeks later, Sands died.

O'Rawe was one of the first prisoners to learn of the death. He and others in his block kept a tiny cylindrical radio that they passed among themselves and, as O'Rawe would later say, hid "up their bums" during searches. That radio relayed the news of Sands's death.

"It was like somebody had just stolen your soul," O'Rawe said. "It was just shattering."

Word spread inside Long Kesh, with prisoners sending the news to each other by tapping in code on pipes in their cells.

In the weeks afterward, more prisoners died. Talks about the demands resumed. The IRA would not relent without a full acceptance of the demands. In later years, this would be portrayed as intentional recalcitrance, a willingness to let people die to show the brutality of the British. But the prisoners wanted what they wanted, and the deaths of their friends emboldened some of them.

"It was all or nothing at that stage," one later said. "The fact that so many people had died made us even more determined."

But some families felt otherwise and succeeded in pulling their sons and brothers from the ranks of those starving themselves. Within prison walls, some people's fervor for the strike waned. By late August, ten men had died, and the Brits agreed to some concessions.

The strike was over, but within the annals of IRA history, it would become a watershed moment. The dead were made into martyrs and celebrated. Films and books would recount their heroism. They would be remembered as the conscience of the struggle.

O'Rawe, however, would have a particularly sour memory of the hunger strike. Years afterward, he would maintain that news came to him in his role as the public relations manager for the prisoners: The British had been willing to accept many of the protesters' terms before six people died, but IRA leaders outside Long Kesh rebuffed the offer because of the growing power the hunger strike had to energize the faithful.

O'Rawe wrote two books about his allegations—claims that have since found some support in historical documents released decades after the hunger strike. But he also became persona non grata to some of his former friends, who believed that he had diminished the legacy of the protest.

Still, when the demands were met, one of the concessions was a return to the original prison sentences for the blanketmen who'd had their sentences lengthened because of their protests. Millar was among those. To get out of prison earlier, he had only to agree to do the menial chores that he and other IRA inmates had refused.

"It was tempting, of course, and the Brits knew this," Millar wrote. "No nakedness, degradation, humiliation; no strip-searching, anal-probing mirror searches . . . forced washing or horrendous beating.

"Fuck it."

Millar's sentence was not shortened. In 1983 he was released from Long Kesh, one of the last blanketmen freed (by some accounts, the very last). He was met outside the prison gates by families and friends. His teenage sweetheart, Bernadette Fennell, had faithfully awaited his freedom.

"Welcome home, kid," his older brother, Danny, said, according to Millar's memoir.

Long Kesh, however, would not be Millar's last incarceration. Instead, he would later return to prison on a different shore.

CHAPTER 8

— — —

When John Henderson reached the Brook House Restaurant the evening of January 5, Tom O'Connor was already in an ambulance, being readied for transport to the nearby Park Ridge Hospital. Henderson— a police officer in the town of Greece, where the restaurant was located—had been tasked with the first police interview of O'Connor, even if he had to do it from the inside of an ambulance.

Henderson joined the emergency medical workers as O'Connor, his eyes slightly dazed, lay on a stretcher, his mouth covered by an oxygen mask.

O'Connor's vital signs appeared positive, but he complained of chest pains. Henderson thought the retired Rochester police officer, a man whom he recognized but did not know well, looked as if he were in mild shock.

Nevertheless, Henderson had a job to do, and he asked O'Connor about the robbery and kidnapping. As the ambulance began its short trip to Park Ridge, O'Connor answered some of the questions, relating what he could from the evening. The oxygen mask slightly muffled his voice, but Henderson could still understand the answers.

O'Connor said that shortly before the robbery, he and his colleagues had struggled to reconcile the count of the money. Eventually, they found an error, and the count was back on track. Once the problem had been resolved, he took a break and left the vault room. Henderson did not know the details of the story from the other Brink's guards—that O'Connor had said he was going to pick up extra money bags from the outdoor shed—but authorities would later use this minor difference as evidence of O'Connor's deceit.

While walking toward the office, O'Connor said, he was overtaken by a gunman wearing a ski mask and a Brink's uniform. The man forced him into the main office, sat him down, and placed a ski mask backward over O'Connor's head. The man stayed with O'Connor, telling him that he would have to answer any phone calls that came in and act as if nothing unusual was happening. Any misstep, any indication of trouble, any attempt at tipping off a caller that something was amiss and O'Connor would be dead, the gunman said.

Even with his head covered, the noises from the garage were unmistakable to O'Connor. Like Dick Popowych and Milton Diehl, he said he could track the activities of the robbers simply by the echoing series of sounds from inside the depot. First, he recognized the vibrating sounds of the garage door moving upward and then downward on its tracks. Then there was the clicking of the wheels of the money carts, constantly in motion, clearly being used by the robbers to move the cash.

O'Connor's story did not come fluidly or quickly. As Henderson prodded him, trying to lead him through the robbery step by step, O'Connor paused—his eyes unmoving, more vacant than staring—before he continued with the narrative. This might have been expected from a man who'd undergone such an ordeal, questioning whether he would live or die. But, in the months ahead, each move and statement O'Connor made on the night of January 5, and much of what he did thereafter, would be dissected and compared to the physical evidence and the statements from the other guards. O'Connor's past—the suspicions of his involvement in the homicide of Damien McClinton and the knowledge that he'd smuggled an IRA guerrilla into the United States—was enough to convince investigators that he'd be willing to help rob Brink's of millions of dollars.

Once the robbery was apparently over, and the garage door had been raised and dropped again, O'Connor was hustled into the back of the truck carrying the stolen loot. Based on the sounds, he said he was sure the vehicle was a U-Haul type truck with a single rear door that lifted up and not out. Henderson did not know this was another discrepancy with the statements of Popwych and Diehl, who were certain that a van had been used for the heist.

Inside the truck, O'Connor sat on a pile of bags that he believed, from the feel of the lumps beneath him, were stuffed with cash. From the movement of the truck he could tell that they were sometimes driving on city streets, occasionally stopping at traffic lights, and sometimes on the highway—likely one of the expressways that linked the city of Rochester with the suburb of Greece. At some point the truck stopped, and he was pulled from the back. He thought then he would be shot dead and left. Instead, the mask was removed, a paper bag slipped over his head instead, and he was ushered into a car. He was driven a short distance more and left only hundreds of yards from the Brook House.

Once at the hospital, Henderson's questioning ended, and the emergency workers wheeled O'Connor in to be checked. They gave him nitroglycerine tablets to try to ease his chest pains.

O'Connor entered the emergency room shortly before 10:00 p.m. His vital signs were largely stable and sound. He continued to talk of occasional chest pangs. There was a history of heart problems in his family, and he feared that genetics and the trauma of the night were collaborating and conspiring against him. He worried aloud about a heart attack, but electrocardiogram readings showed none of the signs necessary for such a diagnosis. O'Connor was stressed but not suffering a heart attack, despite the fears he voiced. A hospital physician recorded a diagnosis of "acute non-cardia chest pain" on O'Connor's medical records. The doctors saw nothing life threatening in O'Connor's condition.

A longtime Rochester police officer, Mark Merklinger, was at the hospital to continue the questioning of O'Connor. Once the physicians had ensured that O'Connor was not at risk, despite his occasional protestations to the contrary, they allowed Merklinger to talk to him.

O'Connor told Merklinger much the same story he'd told Henderson. He said that the robbers seemed to know too much about the operation; he was certain it was an inside job. His mild chest pains continued, he told Merklinger, asking that he be left alone so he could get some sleep.

Around midnight O'Connor was moved into a hospital room. He slept fitfully, his blood pressure occasionally spiking upward. Around 2:00 a.m. he was allowed to take a Xanax and managed to finally sleep solidly, his snoring so loud that one hospital aide noted it in a record when he checked in on O'Connor shortly around 5:00 a.m.

The next morning Merklinger returned. Some of O'Connor's family was now at his bedside. They gave Merklinger a little space but lingered nearby as he resumed his questioning.

The doctors had found nothing to warrant keeping O'Connor at the hospital. Merklinger asked if, after his release, O'Connor could take the police to the exact spot in Greece where the kidnappers had freed him. Also, Merklinger said, O'Connor could help by coming to the Public Safety Building for a more formal and thorough deposition.

Some of O'Connor's relatives heard the requests and stepped in, stating that he would go home now and rest. O'Connor also said he needed to get home and could not make any immediate plans beyond that. Merklinger asked O'Connor to call him once he felt up to it. O'Connor agreed. He never made the call.

Merklinger left and, not long thereafter, O'Connor was discharged after telling the medical staff that he felt better. There was no reason for him to stay. He was healthy—rattled, but healthy.

O'Connor's fiancée, Barbara Saucke, drove him home, where, he hoped, he could find some relaxation and quiet. Instead a crowd of people from the media, who'd been tipped off that he'd left the hospital, awaited him. Saucke hustled him into the house, and O'Connor refused to answer the occasional knocks at the door.

In the days to come, many would want to talk to O'Connor, especially those investigating the Brink's robbery. He would rarely cooperate. For police, this was yet another sign of a man with much to hide.

— — —

As police continued to scrutinize the evidence, they became even more convinced that the robbery had been an inside job and O'Connor was culpable. The night of the robbery they found his handgun on the floor next to his gun belt, laid out almost too neatly—so neatly that investigators later claimed the gun had been placed there as a prop.

Police also found a lockbox that contained keys and firearms ripped from a wall in the depot's front hallway. However, the box had been locked with a padlock that ran through a hasp. The padlock was gone, but the hasp was unbroken. Someone had either opened the lock with a key or bolt cutter, leaving investigators to question why the box had been yanked from the wall—unless it was an effort to mask the fact that the robbers had help from someone on the Brink's workforce.

The discrepancies between O'Connor's initial stories and those of Popowych and Diehl were, while perhaps seeming minor to some people, glaring to investigators. The police were sure a van had been used. Why would O'Connor indicate otherwise unless he wanted to misdirect the state troopers and other cops who had been on the lookout for the getaway vehicle on roads and highways in the Rochester area? The state police had even used helicopters after the robbery, with troopers surveying the highways and the east-west New York State Thruway. But with no reliable description of the vehicle, they could only hope to spot a van with stacks of greenbacks tumbling out of the rear.

Within hours of the robbery, the FBI and Rochester police began collaborating on the investigation, with the FBI taking the lead. There were still bad feelings between the two agencies—especially given the arrest and conviction of the popular police chief, Gordon Urlacher, and the ongoing investigation into alleged brutality by Rochester cops. But Chief Roy Irving had been working hard to ease those tensions. He let the FBI know that his officers would do whatever they could to help. In the coming weeks, he provided the FBI with an office at Rochester police headquarters, so investigators could work closely. He also provided two shifts of cops to assist the agents.

FBI Special Agent Paul Hawkins, who was heading the investigation in the Rochester office, later remembered how some police officers were less than welcoming when he first showed up at police department headquarters. "The scars from . . . Urlacher's case were still fresh," Hawkins said. "He was a popular chief. He was a cop's cop."

As the days passed, a camaraderie grew among the investigators. One of their key targets was O'Connor. FBI agents wanted to hear more from him than he'd been willing to provide in the ambulance or at his hospital bedside right after the robbery.

Once he was released from the hospital, O'Connor holed up in his house, a squat 900-square-foot bungalow near the waters of Lake Ontario. A small contingent of media representatives camped outside the home during some daylight hours, wanting to hear from the former cop whom a number of reporters knew from his days on the force. O'Connor had no intention of talking to the media.

Nor, it seemed, did he plan to talk to the FBI.

Shortly after O'Connor returned home, an FBI agent telephoned him to set up an interview. The phone went unanswered. Throughout the day the calls continued, and the agent left voice-mail messages for O'Connor. No one responded.

Nor did anyone answer when agents knocked at O'Connor's door. The police weren't the only ones wanting some time with O'Connor. Brink's officials also wanted a statement from him: they needed all of the evidence they could amass to make an application to the company's insurer, Lloyds of London, for reimbursement of the stolen millions.

For several days Brink's officials left a half-dozen voice-mail messages for O'Connor, but all of them were ignored. A Brink's investigator went to O'Connor's house. No one answered the door, even though O'Connor was inside, hiding out from much of the outside world.

On January 7, the Rochester *Democrat and Chronicle* reported that there was suspicion that a Brink's employee or employees had been involved in the heist. "Robbery Probed as Inside Job," proclaimed a front-page headline.

"I think it's likely an inside job," one investigator told the newspaper. "There is no forced entry here. And there is this security system . . . that's circumvented."

Also, investigators noted, a videocassette from the security system was missing, the robbers appeared familiar with the depot layout, and, according to O'Connor, at least one robber had worn a Brink's uniform.

The newspaper ran four stories on the heist, and O'Connor was prominent in much of the coverage. One story focused on his appearance at the Brook House and quoted the bartender, Louis Niger, about how O'Connor had appeared "pale, sort of sweaty, shaken."

The theme of another story provided a brief look at O'Connor's police career and was headlined, "Investigators Say Retired City Detective Is Not a Suspect in Brink's Inc. Robbery." The story made clear that while investigators said one thing—that they did not suspect O'Connor—their actions indicated otherwise. O'Connor had briefly stepped out of his house the day before the story appeared, strolled along his street for a few minutes, and then retreated back inside. "O'Connor was followed yesterday by FBI agents when he took a walk near his home," the newspaper story said. (Why the agents, who wanted to talk to O'Connor, did not then approach him is unclear.)

Three days after the robbery, O'Connor had had enough. The house was becoming a prison: the phone calls, the media presence, the maddening knocks on the door were not abating. He wanted out, but he did not want to deal with the FBI or reporters. Inside his garage, he climbed into the trunk of a car and had Saucke drive him the short distance to downtown Rochester.

Two Rochester police officers watched as the car pulled into a small alley off of Rochester's Main Street, the thoroughfare that bisected downtown and had once been a hub for thriving retail establishments before the advent of suburban malls. Saucke opened the trunk, and O'Connor unfolded himself from the car. He quickly spotted the police nearby and did not seem surprised in the least. As he strolled by one veteran vice cop whom he'd known for years, O'Connor said, "I just thought I'd take you guys out for a walk."

O'Connor walked to a nearby bank building, his limbs springing back to life after his time in the car trunk, his stride becoming almost arrogant as he proceeded along Main Street. Inside the high-rise building, he took an elevator to an upper floor to talk to an attorney, George Conaty, who also was a friend. Conaty owned a thirty-foot sailboat called *Bluebird* that was often the site of parties for O'Connor and a group of friends. O'Connor spoke briefly with Conaty, saying he believed that he was a suspect in the heist. Conaty said he would help as best he could, and he suggested that O'Connor consider hiring a lawyer. O'Connor decided to wait and see whether he would need an attorney; perhaps the media attention and the suspicions would pass.

O'Connor returned to the first floor and, in the lobby outside of the bank's entrance, he was met by a Rochester police investigator, Bob Siersma, and an FBI agent, Tom Minton, one of the agents who'd tried unsuccessfully to talk to O'Connor at his home. They'd learned from O'Connor's surveillance that he was now downtown, and they might have a chance to question him further.

Siersma and O'Connor were on friendly terms. Siersma approached O'Connor first, expressing sympathy for all that his former colleague had gone through.

"I heard you had chest pains," Siersma said. "I hope you're all right now."

"It was awful, Bob," O'Connor said, as Minton stepped into the conversation.

"Hi, I'm Tom Minton with the FBI," he said, extending his hand to O'Connor.

The friendly tone of the conversation evaporated. O'Connor's genial nature disappeared, and his tone turned angry.

"What's the FBI doing here?" O'Connor said, refusing to shake Minton's hand.

Minton explained how he and his colleagues had tried, unsuccessfully, to talk to O'Connor and how they needed a fuller statement from him.

"I've already given nine statements," O'Connor said, the exaggeration adding to the growing litany of misstatements that may have been unintentional, but that investigators saw as signs of guilt.

O'Connor said he'd still had little sleep and didn't want to talk. He looked at Siersma and said, "I'll talk to him but not the FBI." But, for now, he continued, he was too weary to talk to anybody.

— — —

After O'Connor's refusal to talk to Minton, the FBI agents realized something: O'Connor did not like them.

But the FBI was the lead agency in the investigation, and its agents had questions they wanted answered by O'Connor. Yes, he was a suspect, but no one wanted to spook him. It was best to treat him as a witness and somehow get him to talk at length about the night of the robbery. In his short talks with Merklinger and Henderson, he'd already revealed some small inconsistencies with what the other guards said. Maybe there was a rational reason; maybe O'Connor was innocent. Either way, innocent or guilty, his steadfast refusal to talk to agents was not helping him. This did nothing but reinforce their suspicions.

Popowych and Diehl had also submitted to polygraphs—the machine determining that each man was honest in reporting what he remembered of the rob-bery. They'd also agreed to go back to the depot for a videotaped reenactment of the heist, a re-creation that helped them remember even more details of the night.

They'd been helpful and cooperative. O'Connor had been neither.

The agents decided that their only hope of talking to O'Connor was to get his former colleagues from the Rochester police to approach him. They drafted several pages of questions they wanted him to answer and asked the Rochester police to drop off the questionnaire at O'Connor's home. O'Connor was free to respond to the questions in writing; the FBI just wanted to get the answers.

The questionnaire would lead O'Connor again through the robbery, prompting him for far more details about the heist and kidnapping than he'd yet provided. A longtime veteran of the Rochester force, Vito D'Ambrosia, was asked to de-liver the questionnaire. D'Ambrosia had joined the force in 1960, only two years before O'Connor, and the pair had worked as patrolmen together in northwest Rochester. While O'Connor had left the force after twenty years, a stint that ensured him the maximum pension, D'Ambrosia was a cop for life. He was now in his second shift with the homicide squad and had been witness to many of the region's major crimes. He had helped try to quell the chaos of the city's 1964 race riots and investigate the notorious serial killer Arthur Shawcross, who'd murdered eleven women.

D'Ambrosia had something else going for him: he'd always been popular with his Rochester police brethren. O'Connor was unlikely to shoo D'Ambrosia away.

On the morning of January 9, D'Ambrosia—accompanied by another inves-tigator, Evelyn Beaudrault—knocked on the door of O'Connor's house. Again, there was no answer at first. They knocked again, and venetian blinds at one window split slightly. O'Connor peeked out and saw D'Ambrosia, a bear of a man with tree-trunk forearms, on his front porch. O'Connor opened the door and invited the two cops in. They stepped into the small hallway of an immac-ulately tidy home.

D'Ambrosia explained that they had a questionnaire for O'Connor. If he could simply answer the questions in writing and call them when he was finished, they would pick it up and return it to the FBI. Clearly O'Connor didn't want to see the FBI, so this could be a compromise, D'Ambrosia said.

O'Connor had other ideas. He'd already been thinking of writing out a state-ment. If D'Ambrosia and Beaudrault stayed, he would answer whatever questions they had. They could write out his statement and take it back to the FBI and any other investigators who wanted it.

Realizing that O'Connor might finally be prepared to talk, the cops asked him to consider going downtown for the statement. He refused. Ask whatever you want, O'Connor said, and he'd answer.

O'Connor led them to his basement, where he had a stylish glass-top bar. For hours, they asked him questions, and he provided his narrative of the events of January 5. He did not disagree with the notion of an inside job. He, too, believed someone at Brink's was involved, he said. But it wasn't him.

"I feel that the persons who committed the robbery knew too much about the building," O'Connor said.

O'Connor took the investigators through his activities on the day of the robbery, beginning with his 10:00 a.m. start and ending with his drink at the Brook House Restaurant. He, Diehl, and Popowych had some issues with the money count that night, he said.

O'Connor said he'd been preparing money for the ATMs and "I stopped doing my order to help Milt because he was short. . . . I think it was $100,000 to $150,000. Milt told me to check the $100 and $50 bills. We checked and checked and finally we balanced out."

Afterward, O'Connor said, he left the vault area to go to the office. He was met in the depot hallway by a man wearing a red ski mask. "Be quiet; don't make any noise," the man said, pointing a handgun at O'Connor that the retired cop said looked like an older police revolver, possibly a .38- or .32-caliber.

The man slipped a wool cap over O'Connor's head, led him to the office, and stayed with him as others loaded the depot's cash into a truck. "Besides the man that continuously stayed with me in the office I would say two or three other people came inside," O'Connor said. "It sounded like an army."

O'Connor had heard the garage door opening and closing shortly after confronting the robber. Once the sounds of the money carts being wheeled through the depot stopped, he heard the door rise again. He was led to the truck inside the garage and gently helped into its rear. "Help the old man into the truck," one of the robbers said to another.

"The talker got in the back with me. I felt it could have been a U-Haul truck-type with the pulldown door. The door was closed and the talker told me that if we are stopped by the cops I better be a good talker or we are all dead."

After the truck backed up, O'Connor said, he heard a door open in front of him, sounding as if there was a front cab in the vehicle—another sign that this was likely a small truck and not a van. As they drove along, the man who'd first taken him hostage sat in the back with him, chatting idly, resuming a conversation about professional football that had started as O'Connor sat with his head covered in the depot office.

"So you're a Buffalo Bills fan?" the gunman asked.

The chatter continued briefly about the Buffalo Bills—a powerhouse in the American Football Conference—before the man fell silent. The drive continued, with O'Connor trying to pay attention to where they might be going.

"We drove for hours," he told the Rochester police investigators. "It seemed like at first some was city driving and then the speed changed and there were curves so I felt like there was expressway driving. We then stopped and the door was opened from the outside. There were at least two guys unloading the truck, moving the money bags.

"When they were done they took me outside. . . . He told me to close my eyes tight and they put a paper bag over my head. I thought I was going to be shot."

O'Connor had reached this part of the story previously with Henderson and Merklinger. Again, he paused, as if still in surprise that he was alive to tell the tale. Twice during his statement he had gone over to the bar for a drink of whiskey. He did so again now.

"Do you see what I'm drinking?" he once asked D'Ambrosia. "You know what I like?"

D'Ambrosia remembered that O'Connor was mostly a beer drinker and remarked that he was surprised at his choice of beverage.

"You know what this means?" O'Connor said.

"Yes, you're nervous," D'Ambrosia answered.

O'Connor downed the small glass of whiskey and returned to his tale.

Instead of putting a bullet in his forehead, his captors then removed his handcuffs, O'Connor said. He was walked to a car and placed in the front seat. His abductors were surprisingly gentle, even thoughtful.

"The guy I first encountered stayed with me all through the ordeal. He was a nice guy. They never touched me or asked me any questions or went through my wallet."

For fifteen minutes they drove again. Despite the behavior of his captors, O'Connor still feared that death was imminent. Why keep him this long unless they planned to dump his body somewhere?

Then, O'Connor said, the man who'd spent hours with him—from the first moments of the robbery until now—allowed him a glimmer of hope. "The only reason I'm not going to kill you is because this is the happiest day of my life," he told O'Connor.

"That was the first time I felt I stood a chance and was not going to die," O'Connor told the investigators.

Moments later the car stopped, and O'Connor's door opened. He was ordered to get out and leave the paper bag on his head. He heard the door slam and the car pull away. With the bag still on his head, he asked anyone close enough to hear, "Are you still there?" When the question hung unanswered, the night's stillness unbroken, O'Connor slipped the bag from his head and felt the trauma of the evening begin to overtake him, his chest tightening. He ran, without purpose until he realized he was near the Brook House, a restaurant and bar he recognized.

Inside, he asked Niger, whom he knew, for a drink and said he felt he was suffering a heart attack: "I told him to call the police. I don't remember anything else after that."

Beaudrault had been writing the entire statement down, as D'Ambrosia asked the questions. O'Connor requested a copy. D'Ambrosia said he and Beaudrault could go downtown, make a copy, and return it. That didn't suit O'Connor. He wanted the copy before the cops left.

Beaudrault agreed to write a copy of the statement, and spent nearly another hour doing so. O'Connor read through one of the copies afterward, nodding in agreement, and initialing each page.

"Anything else I can do?" he asked.

D'Ambrosia had an idea. What if O'Connor let them search the house while they were there? They had no warrant, but the unspoken message was this: O'Connor was a suspect and his cooperation could go a long way toward changing some people's minds about his involvement.

O'Connor agreed without hesitation but asked that he be allowed to alert his fiancée, who was upstairs. He returned moments later and led the investigators through the house. In his bedroom, he pulled up the covers on his bed and encouraged them to look underneath. He then slid open the drawers on an end table.

"Tommy, what I'm looking for won't fit in an end table," D'Ambrosia said. "It would fill up the room."

O'Connor showed them the bedroom closet and more closets throughout the house. He led them into the garage—nothing unusual there either.

There was no Brink's money to be found in O'Connor's home.

Four hours after entering the house, D'Ambrosia and Beaudrault left, holding the only detailed statement that O'Connor would give police about the Brink's robbery.

O'Connor hoped his recollection of the night and the fact that nothing in his house hinted at any involvement in the robbery should convince investigators that someone else at Brink's was the collaborator in the robbery. Instead, within days the media was raising questions about suspicions that O'Connor had been the inside man.

O'Connor had been a cop long enough to know what to do next. He stopped talking to police and called a lawyer.

— — —

Felix Lapine, the attorney O'Connor summoned for help, was well-known in Rochester defense circles. For years he'd been one of the region's most sought-after lawyers, a man with a quick wit who loved little more than jousting with prosecutors.

Also, like O'Connor, he enjoyed an occasional drink. Lapine and O'Connor had both been part of an annual bacchanalian rite on Father's Day weekend in which a bunch of friends—all men—boated from Rochester across Lake Ontario to a Canadian town—often Belleville—where they would overrun the bars.

As many as a dozen sailboats and several powerboats would make the pleasure pilgrimage, with some men who were regulars and some who went no more than once or twice. George Conaty Jr., the lawyer who was O'Connor's friend and a central figure in Rochester's chapter of NORAID, was a regular. In fact, he was one of the founders of the event.

Judges and cops and lawyers participated. Former federal prosecutor Charles Pilato, who would later find himself ensnared in the Brink's robbery case, went once.

"These guys were like the New York Yankees of drinking," he said. "I was like Little League. Alcohol would just disappear."

Called Vikings Revenge, the boating trip involved a Vegas-like pact among its participants: What happened in Canada stayed in Canada.

"It has always been a guys' trip where people can totally relax without fear of stories of drunken revelry and pranks getting back to hamper a career," said one of the participants.

Vikings Revenge started inauspiciously enough, with Conaty and a friend in the early 1970s deciding one day to sail to Canada. They didn't make it very far, recalled Conaty's former business partner, C. P. Maloney, but they still had enough fun—and booze—to decide to make it an annual rite. The next year, a few more sailors joined in, and they did reach Canada. Eventually the numbers swelled to upward of a hundred, and Vikings Revenge became such an institution that an elected official in Belleville made sure that the clubs and restaurants there were welcoming and ready to take cash from the Americans from across the lake.

As the Vikings Revenge founder and one of its heaviest drinkers, Conaty was looked at as the patriarch of the boaters. Conaty loved little more than his sailboat, and when he was going through a divorce he did not care much about what he had to sacrifice—as long as he did not lose the boat.

To be sure he would not part with *Bluebird*, he transferred the boat's ownership to O'Connor, his police friend. Conaty knew it was unlikely that O'Connor would damage the boat. O'Connor didn't sail; he just went on the Vikings Revenge trips for the fun and drinks.

Conaty hoped no one would challenge the transfer to O'Connor. Who else could be more upright and upstanding than a cop?

— — —

Among O'Connor's colleagues in the Rochester Police Department there was a joke about how loath he was to make arrests.

Why?

The paperwork was a time-consuming hassle.

What some of O'Connor's colleagues did not know was that the punchline likely originated with him. When drinking with friends, often on Vikings Revenge travels, O'Connor told them that he only liked to make a bust for the most serious of crimes because he had to complete too much paperwork with every arrest and he did not like to write. His version, in keeping with his jesting character, would be pithy, told with a slight smile, leaving his friends to wonder whether he was joking or not.

For O'Connor, law enforcement was a job, not a calling. He once said after his retirement, "Hopefully, I was an average cop."

What O'Connor was to many people was a puzzle. Some found him friendly and approachable, a decent man quick to help a friend or neighbor, while others believed him off-putting and untrustworthy, an individual whose every act had a motive—and not necessarily an altruistic one—behind it.

O'Connor had joined the force in 1962 after three years in the US Army—much of it spent in Germany—and a year as a meat truck driver. He started as a patrolman, joined the criminal investigation division as a plainclothes officer, and rose to detective—a sign that he was at least adept enough as a policeman to advance through the ranks.

Not long after joining the Rochester police, O'Connor married. He and his wife had two sons. The marriage ended in divorce in the early 1980s, shortly after O'Connor left the police after a twenty-year career.

While with the police, O'Connor had second jobs—driving trucks and working as a security guard—while developing an odd habit with the money he made. He kept most of his cash at home, leaving only a minimal amount of money in bank accounts for those times when he had no choice but to write a check.

"Like paying an insurance company out of town . . . you can't run and pay them money so I would pay them by check," he once said of the rare occasions when he would use funds from a bank account.

Asked where he kept his money, he said: "Mostly in the bedroom. I would throw some in a freezer in the garage."

After his divorce, O'Connor dated several women—some of them active in NORAID and the Irish National Caucus. Whether or not O'Connor developed a more intense interest in the Northern Ireland cause during these years is unclear. Perhaps his passion for the cause was legitimate; perhaps it was a boyfriend's ruse, much like a suitor who falsely claims to share the musical preferences of the woman whom he is dating.

But O'Connor had long been interested in genealogy, and whatever the impetus for his fascination with Northern Ireland, he became a true believer, a man who understood just why factions like the IRA would resort to violence. The United States had used violence to win its independence, and to O'Connor Northern Ireland was no different.

O'Connor became more deeply involved in Rochester's NORAID chapter, which—because of its impressive number of members—was a stop for speakers who were making the national circuit.

One of the speakers supporting NORAID (and the IRA, although this may not have been stated) was Seamus McAloran. As a Catholic resident of Belfast, McAloran lived under what he considered the oppressive thumb of the British. And he had a brother-in-law who'd been imprisoned at Long Kesh and witnessed the oppression there.

That brother-in-law, Sam Millar, was now free from prison, McAloran privately told Rochester NORAID members during a 1984 visit to the city. The British were now harassing Millar so much and keeping such an unrelenting eye on him, that Millar worried that he might end up imprisoned again—even for an offense as slight as jaywalking.

Millar was done with Northern Ireland, McAloran said, and wanted to come to the United States with his girlfriend, Bernadette Fennell. He'd tried to secure a visa but was unable to do so because of his crimes.

Rochester NORAID members saw an opportunity to help on a grander scale than the semiannual dances and pig roasts. They could smuggle an IRA rebel—a hero in their eyes—into the country and perhaps even provide the couple with a life in Rochester. Millar and Fennell would need new identities, but that wouldn't be hard, and the many IRA sympathizers in Rochester could help them settle in the United States.

Ultimately O'Connor would be the person whom McAloran and Millar turned to. O'Connor would later claim that he traveled to Northern Ireland to explore his roots, connected with McAloran, and learned only later that he wanted help in getting Millar into the United States. This is unlikely, and it contradicts what others active in NORAID said in later years.

Instead, O'Connor likely traveled to Northern Ireland in 1984 with one goal in mind—to meet Millar and discuss how they could later get him into the United States.

O'Connor knew that, to some in the NORAID ranks, he was considered a good guy, a friendly guy, but—perhaps because he was a cop—not necessarily someone who would step up to the plate if the cause required the law to be circumvented or ignored.

By assisting McAloran and Millar, O'Connor had a chance to prove that he was as devoted a supporter of an independent Northern Ireland as others in Rochester. He would somehow get Millar into the United States.

CHAPTER 9

The streets of Belfast were unlike anything Tom O'Connor had seen.

The British were everywhere—both the Royal Ulster Constabulary and the army. The police, clad in dark green tunics and trousers, wielded automatic weapons and Smith and Wesson pistols. The military patrolled lower-income areas of Belfast—the most likely locations for IRA members to gather and plot—in armored vehicles on the ground and, occasionally, in helicopters overhead.

"Patrols of up to sixty soldiers, complete with mobile back-ups in armored cars or jeeps as well as helicopter cover, could frequently swamp areas," said a Belfast journalist who lived in the city during the Troubles. "A few police might accompany the patrol, or it might be made up only of soldiers. Such patrols would severely limit the chances of an attack because it would be difficult to get away. That's not to say the IRA wouldn't try. Some soldiers were killed in gun and booby-trap attacks but, on the whole, the saturation patrolling was reasonably effective and relatively invulnerable.

"Security gates with civilian searches, sometimes backed by soldiers and police, surrounded the main shopping area in the center of Belfast. There was virtually no night life in the city."

To O'Connor, the tension in Belfast was palpable, the air seeming damp with fear. Some Belfast residents went about their daily lives as if nothing was out of the ordinary, and the police and military presence was largely centered in the city's working-class neighborhoods, the very areas O'Connor was visiting.

It was spring of 1984 and the Troubles were still festering. Peace talks were well in the future, even with the growing power of the Sinn Fein political party—which later, with Gerry Adams as its leader, would be a primary mover in the march toward peace (though not necessarily reconciliation).

The Long Kesh blanketmen were now free, with the exception of several who had been jailed on new charges. Some remained active in the IRA; others wanted to settle back into a routine domestic life and somehow bury the memories of brutality, suffering, and the starvation deaths of friends.

Sam Millar and others from Long Kesh—men who were well known by the British forces—found themselves constantly stopped and bothered about their comings and goings, no matter how mundane their plans for the day. The daily harassment and annoyances would never match the ugliness of Long Kesh, but they were a barrier for men who longed to find some solitude and sanity now that they were free and home again in Northern Ireland.

As one British army regiment finished its shift, its leaders would pass on to its successor details about individuals worthy of special attention.

"Fresh soldiers would mean a fresh cycle of abuse," said the Belfast journalist. "If someone who was known [by the military] was stopped at a checkpoint, they could come in for special treatment. They could be detained for hours, arrested, and held—maybe even for days. One guy I knew would travel to work in the city from his home in the country by bus. His bus would be stopped en route almost every morning. Some days they would make the whole bus wait while he was taken off and searched. Other days they would make the bus go on without him."

Free from prison, Millar envisioned marriage, having a home and children with Bernadette "Bernie" Fennell. But who would want to raise children in an environment like Belfast?

For Millar, O'Connor would be the solution—the individual who would help Millar escape Belfast for a country with more freedom, peacefulness, and opportunity.

Millar and O'Connor would later claim that Millar's very life was at risk in Belfast, whereas the truth, most likely, was that he was exhausted by the frequent police attention. "I know he was in constant danger," O'Connor later said of Millar.

O'Connor had traveled to Europe with Colleen Dunham, whom he knew from the Irish American circles in Rochester. Whether they were seriously dating is a question that might be answered differently by the two: O'Connor had feelings for Dunham, but they were not reciprocated with the same intensity from her.

Shortly after landing in England, they went their separate ways, with plans to reconnect several days later in Belfast. Dunham traveled in England, while O'Connor headed into Belfast to meet with Seamus McAloran.

While in Belfast, O'Connor stayed with McAloran's family. McAloran watched out for O'Connor, who—though he'd been aware of the tensions in Northern Ireland—was shocked at the scope of the military presence. "I stayed close to the people that could make sure I didn't go to the wrong places there," O'Connor later said.

McAloran introduced him to Millar and Fennell. Over pints at local pubs and meals they plotted how to get the couple into the United States (O'Connor would later say that an Irish breakfast he shared with the McAloran family was highlighted by "the biggest plate of food you ever saw in your life"). Unlike Millar, Fennell could get a travel visa. But Millar needed another route into the United States—an illegal one.

O'Connor showed no hesitancy; he agreed to help out however he could.

Dunham, who also knew McAloran through NORAID, joined O'Connor in Belfast after about a week. They now had a pact with McAloran: O'Connor would get Millar into the United States.

— — —

In late 1984, O'Connor was dating a new woman, Jean Arena, who was also active in causes connected to Northern Ireland. She had arranged McAloran's earlier speaking visits to Rochester and knew that he was looking for help for his brother-in-law.

She knew that O'Connor had promised to be Millar's US connection, and in August 1984, she drove O'Connor to the international airport in Toronto, Canada, to meet Millar, who'd flown in using an alias.

After meeting Millar at the airport, Arena drove back to Rochester without the two men. O'Connor insisted that he had solid plans to cross back into the United States with the illegal immigrant. "My understanding was that they were going to rent a boat," Arena later said.

This was a surprise, but she asked no more questions. Arena thought that O'Connor knew little about boating, though he had made the Vikings Revenge trips with some people who did. O'Connor's friend, Conaty, had his beloved sailboat, *Bluebird* (the boat whose ownership would later transfer to O'Connor); perhaps Conaty planned to somehow smuggle Millar into the country in the sailboat.

O'Connor would later claim that, days before going to Toronto, he drove his own car to the Canadian airport, left the vehicle there in a parking lot, and caught a bus back. After Arena left the airport, he said, he drove Millar back across the border, stopping and reversing course several times out of fear, before finally entering New York at the Niagara Falls border. This may be true; it may not. If Conaty was involved, he kept the fact secret from most of his friends—

even though many continued to suspect that, despite O'Connor's claims to the contrary, Conaty did sail to a Toronto marina and bring Millar and O'Connor back by boat.

In Rochester, Millar had no shortage of new friends and admirers ready to provide him with a home and work. Fennell had also traveled to Rochester with her visa, and she was reunited with Millar. O'Connor became especially close to the couple. So did his friend, Cahal Magee, an electrician who also very active in NORAID and who hired Millar—off the books, of course—to help with some jobs.

For several weeks the couple lived with O'Connor in his apartment. O'Connor became a surrogate brother to the couple, assisting them as best he could. He helped Millar and Fennell find an apartment, which was not rented in their names. He taught Fennell how to drive, though she did not take naturally to it. He spent so much time with the couple that it began to annoy Arena. Then in her early thirties, she had resumed her education and was in college; she would later get a law degree. She lived separately from O'Connor. Millar and Fennell—sometimes with O'Connor, sometimes without him—often showed up at her apartment at times when she had plenty to do other than entertain them.

"I was beginning to feel that the time that I was spending with Sam and Bernie and having them over as frequently as I did was beginning to encroach upon my study time," she later said.

Still, Arena was part of a group of Irish Americans who, with some Irish immigrants, became a second family for Millar and Fennell. Some of them had been involved in McAloran's planning to get the couple into the United States, and now they wanted to protect and shelter the couple and ensure that they could have the golden life they wanted, even if they were living illegally.

"We all felt, I think, a certain degree of responsibility for Sam and Bernie's well-being," Arena said.

— — —

After her split with O'Connor—if she even considered the relationship serious enough to call its ending a split—Dunham began dating an Irishman, Damien McClinton, who had separated from his wife.

McClinton, his wife, and their four daughters had moved from Belfast in the late 1970s to escape the daily uncertainty of life in a world where bombings and violence, though usually targeted at the British or the IRA, could claim civilian casualties.

"He loved Ireland and was very proud to be Irish, but my mum and dad decided to leave due to the war," said McClinton's eldest daughter, Joanne. "However, he never forgot his roots and he didn't let us either."

In late 1976, McClinton moved to Rochester, where his older brother had settled and made a decent life for himself at Xerox, the thriving copy machine manufacturer that had been founded in the city.

The family followed months later. "We followed him on January 3, 1977, a date I won't forget, as it was my fifth birthday and first time on an airplane—so it was very exciting," Joanne recalled.

The marriage was not to last, however, and seven years later McClinton and his wife split. She returned to Belfast with the children, but McClinton stayed in Rochester, which he now considered home.

"We didn't have a phone when we moved to Belfast. Not many people did at that time, but my mum's friend who lived around the corner did, and he [McClinton] would ring us every Sunday at a prearranged time," Joanne said. "It was great to hear his voice for that brief time."

With a perpetual smile and gregarious nature, McClinton had the ability to turn anyone he encountered into an immediate friend. Bushy-haired and mustachioed, he was also known for his ability—one that he'd mastered—to charm most women he met. As one friend would say, he was the kind of man "who'd be dancing with one woman and eyeing another."

McClinton ingratiated himself with the active Irish community in Rochester. He found like-minded friends, men and women who wanted to advance the cause of a Northern Ireland free from the British. He drove a bus with city and suburban routes for the Rochester Transit System and was later hired by the Genesee Brewing Company, where he worked shifts as a security guard before moving into management. And he found Rochester's popular Irish bars, such as McGinnity's, Carroll's, and Molly Malone's, to his liking.

He also met Colleen Dunham and began a serious relationship with her.

Like so many others supportive of the goals of the IRA, if not always of its violent tactics, McClinton joined Rochester's NORAID chapter. While Dunham was not as sympathetic as McClinton toward the more militant ranks of NORAID, she became active in the organization as well. She had once been one of the leaders of the Irish National Caucus in Rochester, but NORAID, with its social activities that were as important to some people as its mission, had completely supplanted the caucus. By 1986, if one wanted to be active in a Rochester organization promoting an independent Northern Ireland, NORAID was the sole significant option.

Dunham and McClinton, along with Cahal Magee, Conaty, and their spouses, were among the people who were often with Millar and Fennell—a protective tribe for the IRA insurgent and his girlfriend. They sometimes traveled together to New York City for statewide NORAID events. Dunham and McClinton were a close couple, their affection for each other clear to those who traveled with them.

O'Connor may still have had some feelings for Dunham. Some police officers would later surmise that O'Connor was jealous of McClinton, and that he could not control that emotion.

At least, that would be one theory—there would be others, including the involvement of the IRA—when O'Connor became a suspect in a homicide. As one of McClinton's friends later told the Rochester police, "Tom totally disliked Damien, who had taken his girlfriend."

CHAPTER 10

— — —

The last words Colleen Dunham heard from her boyfriend were the ones she'd often heard before: "I'm on my way."

Damien McClinton, a distribution supervisor at the Genesee Brewing Company, was closing up the beer operation's warehouse for the night. The night—December 3, 1987—was chilly, with intermittent snow. New to the security supervisory job, McClinton had to lock the warehouse's chain-link fence after the last beer-delivering trucks pulled into the lot and the drivers headed home.

McClinton had a routine: he'd call Dunham to alert her that he'd see her soon, set the warehouse's security alarms for the night, drive his car outside of the gates, and then lock up the warehouse grounds. If all went as usual, McClinton would be downtown within fifteen minutes. The brewery's warehouse was on the west side of the city, and what slight traffic there was in Rochester had typically dissipated by 6:30 p.m., when Dunham expected McClinton to arrive.

But 6:30 came and went, and McClinton hadn't shown up. Dunham waited, assuming McClinton had gotten held up by something at the warehouse. By 7:15, when he had still not arrived, she became worried. Dunham telephoned a nephew of McClinton, who was not home. However, his roommate, Mark LaPiana, was, and he agreed to take her to the warehouse.

He picked Dunham up and they drove the route McClinton would typically have traveled in the opposite direction. They looked for his car, thinking it might have broken down along the road, but they did not spot it. The drive to the warehouse took just under fifteen minutes; they saw no sign of McClinton along the way.

A light coat of snow dusted the warehouse lot, providing a natural touch of illumination at the poorly lit front gate. McClinton's car was not nearby. The gate, oddly, sat half open. McClinton surely would have secured it before he left.

LaPiana and Dunham simultaneously spotted McClinton's body, lying face up, between the two gates. There was a small pool of blood next to his head.

LaPiana left his car. Dunham sat inside, frozen. She realized that whatever had happened to her boyfriend, he was likely dead.

LaPiana held onto a slight hope that McClinton was alive. Perhaps he had been struck by a car, LaPiana thought, but with the warehouse slightly isolated, set off from major thoroughfares, this seemed unlikely.

Once he saw McClinton up close, LaPiana knew his friend had not been hit by a car. And he knew McClinton was dead. As well as the blood dripping from a gunshot wound to McClinton's head, there were other splotches of maroon alongside the body. They were hard to miss, their color highlighted by fresh snow.

McClinton had also been shot in the midsection and, according to LaPiana, in a knee.

(LaPiana remains insistent that McClinton was shot in the knee, and a police officer on the scene that night said the same thing, wondering whether the shot was meant to mimic a violent IRA tactic known as kneecapping. The tactic, however, was used to wound individuals who fell out of favor with the IRA, leaving them hobbling with an injury that served much like a scarlet letter. Current police investigators say that McClinton was not shot in the knee, and the autopsy report, which might have provided a definitive answer, was unavailable for this book's research.)

LaPiana figured that the killer had started with the knee and moved upward, only then firing the fatal shot into McClinton's head. How long the killer had taken between the shots could not be discerned, but McClinton had surely suffered—perhaps for seconds, perhaps for minutes. "Whoever killed him let him know he was killing him," LaPiana later said. "It was an execution."

There was no saving McClinton. LaPiana and Dunham drove to a truck maintenance shop only minutes away and found workers in the main office. Finding the door locked, LaPiana pounded on a window, yelling at them to call the police. Finally, they did.

When the police arrived at the warehouse, LaPiana and Dunham were there, waiting alongside McClinton's corpse. They'd looked for McClinton's car nearby but hadn't found it.

"He's dead and his car's gone, too," LaPiana told police. The car would be found later that evening, abandoned about a mile from the warehouse.

There was no evidence that McClinton had struggled with the killer. Instead, he'd either been overtaken by surprise—which seemed unlikely to the police, given the expanse of the warehouse parking lot—or was killed by someone he knew.

— — —

In the years before his killing, McClinton had become active in the leadership of the local NORAID chapter, propelled there by his popularity and ebullient nature. The crowds at the annual fundraising dances grew. Who could say no to McClinton?

Though thriving, the Rochester chapter of NORAID was never known for its organizational prowess. It religiously sent money to the state and national operations, but there was little in the way of reliable accounting safeguards. Like siblings squabbling over whose turn it was to wash the dinner dishes, NO-RAID members—in particular, the chapter's officers—sometimes engaged in finger-pointing over who was responsible for what.

By the mid-1980s, McClinton had moved into the top leadership position of the NORAID chapter, which landed him squarely in the center of its infighting. And in 1985, what began with internal questions about the chapter's bookkeeping ballooned into a full-blown internecine skirmish, with allegations of malfeasance and misappropriation and, later, suspicions that the contentiousness could be the roots of McClinton's homicide.

"I cannot and will not work with an organization that lets one member spoil the fun for everyone," the chapter's corresponding secretary wrote in an October 1985 letter to McClinton. The woman announced her retirement, claiming she'd been the target of venomous rumors over the accounting of funds used for a chapter newsletter.

"It's too bad that it had to come about this way," she wrote to McClinton. "You know I have always trusted you. Also, I still believe firmly in the Republican Movement and the IRA's right to defend it. That will never change."

Conaty, as one of the chapter's founders, was also embroiled in the dispute. He had ceded the leadership to McClinton but was now being encouraged to again take the reins. He and others were challenging the chapter's bookkeeping.

Conaty decided that a cursory look at the chapter's financial statements showed numbers that could not be reconciled with the fundraising efforts, especially with the tickets sold for the dance that year. Money was missing, he maintained. He tried to set up meetings with the officials responsible for accounting but was constantly stymied.

"I will no longer go begging and pleading for this to happen," he wrote in a 1985 letter to a Rochester NORAID official. "I have had enough of end-runs, missed and changed meetings, forgotten records and prevarications."

The dispute centered on no more than $700 to $1,500, but the bitter fighting made its way to the statewide governing body of NORAID, and leaders there decided McClinton had to go. They'd heard multiple stories of his inadequacy as a chapter chairman, and though the stories varied in the specifics, they all painted McClinton as an unreliable leader, a man whose charisma had secured him the chairmanship but who found the organizational and managerial parts of the job tedious and even unnecessary. Some of those who reported having problems with McClinton believed that he had pocketed the allegedly missing money; others simply thought his personality-based leadership style was inadequate for the job.

In December 1985, the New York office of NORAID ordered that McClinton and Dunham, who had also stepped into a leadership post despite her earlier issues with NORAID, relinquish their positions and "turn over all committee information to Conaty."

(Years later, some former NORAID members would find a particular irony about Conaty's being trusted to manage money. He was twice charged with failure to pay his taxes and was jailed for three months after a 1990 conviction. His defense was that he had forgotten he had to pay taxes.)

In December 1985, Conaty wrote McClinton, demanding the keys to the chapter post office box, membership materials and address lists, and the Irish National Aid rubber stamp. Dunham had carried the post office box key but had lost it when her purse was stolen. If Conaty did not believe her, she referred him to the specific number of the police crime report about the theft.

"There was a second key to the post office box," she wrote to Conaty. "I don't know who holds that now."

Two years after writing that letter, Dunham would find her boyfriend fatally shot—and police investigators would look to the NORAID dissension to see whether it could provide any clues.

— — —

As the police dug deeper into McClinton's murder, his history with NORAID—and, some suspected, the IRA—could not be ignored in the search for the possible causes of his killing. Indeed, one witness told the police, "On one occasion Damien had purchased guns with the organization's money to send back to Ireland."

Homicide investigators turned to the two-year-old financial issues of the NORAID chapter as one lead. They interviewed Conaty and others active in the NORAID group, trying to determine whether McClinton had in fact pilfered from the NORAID coffers and whether such a transgression would be serious enough to get him killed.

As they questioned members of Rochester's Irish community, more stories came to the fore. They investigated the gun-running allegations but found no solid evidence that McClinton was shipping firearms to Northern Ireland.

The allegations of an IRA-orchestrated hit became so prevalent that Rochester police officers even received a telephone call from a student at the local liberal arts college, St. John Fisher, who told of overhearing two classmates talking about the homicide. "The schoolmates were talking about the victim being involved in IRA activities and that with family in Ireland the victim may have been killed for activities related to the IRA in Rochester," according to a police report on the telephone call. The student did not know who the classmates were.

The police weren't the only ones hearing rumors that McClinton may have been more active with the IRA than many people knew. Only days after the homicide, the *Democrat and Chronicle* received an anonymous telephone call, claiming that McClinton had "very close ties" with the IRA—so close that he occasionally ran guns between the United States and Northern Ireland. The reporter who took the call noted, "Caller suggests that this was a 'hit' of some sort that is related to IRA activities."

There were more mundane theories for police to explore: drugs and romance.

A close friend of McClinton's, who tended bar at Irish pubs, had developed a serious liking for cocaine, which not only incapacitated his judgment but led to a mountain of debt to men who did not like to absorb too much debt. McClinton's friend could not pay the money back. He realized that McClinton also knew the men and asked McClinton to intervene on his behalf. Perhaps McClinton's charm could buy more time.

Or, as some would later surmise, perhaps it got McClinton killed.

Only days after the homicide, McClinton's friend quickly packed up his clothes and left his girlfriend and Rochester behind, moving to South Carolina. His girlfriend would later tell police that he was "like a caged animal" in the days before the killing and "inconsolable." Interviewed later about McClinton's homicide, the man provided little helpful information for the police.

Dunham added another suspect to the mix of drug dealers and IRA hitmen. She was convinced that O'Connor had never completely gotten over his feelings for her, and that his disdain for McClinton was evident. His jealousy was amplified by the fact that McClinton had only recently been promoted to a supervisory role at Genesee. Dunham and some of McClinton's colleagues there suspected that O'Connor, a brewery security guard after his retirement from the Rochester police, thought he deserved the job that had been given to McClinton.

Dunham encouraged police to look hard at O'Connor as a suspect. McClinton's schedule had changed only days before his murder, and Dunham believed that only someone with knowledge of the change would know just when to lie in wait for McClinton. As a colleague of his at the warehouse, O'Connor would know of any schedule changes.

For investigators, there was one problem with O'Connor as a suspect: he had an alibi, one provided by a Rochester cop.

The cop said that he'd bumped into O'Connor at a strip mall parking lot the night of the killing, and they had sat and chatted for almost two hours, reminiscing about old times and interesting criminal cases and colleagues who, like O'Connor, had retired. The cop was unwavering with his story and the alibi, specifically remembering that he'd gone to a drugstore at the strip mall because "my ass hurt" and he needed some Preparation H.

The conversation took place at the same time that someone was filling McClinton with gunshot miles away. Some investigators found the chance meeting too convenient; others found the story plausible.

Dunham did not. She was insistent that she knew who killed McClinton, and she could only wonder if the police, united in the brotherhood of blue, were unwilling to acknowledge the truth of what she believed: a retired Rochester cop was the murderer.

She had letters she and O'Connor had exchanged, which she believed provided evidence showing just how strong O'Connor's feelings for her had been. She gave the letters to the police. She told several investigators and even the chief of police of her suspicions. Some of them tried to convince her that a drug dealer and not a former cop was the lead suspect.

Years later, investigators would reopen the McClinton killing. Surprisingly, the files did not contain the information Dunham had passed on to the police. Dunham, who had moved to the West Coast, was questioned again. She was still sure that someone in the police force was protecting O'Connor, the retired cop.

O'Connor left his job at Genesee not long after McClinton's death. He went to work as a security guard at a downtown Rochester bank, before landing the job as a guard at the Brink's depot.

When O'Connor's name later came up as a suspect in the Brink's robbery, the media also looked back at the McClinton homicide, discussing two common factors it had with the robbery—suspicion of O'Connor and allegations of IRA involvement. And the media also reported on another homicide that O'Connor had once been questioned about.

In 1980, a resident of the Rochester suburb of Gates had been fatally shot. The man, Alisandro Delhoyo, was in the midst of a contentious divorce proceeding with a relative of O'Connor.

Weeks before his death, Delhoyo was visiting Washington, D.C. There, a Washington cop allegedly shot up Delhoyo's car's engine, disabling the vehicle. Delhoyo accused O'Connor's brother, a Washington police officer, who was temporarily suspended from his job after the allegations.

Gates police contacted O'Connor about the Delhoyo homicide. He said that he knew nothing about it, and police could find no evidence of his involvement.

The case went cold and, like the McClinton homicide, would remain unsolved.

CHAPTER 11

— — —

FBI Special Agent Richard Vega was working on an organized crime investigation in New York City when he got a call on February 8, 1993, from a Rochester-based colleague, Paul Hawkins.

Hawkins, nicknamed "Hawk" by his colleagues, had been one of Vega's teammates when the two had both been working in Rochester. Hawkins had even done the background check on Vega when Vega, a seven-year veteran of the Rochester police force, applied for a job with the FBI.

Hawkins was now the lead agent in Rochester on the Brink's case, and he was following up on some advice from another colleague, Bill Dillon. The investigation had run into one dead end after another, but Sam Millar was still out there. The more the FBI researched his past and the more agents learned of Millar's years with the IRA, the more they wanted to find him.

The FBI and some Rochester police investigators were certain that Tom O'Connor had been the inside man in the Brink's heist. He'd been uncooperative with police; his story about the robbery was inconsistent with those told by the other guards; and now he'd hired a lawyer.

An internal FBI memo, written within twenty-four hours of the robbery, shows just how quickly O'Connor was targeted as a suspect: "Investigation to date at Rochester, NY indicates numerous inconsistencies in . . . the account of Thomas O'Connor. It is noted that O'Connor is a retired RPD [Rochester Police Department] officer who has a history of suspected improprieties and illegal activities."

Within a week of the robbery, O'Connor's alleged affinity for the IRA was also under investigation. "Prior background by the [western New York] division has determined O'Connor has been linked to the Provisional Irish Republican Army [PIRA] and has attended PIRA fundraisers in the Rochester NY area, as well as having associated in the past with PIRA members," an FBI investigator wrote.

The FBI alerted authorities in Great Britain about the heist and the possibility—remote as it might seem—of IRA involvement. All other investigative steps had produced nothing. Investigators had checked every storage unit in four New York counties in the Rochester area that had been rented in the months before the robbery. They checked the records of hotels and motels in Rochester and the surrounding region. They interviewed current and past Brink's employees.

Hundreds of hours had turned up very little information. The one lead that needed to be pursued further was Millar. He had to be found.

Following up on the information that Dillon provided the night of the robbery, investigators gathered some intelligence as a possible starting point. As the police knew, Millar's girlfriend, Bernadette Fennell, owned a gray Plymouth Voyager minivan. The car was still registered at a Rochester-area address, with the New York license plate number MLY843.

State education department records showed a Kelly Millar attending Public School (PS) 69, a high-rise red-brick elementary school in the Jackson Heights neighborhood of Queens. The girl appeared to be the right age.

Hawkins told Vega of the connections between Millar and O'Connor. Vega knew O'Connor from the days he'd worked in Rochester, and he wasn't surprised to hear O'Connor was a suspect in the heist. When Vega was new to the Rochester force, a superior officer had told him to keep his distance socially from O'Connor. The supervisor didn't explain further, but in 1987, when O'Connor became a suspect in the Damien McClinton homicide, Vega realized how wise the advice had been.

The more Hawkins revealed in the telephone call to Vega, the stranger the tale got. There'd been undertones of IRA involvement in the McClinton killing, but those leads had gone nowhere. Now there were similar undertones in the Brink's robbery, and O'Connor's name was again in the mix of suspects.

The FBI wanted to find Millar, simply to decide whether he could be connected to the robbery at all, Hawkins said. They didn't want to question him, just watch him for a while and see how he acted, see if perhaps he might be carrying around a few extra million dollars.

"How soon do you need this checked out?" Vega asked.

"I need this done like yesterday," Hawkins said.

Vega got a kick out of the urgency, and even more of a kick out of Hawkins's next request: "Can you find the van Bernadette Fennell is driving, and check the tire width?"

"Paul, this is New York City," Vega said. "This isn't the northeast [police] section of Rochester."

Vega was then working undercover surveillance for the FBI, tracking organized crime figures. He and his team—dressed in T-shirts or sports shirts and jeans—blended in wherever they went, the antithesis of the buttoned-down G-man so easy to spot as a federal law enforcement agent. They drove cars that disappeared into New York City traffic—sporty Mustangs and slightly aged Monte Carlos. Vega had a navy blue Camaro.

For Vega, surveillance was the perfect job. He hated to be in an office. He hated to wear a suit and tie. And he loved the cat-and-mouse nature of surveillance work.

That afternoon, Vega, working solo on his own time as a favor to Hawkins, went to PS 69. He strolled into a first-floor administrative office and said that he needed to speak with a high-ranking school official.

A vice-principal came to the counter. Vega showed his FBI identification and asked if he could see the school's student registry. The FBI was trying to locate a young girl, and she could be a student at the school, he said.

"Do you have a subpoena?" the vice-principal asked.

Vega did not, and he said he could come back the next day if necessary. But, he said, it would be helpful if he could see the information without the court order.

"You have to have a subpoena," the vice-principal replied, as he removed a bound book and set it on a counter in front of Vega. "But wait a minute as I go to my office."

With the man temporarily in his office, Vega opened the book—a registry of students—and scrolled through, eventually finding the name of Kelly Millar.

The administrator returned, again reminding Vega of the need for a subpoena. However, he showed a willingness to return to his office for a few more minutes if necessary. His expression—that of a man who believed that he was clandestinely serving his country—sent a quiet message: don't tell anyone I did this.

For the benefit of the other school officials in the office who'd begun to listen to the exchange, Vega said that, if necessary, he'd come back with a subpoena. He left, having found a Kelly Millar whose age matched that of the daughter of Sam Millar and Bernadette Fennell.

— — —

With this lead and the possibility that Sam Millar could well be in Queens, Vega decided to bring his team aboard. The message went out to the surveillance squad to join Vega in Jackson Heights on February 9.

As the school day came to an end on that date, FBI agents gathered near PS

69. They knew they were hunting for a Plymouth Voyager van, and Vega had provided them with a likely license plate number. The agents then blended into the scenery.

Even Vega was surprised that it didn't take long for one of his team to spot the van, which was parked only a block from the school, on 37th Avenue. The van was empty, and the agents had seen no one come or go near it. Vega couldn't believe his good luck. He'd joked with Hawkins that locating the van amid the thousands of vehicles that commuted through the Jackson Heights neighborhood—if it were even there to begin with—would be like finding the proverbial needle in the haystack. Yet somehow, the needle had been found, and found quickly.

Vega walked to the van. Hawkins had asked for information about the tires if it was found. From a distance, Vega could tell that the tires were older; the white-walls had lost some coloring and that tint of blue, common on the whitewalls of new tires, had long faded away. Vega crossed the street and passed the van, glancing down so he could check out the tires on both sides. There were three manufacturers for the set of tires, which had obviously been put on at different times during the life of the van.

Vega didn't want to risk taking more specific measurements of the tires, since its driver could appear at any minute. He returned to the pay phone on the street corner that he'd used to contact his bosses and called Hawkins at Rochester's FBI office.

Hawkins picked up the phone, hoping the news was good.

"We found the van," Vega said. As for the driver, there'd been no sign of Millar or Fennell or anyone else with the Plymouth Voyager.

Vega again surveyed 37th Avenue as he and Hawkins discussed their next steps. Vega now figured his team was in for the long haul. They were in the midst of an organized crime case, but this surveillance had a certain urgency to it. They had Millar's van, and they'd likely located his daughter. Millar probably was close by, living in the neighborhood.

"Wait a minute," Vega said, interrupting the brainstorming with Hawkins about how best to proceed.

Walking on the opposite side of the street was a man about five feet eight inches tall, with a medium build and reddish-brown hair. He was with a young dark-haired girl. The man matched the description of Millar, and the youngster appeared to be about the same age as his daughter, Kelly.

Vega told Hawkins the news. Maybe they'd found the IRA renegade whom the Royal Ulster Constabulary (RUC) and some elements in the FBI had once been so worried about. Maybe they'd even found the man who'd made off with $7.4 million a month earlier and three hundred miles away.

Vega hung up, pulling his jacket around him as he found a spot where he could keep an eye on Millar. He and his agents continued to blend in like ghosts, some walking about as if occupied by the quotidian details of life, others sitting in their cars as if waiting for a friend.

Another member of the surveillance team also saw the man. Deciding that he was a match for Millar, she quickly snapped a photo. Years later, Hawkins would still remember the clarity of that shot and how it left no question: Millar had been found.

"He was looking right at the camera," Hawkins would say. "He had no idea."

The man and girl walked right by the van and sauntered another two blocks, going into a travel agency. Ten minutes later they emerged, walked to the van, got in, and drove away. Members of the FBI team picked up the tail one by one.

The drive lasted only minutes, as Millar headed north on 37th Avenue, turned left only a mile away, and then stopped at an apartment complex. He and the girl walked into one of the apartments. From the front seat of his Camaro, Vega was not close enough to pick up the exact address, but he was able to narrow it to one of two apartments.

Millar was only at home for a short time before he came out with the girl, who Vega felt sure was Kelly, another young girl, and an infant. With Millar and the children was a petite blonde, likely Bernadette Fennell.

Back into the van the family went, and the FBI followed them to a laundromat and then a hospital. The agents again became invisible, like any other visitors in the parking lot. Twenty minutes later, Millar left the hospital with one child and drove away. Bernadette and the other children followed fifteen minutes later, taking a cab back to the apartment building on 24th Avenue in Jackson Heights.

It was early evening, and Vega and the rest of the team left the tail to let Hawkins and FBI leaders know of the day's activities. They couldn't continue to track Millar without authority from above. Vega now wanted a piece of the action. Like any driven cop, Vega hated to start an investigation that had such promise—and so many questions to be answered—and not finish it.

— — —

The following day Vega got word on the investigation's next steps. He and his team were to return to their organized crime case. The joint terrorism squad, which included law enforcement from the FBI and police from New York City

and New York State, would take over the surveillance. If there was an IRA connection—especially if Millar had channeled millions of dollars to the paramilitary
organization—the FBI wanted its terrorism agents on the hunt.

Angry, Vega confronted a supervisor about the decision. Vega felt that his
agents had long ago proven their surveillance bona fides. They'd been involved
in the continuing surveillance of the mob boss John Gotti and his murderous
underling, Sammy "the Bull" Gravano, whose testimony eventually led to Gotti's
conviction and imprisonment. There had been moments of high humor during
that surveillance. Gotti was certain he was being watched but never seemed to
know from where. More than once he got out of a car and began shouting at the
driver of another vehicle stuck behind him in traffic. "I know you're following
me," he yelled at one. The drivers would shrink into their seats, possibly recognizing the violent organized crime figure of New York tabloid fame. Meanwhile,
the agents who were actually tailing Gotti chuckled.

Vega's supervisor told him the decision was out of his hands. The terrorism
squad was taking over—immediately, in fact.

Vega was sure of one thing: he and his colleagues had done their job well. His
squad had found Millar. The FBI could have dragged Millar in right then, had
him deported by immigration officials, and let the RUC decide what to do with
him in Northern Ireland.

But unlike the situation nearly a decade before, Millar's immigration status
was not what the FBI was concerned about now. The missing $7.4 million was.

— — —

The terrorism squad wasted no time acting on the legwork of Vega's team. The
squad had its own surveillance team—known as S09—that it operated jointly
with the New York City police and New York City transit police.

By the afternoon of February 10, the team had the basic information about Millar, his residence, and the possibility of his involvement with the Brink's robbery.
That afternoon, the van was still parked outside of the 24th Avenue apartment.

Kevin Frazer, a New York City cop, was the first member of the team to see the
van. He, too, had been told that investigators wanted to check the width of the
tires. This wasn't the time—Millar or his wife might emerge from the apartment
at any moment—but he could do some elementary canvassing.

Frazer walked by the van, jangling his car keys in his hand, then dropped the
keys next to the van's front passenger tire as if by accident. He bent over and
noticed that the tires seemed new, with the whitewalls still shaded blue.

He walked for a moment more, turned around and again passed the van, stopping this time at the rear tires to tie his shoes. These tires were also new, matching those in the front. He committed the make and manufacturer's name to memory and continued on like any neighborhood pedestrian.

The surveillance team from the day before had also checked out the tires and observed something entirely different. Vega had spotted older tires, their whitewalls discolored and their tread low. Now, not even twenty-four hours later, the van was adorned with a brand-new set of Goodyears. Whether this was important or not, Frazer didn't know.

Sometimes cops are good, sometimes they are lucky, and sometimes they are both. Through Dillon's initial tip and the legwork of Vega's surveillance team, the Brink's investigation had located Millar and the van his wife owned. And the investigation was about to be blessed with yet another bit of good timing.

— — —

Late that afternoon Millar left his apartment with his infant child, whom investigators would later learn was a son named Corey. Frazer and other cops and agents shadowed him as he drove away in the van.

He stopped at a gas station, filling the tank. He then headed for McDonald's for an early dinner with his child.

Frazer and colleagues continued the tail after McDonald's. Thus far, this wasn't amounting to much of interest, save for the fact that Millar apparently didn't have a job that required him to be somewhere that day.

The van returned to the 24th Avenue apartment. But before parking, Millar made a U-turn and maneuvered the Voyager into a nearby vacant lot. He parked the van, stepped out, and opened the rear hatch.

Frazer watched as Millar pulled two tires from the back of the Voyager, dumped them in the vacant lot, then drove back to his apartment and parked outside.

Frazer waited until he was sure that Millar and his son were tucked inside their home for the evening. He went to the parking lot, picked up the tires, marked his initials on the whitewalls in case they were ever needed for evidence, and handed them in at the FBI's New York City headquarters for safekeeping.

Later, when measured, the tires would turn out to be a good match for just what the Brink's investigators were looking for. Had the police started their surveillance two days later, they likely would never have found the tires.

— — —

Surveillance is an art, requiring multiple men and women so the target is not surrounded by the same faces daily. When tailing a car, one person takes the task for a short time and then turns it over to another. The "eye" of the surveillance team—the person with the target in sight—fluctuates regularly.

Millar's travels were so short, and so restricted to the same few blocks of his neighborhood, that his trackers did not even have the time or distance for significant rotations. Yet the surveillance continued, with Millar remaining unaware of his new friends.

A decade before, he'd fled Northern Ireland, fearful that he would not escape the eye of the RUC. But now, in the new country he considered home, he was the focus of surveillance far more intense even than what he had encountered in Belfast.

The investigators still didn't get the sense that Millar had a job. Nor did Fennell seem to be employed. In the very first day of the S09 surveillance, she'd left the apartment alone and taken a cab to LaGuardia Airport. Investigators checked flight logs and found that she was traveling back to Rochester for a short visit. She was scheduled to return only days later.

Over the weekend, the cops noticed something in particular about Millar's travels around Queens. He apparently liked comic books. He made several stops at a comics store—the Strike Zone—chatting up whoever was at the counter and perusing the stacks of comics. He often didn't buy but just flipped through different comics. Occasionally he stopped at a collectibles store in the neighborhood and strolled up and down the aisles. With his wife away with their youngest child, he took his two daughters along on his travels, doing just what parents do. While there were questions about his employment, he didn't seem to be spending money extravagantly. This was just a dad with an aging van and children to keep occupied.

On February 13, Fennell left Rochester to return to her family. On her hour-long flight back to LaGuardia, holding sixteen-month-old Corey, she struck up a conversation with the woman next to her.

The two talked about their homes and their families. Fennell said she had a husband and two more children—seven-year-old Kelly and three-year-old Ashley—at home in Jackson Heights. She was a full-time homemaker, she said. She said nothing about whether her husband worked.

The two women enjoyed each other, talking amiably. Fennell's neighbor, a slender and petite woman with brown curly hair falling to her shoulders, was someone Fennell sensed she would like to know better. She was chatty and friendly, the kind of neighbor one hopes for on a flight if in a talking mood.

Fennell gave her new friend her telephone number. They got off the plane together, and there at the airport were Fennell's husband and the two young daughters she'd mentioned.

The two women said goodbye and promised to get in touch again one day.

As Fennell and her family walked away, Caryl Cid, who had been an agent with the FBI for fourteen years, pulled a notepad from her purse and quickly scribbled down all of the information she'd committed to memory from her conversation with Bernadette Fennell. She then forwarded that information to the hub of the New York City portion of the investigation.

Millar and Fennell were getting more interesting with each passing day. They had no apparent jobs but the financial wherewithal to raise three children in Queens. The rents in their apartment complex were average for a working family, but this family did not seem to be working.

Then there were those discarded tires. Why unload them in a vacant lot?

The surveillance would continue. Millar had lived in the United States for years now, and as far as the police knew, he had caused no troubles for anyone. His immigration status was of far less concern than the missing millions—and the question of whether the money might land in the hands of the IRA.

— — —

Around noon on February 26, as FBI agents and New York cops continued their watch on Millar and his family, Eyad Ismoil pulled a yellow Ryder rental van into the basement parking lot at the towering World Trade Centers in Manhattan. A Jordanian citizen who'd come to the United States to study on a student visa, the twenty-two-year-old man had become enamored with the preaching and teaching and strident anti-Americanism of a group of radical Islamists.

The van was loaded with nearly 1,500 pounds of explosives. Ismoil and a criminal colleague lit twenty-foot fuses connected to the bombs, then stepped into a waiting car, and quickly exited the garage.

At 12:17 p.m., the van erupted, exploding in a terrorist attack—a precursor of what the country would witness in the next decade. The World Trade Center towers withstood the blow, but some floors were heavily damaged, and the dense, suffocating smoke that drifted upward was too much for some tower workers to bear. Six people died, including one woman who was pregnant. Nearly a thousand people were injured.

While there had been law enforcement warnings about this new breed of radical Islam and its anti-American venom, few people had imagined an assault as bold as this. FBI agents in Manhattan, along with a significant portion of the New York City police force, were pulled into an investigation to locate the terrorists and try to ensure that there were no more targets and no more attacks on the immediate horizon.

Millar, the missing $7.4 million, even the suspicions that the money was being routed to the IRA—all of that could wait. Terrorism had visited the most vibrant city in the United States and had struck at the 110-floor towers that represented American ingenuity and pride.

The terrorism surveillance team was pulled off of the Millar case and put to work on the World Trade Center bombing investigation. It would be months before they would return, with some members fearful that the money—if Millar had any of it—would be long gone.

Instead, they would find the supposedly tough-as-nails IRA freedom fighter indulging himself in one of his lifelong passions, the same passion that had been revealed in his visits to the Strike Zone: this terrorist really liked comic books.

CHAPTER 12

— — —

The Brink's investigation was dormant.

No, it was worse than dormant, FBI Special Agent Paul Hawkins realized in the months after the World Trade Center bombing. The Brink's investigation was dead.

Before February 26 and the explosion that had killed six and had transformed lower sections of the World Trade Center's North Tower into mountains of rubble, the FBI's New York City–based antiterrorism unit had shown a particular zeal for the investigation into Sam Millar and the Brink's robbery. The surveillance had been extensive, increasing the suspicions that Millar was involved in the heist. How else to explain his and his wife's lack of employment and ability to provide for their family?

But the FBI was less concerned about the IRA than it was about the likely masterminds of the World Trade Center bombing. That investigation quickly zeroed in on Islamic jihadists who had now shown a willingness and ability to strike on American soil. American citizens were not at risk from the IRA. In fact, many US citizens and politicians supported the paramilitary organization, seeing its members as freedom fighters.

The jihadist threat had to be dealt with immediately. Otherwise, it could turn into something worse, something even more deadly.

Within the FBI, other ongoing investigations were moved to the back burner. Nearly 700 agents from around the world focused on the World Trade Center attack. Other federal law enforcement agencies, as well as the antiterrorism cops on the New York City force, joined the hunt for the killers.

A Ford Econoline rental van discovered in the rubble, with its frame and mechanical systems splintered and shredded, appeared to be the epicenter of the explosion, the likely vehicle used in the bombing. And its identification number was still intact.

With that number, investigators traced the van to a New Jersey Ryder rental agency, and, as is often the case, found that the criminal was more dimwitted than shrewd. Mohammed Salemah, who'd rented the van, was not content with his success in helping pull off the bombing. Instead, he reported the van stolen and insisted on a refund for his $400 deposit. Days after the bombing, Salemah returned to the rental agency to receive the refund he'd been promised. FBI agents, who'd been posing as workers, arrested him.

Within weeks, the FBI arrested five more Muslim fundamentalists for the bombing and murders. The investigation continued into the summer months, as the FBI worked to ascertain the scope of the jihadist organization. Some agents returned to their earlier investigations—organized crime, white-collar theft, and international drug trafficking—as the World Trade Center terrorism required fewer investigators.

In Rochester, Hawkins waited for word that the Brink's investigation would resume in New York City. He and his colleagues in western New York State had chased various leads, but none seemed as fruitful as had the earlier tail on Millar.

The FBI had received dozens of tips about the robbery, some of them bizarre and unreliable, but others worth pursuing. Shortly after the robbery, the FBI sent a notice to all of its divisions, encouraging agents nationwide to see if they could uncover any information about the robbery. One man in Portland, Oregon, who'd helped solve a bank robbery in that region, claimed to know the criminals, but he would offer no information unless he was paid $50,000 and had a pending prosecution against him dropped. The FBI declined his proposition.

An inmate in a New York prison claimed that the robbery was the handiwork of the Gambino crime family, and that a mobster connected with the family had been sent to Rochester to collect the $7.4 million only days after the crime. The FBI decided that the inmate was not credible, nor were the alleged mob connections.

Agents eyed some Boston-based gangsters who were known to pull off major heists for a living but ruled them out. In fact, during the winter and spring of 1993, they ruled out almost every theory, except the one with Tom O'Connor at the center.

"We figured Tom was the key," Hawkins later said. "We tried to talk to people who knew him a little but not enough for them to tell us to go eff ourselves."

What investigators learned was that O'Connor did not talk to a lot of people. The FBI had an informant they thought could get close to him, but the man had no luck. "Tommy was a smart guy . . . and he would smell an informant a mile away," Hawkins said.

O'Connor lived on a short street, which made it nearly impossible to watch his home without being noticed. The FBI placed a small surveillance camera on a nearby telephone pole, but within days the agents were sure O'Connor knew it was there. "He just kept looking right at it" when he'd leave the house, Hawkins said.

O'Connor had some local friends—Cahal Magee, and his brother, Liam—who'd also been active in NORAID. After the robbery, the Rochester office of the FBI launched intense surveillance of Cahal Magee, a local electrician, especially after determining that Magee had also helped harbor Millar and Bernadette Fennell when they lived in Rochester. Fennell's driver's license used an address that was actually Magee's home. But the more agents followed Magee, the less they suspected him of involvement in the robbery.

The agents also found out that it was hopeless to try to talk to either Cahal or Liam Magee. Neither was willing to cooperate.

Millar was something else altogether. Too little was known about him. Hawkins wanted to know for sure that Millar was not a player in the robbery—or that he was. If evidence pointed to the latter, then the expansive surveillance that had been in place before the World Trade Center bombing would again be needed. But while the FBI's Rochester office continued to focus on the Brink's robbery, the downstate branch of the FBI did not show the same interest.

In June, Hawkins had had enough. He went to the Buffalo FBI office, which oversaw the Rochester branch, and pleaded with his supervisors there to ask that the investigation into the depot robbery be resumed. He was joined by Dale Anderson, who ran the Rochester office. Hawkins had a proposal: Stop considering the Brink's case a terrorism investigation. Instead, assign it to the New York City agents who focused on bank robberies. The antiterrorism units had their hands full with the aftermath of the bombing, Hawkins said. Find some agents who could devote the necessary hours to tracking Millar.

Hawkins's supervisors agreed. Brink's was the fifth largest robbery of an armored car company in the nation's history, and it made no sense to abandon a likely investigative lead—namely, Millar.

Hawkins, Anderson, and an FBI supervisor from Buffalo flew to New York City to encourage the FBI leaders there to find agents who could jumpstart the tail on Millar. They carried with them the history of the case, and they reminded their New York City counterparts about the many questions still unanswered from the February surveillance of Millar and his family.

Hawkins knew he could not sway the FBI in New York City by himself. But the involvement of the Buffalo and Rochester leaders made a convincing case. The New York office promised that the tail on Millar would resume. Not only that, but the bank robbery squad would not be needed. The antiterrorism cops and agents who'd handled the surveillance months before would return to the case, at least long enough to rule Millar in or out as a suspect. If no evidence of his involvement materialized, then the Immigration and Naturalization Service could take over and ship him and his family back to Northern Ireland. There, the Royal Ulster Constabulary could worry about him.

Hawkins was elated but also wary. Who knew if Millar was still in Queens and, if he had had a hand in the robbery, whether he'd still have any of the cash with him? Months had passed, months during which Millar could have found ways to transfer the money to his IRA buddies in Northern Ireland. Time could often be an enemy for the police. Evidence vanished, and the memories of witnesses dimmed. But time could have its advantages, emboldening criminals who thought they had escaped the net of law enforcement.

Maybe, just maybe, Millar belonged in the ranks of criminals who believed themselves invincible—a superhero of the law-breaking variety. Millar liked superheroes; he had since he was a kid. His love of comics had helped him survive his tumultuous childhood and the horrors of Long Kesh. Millar could relate to troubled superhero characters like those in Marvel Comics. He'd survived the worst that humanity could throw at him, and for the noblest of reasons and causes: freedom for Northern Ireland.

What could be more superheroic than that?

— — —

Gaetano De Agostino had been dealing in comics since he was right out of college. Now in his midtwenties and a collector of both the popular and the lesser known comics, he had dozens of valuable and original comic book covers and inside page art. As a teenager, he'd worked in an art museum, where a fellow worker convinced him that comic books could be both artistically exquisite and—if preserved and historically noteworthy in the genre—valuable. He started collecting comics arts in his early twenties and then realized that, to feed what he jokingly called his "addiction," he also needed to sell some.

In the summer of 1993, he offered for sale original covers and internal art from the Silver Surfer comic series. He advertised the artwork in the premier collector publication, *Comics Buyer's Guide*. The ad prompted a quick call from a comics dealers in Queens, New York.

The possible buyer, who identified himself as Andre Singleton, clearly knew his stuff about the Silver Surfer, one of the less-recognized action figures in the Marvel universe yet one of the most compelling. Artistically, the Silver Surfer— with his gleaming metallic skin and his space-traveling craft shaped like a surf-board—was unique among the legion of Marvel warriors for good and evil.

Singleton had only recently opened a store called KAC Comics, and he was building a collection both for sale and for his personal enjoyment. He was a major fan of the Silver Surfer, and he wanted to add the art to his quickly expanding and eclectic array of comics and fanboy art.

De Agostino was accustomed to haggling with other collectors. Bartering was simply part of the process—almost entertaining. He could volley offers and counteroffers with the best of them, until either an agreement was reached or he recognized that the would-be buyer had no intention of proposing a realistic price.

Singleton discussed the art in one conversation with De Agostino, and the two agreed to talk prices in a later telephone call. The next time the two spoke, De Agostino proposed $3,125 for all of the Silver Surfer art he was selling. The game was on; he waited for Singleton to toss back a price of his own.

Singleton immediately agreed to pay the $3,125. De Agostino was surprised, but pleasantly so. Still, he wanted to be sure he hadn't missed something in the conversation.

"You don't ask for a discount?" he said.

"No."

De Agostino asked again and was rebuffed again. Singleton would pay the full price.

The sale was consummated in the fall of 1993, after Singleton sent the payment. Singleton later called De Agostino to talk about some more art De Agostino wanted to sell. De Agostino recognized the caller immediately. He thought Singleton sounded like Christopher Lambert, a French-born actor in a film De Agostino had watched that year, *Highlander*. Or, De Agostino thought, the lilt might have a touch of Sean Connery's accent.

This time Singleton was interested in some obscure comics art De Agostino advertised for sale—Gene Colan's *Tomb of Dracula* series and drawings by the famous comics graphic artist Jim Steranko, who'd helped design scenes for the film *Raiders of the Lost Ark*. Singleton also was ready to buy some more Silver Surfer art that De Agostino was selling.

Again no haggling, and the two agreed on a price of $1,100. De Agostino waited for the payment, but it didn't come. He called Singleton, who was surprised that the money order he'd put in the mail had not reached California. Maybe it had gotten lost. Singleton said he'd send the money again.

De Agostino never saw the money, and he never sent the art.

— — —

The single-story comics and collectibles store on 25th Avenue in Queens was unassuming. Outside the store, its signage touted the operation as a home for comics of the golden age, the era that gave birth to superheroes like Batman, Superman, and Captain America, as well as more recent vintage comics from the silver age, when Stan Lee's troubled and irreverent protagonists sprang to life in Marvel Comics. Also, the KAC signs proclaimed, original art comics were for sale for the serious collector.

Inside, separate rooms were connected by a single narrow hallway, which was narrowed even more by the boxes of comics lining each side. About fifty boxes, each brimming with old and new comic books, were crammed into the hallway.

The front room featured comics displayed in a glass counter, but a second room, at the end of the hallway, was the prize destination for collectors. Racks there overflowed with comics, some of them vintage publications costing hundreds of dollars. The customer who wandered back there was typically accompanied by the reserved but friendly storeowner, Andre Singleton, or one of his teenage employees.

Still, despite the bevy of comics for almost all tastes, traffic was minimal—a few teenagers here or there and the occasional older comics hoarder. On many days, no more than five people wandered into the store.

Singleton paid the teens who worked for him in cash and kept what money the operation had in a desk drawer. When a workday ended and it was time to pay the teenagers at their $3 hourly rate, he would inevitably pull out his wallet, count out a stack of $1 bills, and hand over the wages.

Store transactions were also typically in cash. Rarely, if ever, was a sale recorded in any way.

Singleton seemed to have cash to spare. He bought comics by the hundreds, piling more and more into the store. Some collectors in New York City's suburbs came to know him. When they had something for sale that he wanted, he'd come to their home and make the purchase, typically carrying thousands of dollars in cash—sometimes in $20 bills.

Some weeks a United Parcel Services truck pulled up in front of the shop and delivered new boxes of comics—often dozens in a delivery.

Singleton sometimes gave free comics to the poorer kids in the neighborhood. He appeared to have an empathy for youngsters stuck in unstable homes who found refuge in comic books.

These gracious acts made Singleton popular with the neighborhood kids. They also got a kick out of his Irish accent. Yes, the neighborhood had its ethnic mix, but the singsong melody of Singleton's voice—at least when he was inclined to say more than a few words—seemed especially foreign.

Singleton occasionally acted as protector of the kids who found their community particularly hard-edged. One slight eleven-year-old African American boy was once chased on his bicycle by three bullies who caught him, shoved him off the bike, and then ran away.

Singleton came upon the boy as he was dusting himself off. The youngster, who frequented KAC Comics, told Singleton about the neighborhood bullies. Singleton secured the bicycle and then drove the boy around the neighborhood looking for the trio. They did not find them—and the boy was unsure just what Singleton planned to do if they had—but it was an act that the boy would not forget.

There was a mystery to Singleton. One fifteen-year-old boy who worked at KAC in the evenings and on weekends occasionally asked Singleton about his life. The boy was himself a comic book aficionado, and he wondered what Singleton—who he assumed hailed from Ireland—had done to be able to finance and open a store.

The teenager had collected comics since he was in the fourth grade. He enjoyed the talks with Singleton about comics, and on several occasions he had gone with Singleton to his nearby apartment, where more boxes of comics were stored. Once, Singleton asked the teenager to help him carry a safe into the Queens apartment.

Several times Singleton told the boy a bit about his past. However, each time the outline of the biography changed. Once Singleton said that he had been born in Canada to a Canadian mother and Irish father. Another time Singleton said he grew up in Belfast.

A third version of Singleton's pre-Queens life seemed the most complete, yet the oddest. According to Singleton, he had grown up in New York City, had been a comic book vendor since he was a teenager, and once owned a comics store while living in Rochester. While he was running that store, Singleton said, an employee had stolen from him. As payment, Singleton said, he had found a few thugs who beat up the thieving employee.

The boy didn't know if the tale was true, apocryphal, or simply a warning not to walk off with comics. Nonetheless, he didn't worry too much. Singleton seemed like too nice a guy to associate with hoodlums.

Ironically, the versions of Singleton's life all contained truthful tidbits: he was a Belfast native, smuggled into the United States via Canada, who had lived in Rochester. He never had a comics store there, though he had dreamed of doing so.

And now Sam Millar—who'd used multiple aliases over the years, including Andre Singleton, Frank Saunders, Sam Campbell, and Tom O'Connor—did have his own comic books establishment. The name of the shop, KAC Comics, honored his children: Kelly, Ashley, and Corey.

This was the life he'd only imagined while surviving the horrors and brutality of Long Kesh. This was why he now loved America. Where else could he make a life like this?

— — —

The surveillance on Millar resumed on the final day of June 1993. Agents started at his home in Queens, hoping he had not moved in the four months since they'd last followed him and his family. Sure enough, Millar still lived in the same apartment—but something was new, expensively new.

On the morning the surveillance returned, the agents and New York cops realized that the Millar family van was nowhere to be found. Instead, Millar was now driving a Ford Explorer, and a very nice new cranberry red Eddie Bauer Explorer at that—a sports utility vehicle (SUV) that retailed for more than $25,000. Millar and Bernadette Fennell apparently still had money to spend.

A check of motor vehicle records showed that the Explorer had been purchased by Patrick Moloney, a priest who lived in the Lower East Side of Manhattan and ran Bonitas House, a nonprofit operation that helped troubled and homeless teenagers.

Agents set this nugget aside for later exploration. They assumed that Moloney was a friend of Millar who'd taken Millar's money and bought the SUV for him. If so, this would be money laundering, plain and simple. But the agents could return to that later. First, they needed proof that Millar had money—Brink's money.

Alternating cars to keep the Explorer in sight and navigate the traffic in Queens, the agents followed Millar for less than a mile, until he pulled up to a single-story business on 25th Avenue—KAC Comics. Millar walked to the door, pulled keys out of his pocket, and opened the store, unlocking and rolling up the security screen commonly used for protection by street-front businesses. From outside, agents could see him preparing the business for the day ahead, arranging some of the shop's display comics on front shelves.

The surveillance team was unsure whether this was Millar's new job, or whether he was the proprietor of KAC Comics. As the hours passed, teenagers strolled in and chatted with Millar, clearly knowing who he was.

Is this what former IRA guerrillas did—move to the Big Apple to sell comic books to pimply teens? In the world of crime, there was little that could surprise the FBI and New York City police, but this represented a particularly odd chapter in Millar's stormy life.

Whatever the case, whatever Sam Millar was now up to, the surveillance would continue.

And continue it did, into July. Day after day, Millar went from his apartment to the store and then, in late afternoon, back home. Sometimes he or Fennell would go to the laundromat, take the kids to McDonald's, or visit the grocery store. This surveillance routine was monotonous and, were it not for the questions about the source of Millar's money, it might well have been brought to an end within weeks after it resumed.

But, with surveillance, patience often pays off, and days in the doldrums can be the price paid for an investigative lead.

On the morning of July 13, two weeks after the resumption of the surveillance, Millar and Fennell left the apartment in the Explorer. FBI Special Agent Michelle Millane, who'd been involved in some of New York City's major mob investigations, picked up the tail.

Millar drove several blocks from home, parking on 37th Avenue at a travel agency, 747 Travel. Millane watched as Fennell went inside and talked to a woman through a plexiglass window. Fennell pulled a stack of bills nearly two inches thick out of her purse and counted out some money. She handed it through an opening in the window to the travel agency employee, who counted the money herself. Apparently satisfied, the woman handed Fennell a receipt, and she returned to the Explorer. She and Millar drove back to the apartment, then Millar headed off to KAC Comics.

Later that day, another FBI Special Agent, Deborah Flor, went to 747 Travels and spoke with the woman who'd taken the money, who turned out to be the agency's owner.

The owner still had the money in hand, and most of it—more than $3,200—was in $20 bills. Flor examined the bills, which appeared to have been well circulated and unlikely to be traceable with serial numbers, whether or not they were part of the money stolen from Brink's. But the agent asked to take the money, promising reimbursement.

Fennell had purchased a trip to Hawaii—complete with flights and hotel stays—for herself, two children, and a woman named Margaret Booth, whom she identified as an aunt.

The trip had a rush order, requiring that the tickets and hotel information be sent to the family by Federal Express. They planned to travel on July 16, only days after purchasing the package.

A hurry-up job wasn't unusual for travel agents, but there was something odd about the transaction, the owner told Flor. Fennell first inquired about traveling to Puerto Rico and appeared ready for that to be the family's vacation destination. However, once the agency owner told Fennell about travel requirements—the need to carry US residency or citizenship papers—Fennell changed her plans.

Instead, they would go to Hawaii—a more expensive trip, but one that could easily be covered by the wad of cash Fennell carried in her purse.

— — —

On July 22, Fennell, her children, and Booth returned from their week of frolicking in Hawaii. FBI agents had watched them fly out the morning of July 16, taking United Airlines through Chicago to Hawaii, and agents were again waiting at LaGuardia Airport when they returned.

Millar picked up the family and drove home. The next day, he drove Booth to John F. Kennedy International Airport, where she was scheduled to board an afternoon Virgin Atlantic flight to London.

The FBI confirmed her flight information and reached out to a customs agent, Mary Zinck, whose job was to alert international travelers about currency restrictions. The agent met Zinck at the airport and pointed out Booth in a line of travelers waiting for their flights.

Zinck approached Booth and told her of the currency rules—no more than $10,000 in cash could be carried out of the country. She told Booth that she had been randomly selected to be alerted to the rules.

Zinck handed Booth a government form—CP 503—that further explained the regulations and asked Booth to put down how much cash she had. Booth wrote that she was carrying $120.

Zinck said that she needed to search Booth's two carry-on bags. Again, she explained, this was a purely random process and Booth happened to be the unlucky person chosen. Booth appeared nervous, not speaking or objecting as she opened the bags.

Inside one bag Zinck found, amid clothes, toiletries, and traveling accoutrements, several thick stacks of $20 bills—clearly much more money than Booth had said she had on hand. Zinck told the woman that she needed to talk to a supervisor; another customs agent joined them and carried the bag aside.

The FBI had provided customs with a list of some serial numbers of the stolen Brink's money. Zinck's colleague quickly leafed through the bills—totaling $4,000—to see whether any were a match. None were. She gave the bag and money back to Zinck, who returned it to Booth.

Why all the money, Zinck asked.

Booth said that she had forgotten about the cash. She told Zinck that she had just returned from a trip to Hawaii with family, and her niece and nephew had insisted on paying all of the costs. The money she'd brought for expenses had sat in her bag, untouched during the vacation week.

Decision time was at hand. Customs or the FBI could take Booth aside and press her further about the origin of the cash. But she could easily stick with the answer she'd given, and perhaps it was honest. The $4,000—a pittance of the stolen money—was just too little to worry about. Booth's explanation was relayed to the FBI, and the agents decided to let her go.

Zinck gave Booth a mild perfunctory warning about forgetting to record the cash on the customs form. If Booth was surprised that she'd walked away with a minor rebuke, she did not show it. Nor, apparently, did she tell her family who now lived in Queens. If so, they might have begun to wonder whether they were under a vigilant eye.

Instead, they remained unaware of the surveillance teams following them morning, noon, and night.

Their next-door neighbor, meanwhile, had noticed the cars that sometimes parked nearby for unusual lengths of time. "We always used to see a lot of cops on the corner with binoculars," the neighbor later said. "Everybody in the neighborhood saw the police. But [Millar] never seemed to notice."

The neighbors did not alert Millar that he seemed to have new friends. The family was thought to be too decent and too wholesome to be involved in anything nefarious or criminal, regardless of the apparent interest in them by law enforcement officers.

"They were a very nice couple," said the woman who owned the apartment that Millar and his family rented. "They went to bed early. I saw the husband taking the kids to school, McDonald's and the movies. They had a very good family life."

The man who rented the KAC Comics space to Millar said that the Irishman "could have been father of the year."

— — —

Once Fennell and her children had returned from Hawaii, the routine resumed: Millar went from home to KAC Comics in the morning and back to the apartment late in the day. There were the occasional domestic stops at grocery stores, banks, and pharmacies and the trips to McDonald's, clearly a popular dining spot for the children.

The routine was so fixed and so reliable that Deborah Flor noticed when, on July 25, Millar made a slight deviation from his typical day.

All it took was for Millar to walk out of his shop and head east. Flor took note. She knew that east was away from Millar's vehicle and home, and that he usually did not go that direction when he left the store. She alerted her colleagues.

Not far from the shop, Millar approached a parked two-toned green van. He climbed in the passenger's side.

In the driver's side was a sprightly white-haired man with a thin beard and wire-rimmed glasses. The two hunched over as they talked, occasionally peering at some object between them.

After ten minutes, Millar stepped out of the van, carrying a small cardboard box. The mystery man did a U-turn and drove away. The surveillance team was intrigued, and some of them followed the van as it made its way out of Queens and into Manhattan's Lower East Side.

There, the driver parked and entered a five-story brownstone called Bonitas House, the home for wayward teenagers.

The van, records showed, was owned by the Rev. Patrick Moloney, who also happened to be the individual in charge of Bonitas House—and the same person who had bought the Explorer that was now being driven by Millar. Moloney even had an odd connection to Rochester. The van he now owned had been transferred to him by Cahal Magee, a friend of Millar in Rochester and an Irish American active in NORAID.

Moloney was becoming increasingly interesting to the investigators. They decided to dive deeper into his past, looking at any business records, nonprofit records, motor vehicle records, and criminal records they could find.

The background check revealed Moloney to be an individual active in anti-poverty causes and willing to fight for those on the fringes of society—men and women struggling for life and livelihood as some Manhattan neighborhoods were becoming more gentrified. He was beloved by many, a good Samaritan with a bit of the anti-establishment rebel in him.

Moloney also had a reputation as a firebrand speaker with a fierce hatred of British control over Northern Ireland. NORAID chapters sometimes asked him to speak, including the one in Rochester. There, Moloney had befriended Cahal Magee and his family, and Magee had given Moloney the van for him to use at Bonitas House.

There was something else in Moloney's past that could not be ignored. He and his brother, John, had once been arrested in Ireland and accused of running weapons for the IRA.

Apparently, the good father and Millar shared a common passion—for the IRA.

CHAPTER 13

— — —

In 1984 the IRA had a nagging problem it wanted to disappear for a while: Liam Adams, the brother of the popular politician Gerry Adams.

A survivor of Long Kesh prison, Gerry Adams had recently been chosen to be president of Sinn Fein, the IRA's political party. Adams appeared to be an up-and-coming man who could walk the fine line between the angry activism of some supporters of an independent Northern Ireland and the staid political circles where the important decisions about the region's future would be decided.

Liam was the polar opposite of his brother. Gerry was charismatic, handsome, and charming; Liam was rumpled, slovenly, and unreliable. If Gerry Adams was the future of the movement, Liam Adams could well be its albatross.

Liam's marriage had collapsed; years later he would be convicted of the sexual abuse of a daughter from the marriage. Liam had a new girlfriend whom he wanted to marry—a plan that ran into opposition from the Roman Catholic Church—and the IRA decided not to risk the likelihood that Liam would create headlines and headaches for his brother. Instead, the IRA quietly sent Liam to New York City, where a friendly priest who was an ally to the movement was known to shelter IRA members and others in need of hiding or new identities.

Indeed, Father Patrick Moloney did not hesitate when called on to take in Liam Adams, as well as Liam's new girlfriend. "He was just a loose wire in some ways," Moloney said of Liam. "And they were also a little bit afraid of him. How shall I put this? He was a weak link in the chain. I don't think they trusted him."

A priest who ran a home for troubled teens in a New York neighborhood mired in poverty, drug abuse, and crime, Moloney had been an occasional resource for the IRA and its sympathizers. His Bonitas House was a refuge.

Ed Moloney (no relation to Patrick Moloney), who has written extensively on the history of the IRA, once wrote of the priest's home: "During the worst years of the Troubles, Bonitas House became a port of call for indigent IRA men, refugees on the run from the authorities back home, or who wanted a break from Belfast or Derry and were in need of a fresh identity and a start in New York away from the prying eyes of the FBI.

"For [Father] Moloney, this was a natural extension of his republican views and background. When the Troubles erupted, he had gravitated towards support groups that sprang up in New York. . . . In later years, he said the prayers at fundraising events organized by the largest pro-Provo group, Irish Northern Aid, and he had what can only be described as a colorful association with the sharper end of the IRA."

Like Sam Millar, a man whom Father Moloney would meet and befriend in New York City, Moloney had grown up in a home ripe for the cultivation of IRA sympathies. But Moloney's home was different from Millar's. Where Millar gravitated to the IRA because of the stability it provided, even if among a criminal element, Moloney was born into a home that buzzed with passion for the movement.

Moloney's father, a cabinetmaker, was a freedom fighter during the Irish Civil War of the 1920s. An opponent of the Anglo-Irish Treaty—a pact that some people considered an abandoning of independence for Northern Ireland—Moloney's father was imprisoned for three years in the Curragh, a military facility transformed in part into an internment area for IRA rebels.

With five children—Moloney's mother had two miscarriages before the oldest surviving child was born—the couple struggled financially. Living in a cramped single-room tenement apartment in Limerick, Moloney would later say, was comparable to the Irish poverty brought to ugly and visceral life in Frank McCourt's bestselling *Angela's Ashes*.

Still, Moloney's household was a loving one. His mother was a housewife who'd come from a higher social echelon. "It was like a step down to marry a carpenter," Moloney said.

The Moloneys made sure that their children were cared for and educated. The children attended Catholic schools, run by, as Moloney would later jest, "the merciless Sisters of Mercy." He also studied in middle schools headed by the Irish Christian Brothers. "They would beat the knowledge into you if you let them," he said.

The tough edges of the religious school instructors did not deter Moloney from an interest in the Catholic faith. Instead, he found in religion a source of hope and a way to better the lives of those in need. He saw the British oppression in his own neighborhood and read avidly about the civil rights movement in the United States.

Moloney's interest in religion was fostered by his grandfather, a Protestant who as a young man had been known for repeated drunkenness.

When Moloney was a young boy, his grandfather told him how religion had saved him from alcoholism. Once, when he was in his twenties he heard the tolling of bells from a great distance. The sound captivated him, and even though he was staggeringly drunk at the time, he walked toward the bells, as if summoned by something more powerful than the mere music. He claimed he walked a great distance to reach the bells and their home—a monastery run by Trappist monks.

Realizing their visitor's besotted state, the monks asked him if he wanted to be clean. He agreed to stay, and, in a "cold turkey" treatment mixed with prayers and regular meals, he beat his alcoholism.

The story fascinated young Patrick Moloney, especially the monks' ability to speak only when necessary. There was no idle chatter, just a silent union with God. As a young teenager he decided that he too would be a religious hermit, a monk dedicated to God.

But the opportunities in the United States appeared grander (and Moloney was not inclined toward silence). There, in the land of the supposed free, Moloney decided he could make a difference.

"I almost spent part of my life as a hermit monk," Moloney said. "God didn't want me there."

In the mid-1950s, Moloney, in his early twenties, immigrated to the United States and took up residence in New York City. He planned to study for the priesthood at his own pace. He eyed a monastic community in Vermont and moved for a short time to Baltimore before returning to New York City to study at St. John's University.

Though he knew of the oppression of blacks in the United States, he was surprised at the depth of poverty in the country, especially in New York City's Lower East Side.

"It was a bit of a shock because I certainly thought America was the land of milk and honey, the land of plenty," Moloney said. Instead, he found poverty there to rival that in Limerick.

He settled into an apartment he rented for $11.50 a month in Alphabet City, a Lower East Side neighborhood that was known as a longtime enclave for

European-born immigrants. Just as in Limerick, he encountered street urchins on the single-letter avenues that gave the neighborhood its name.

The children were an impoverished ethnic mix, and many had fallen into gang activities.

Moloney worked with the Staten Island–based Sisters of Mercy, introducing the youngsters to worlds that were foreign to them. Occasionally, he'd take them beyond the high-rise confines of Manhattan to a camping area on Staten Island. Dorothy Day, the cofounder of the Catholic Worker Movement, helped Moloney provide new opportunities for the children. "Nobody but a woman like Dorothy would have tolerated the kids we had to work with," Moloney said.

With the assistance of the *Catholic Worker,* a publication of the Catholic Worker Movement, he and the poor children traveled to fourteen acres in rural New Jersey—property that included a Civil War–era home. With volunteers and donated materials, they renovated the deteriorating house and established a summer camp on the property.

He befriended the youngsters and their families and looked for other ways to help them. At St. John's, he found other young idealistic people willing to pitch in and created Bonitas Youth Services. They opened a storefront center at 713 E. 9th Street—between Avenues C and D—designed to help needy youngsters.

In 1961, a fire destroyed the New Jersey property—a blaze some supporters of the project suspected was the handiwork of a racist element in the neighborhood. The news coverage of the fire brought attention to Moloney's small volunteer network, and its ranks began to grow. To this day, Moloney is unsure of the fire's cause, and he thinks it could have been accidental.

Some wealthy liberal Manhattanites, disturbed by the fire, also wanted to help.

The Bonitas volunteers eyed a home for sale at 606 E. 9th Street. Moloney approached a partnership of investors that had purchased the home with hopes of flipping it. Instead, they sold it to Bonitas Youth Services for a small amount of money that included a $1,500 down payment provided by a Bonitas supporter.

That was one of the few monetary donations that Moloney used. He wanted materials that would help, not money.

Moloney again enlisted volunteers and, using donated construction materials, transformed the house into a refuge for runaway and homeless teens and youngsters referred there by juvenile courts. The home, always willing to feed the hungry, was a beacon in a blighted neighborhood. It took the name Bonitas House, befitting a charitable operation working to pull a community out of a downward spiral.

Neighborhood residents wanted to help, but Moloney was hesitant to accept money from working-class families, most of whom were struggling just to get by. Instead he asked them for furniture and art and books—anything they'd stored in an attic or closet and were unlikely to use again.

"I was kind of a very good beggar," Moloney said.

Clothes also were helpful, Moloney said. Perhaps you've put on a few pounds, he'd tell a supporter of Bonitas House—somehow the smiling Moloney could get away with such a remark—and were unlikely to slip back into your old clothes. Moloney used the donated clothes for the young men at Bonitas House, or sold them to raise money for the house.

Meanwhile, Moloney completed his training for the priesthood, opting to be ordained within the Melkite order, which followed the traditions of Eastern Catholicism.

With a mischievous gleam in his eye and a willingness to thumb his nose at authority figures of any type, Moloney assumed a near-folk-hero status on the Lower East Side. He was the subject of admiring profiles in newspapers that reveled in his unceasing activities for the poor. He was especially well known among the homeless and drunks who had transformed Tompkins Square, a ten-acre park only blocks from Bonitas House, into their own community—much to the irritation of City Hall and the police.

When the park became a shantytown, with protesters angry that the police were trying to force the homeless out, Moloney stepped right in the middle of the dispute, joining those who were arrested.

"The protesters are a loose coalition of squatters, anarchists, Marxist ideologues, mainstream liberals and others who see the city's effort to clean the park and demolish squatters' buildings as a concerted plan to push the homeless and poor out of the neighborhood, so developers can reap a profit from rehabilitating buildings," the *New York Times* wrote.

Moloney always wore his IRA sympathies on his sleeve. As the *Times* wrote, "Father Moloney is the son and grandson of I.R.A. fighting men, and he keeps his father's Fenian rifle nearby and Irish nationalist posters hanging in his room. Above his headboard is a postcard for the Provisional IRA and a snapshot of himself at a protest supporting the hunger striker Bobby Sands in 1981."

Moloney was often asked to speak at NORAID events, where, while not advocating the use of violence as a solution for Northern Ireland, he never quite condemned it either. As he told *City* newspaper, "I deplore any civilian violence. I want to be very clear on that point. There should never be a civilian target.

"But I quote—and I hate to quote the likes of him—Ronnie the rogue, former President of the United States, when challenged on what happened in Grenada where . . . people were killed in a mental hospital, some of them children. Reagan's response was that there will necessarily be civilian casualties in war."

This attitude made Bonitas House, under the watchful eye of Moloney, a natural hiding place for IRA rebels on the run. And this attitude made it easy for British and American authorities to believe that Moloney would go to any length to assist the IRA—even engaging in criminal activities.

— — —

In 1982 an FBI agent infiltrated the ranks of the so-called Provisional IRA in America, men living in Boston and New York City who were finding ways to move money and weaponry from supporters in the United States to the frontline warriors in Northern Ireland.

The undercover agent was so successful that he was able to participate in the planning of a major arms shipment to Northern Ireland—nearly $4 million worth of explosives and guns. Federal authorities arrested some of the American-based Provos after seizing twelve containers of arms in Newark on their way to Northern Ireland.

The FBI worried about allowing the containers to continue their journey. What if the agents lost track of the weapons and they ended up in the hands of the IRA? "We were getting a lot of heat from headquarters because they were afraid," said Lou Stephens, who was the lead agent in the investigation.

Authorities decided to let one carton go through. Containing a mix of roller skates, bullet-proof vests, ammunition, and a rifle, the carton was destined for John Moloney, an American-based importer and exporter who also had a home in Ireland.

The container was scheduled to arrive at John Moloney's home at the same time he was there along with his brother—Father Patrick Moloney—to celebrate their father's eighty-seventh birthday.

On the day the container arrived at the low-income housing complex where the Moloney patriarch lived, a carful of Garda—the local police force—arrived almost simultaneously. John Moloney and two friends—Patrick McVeigh and Michael Henniger—were prying the lid off the container when the four police officers swarmed in. One of the Garda fired a shot into the air.

"There's gangsters here," Henniger yelled to his wife, not immediately recognizing the police. "Get the child in."

Parents scurried to gather their children, who were playing in a worn field in the complex.

"What are you doing?" a neighborhood woman yelled at the Garda.

"We are blasting," an officer answered, braced for a possible exchange of gunfire. "Clear the children."

McVeigh, a longtime IRA activist who'd once been the target of an assassination attempt, sprinted off. A few blocks away, an officer captured him.

The police arrested John Moloney for possession of the weapons and McVeigh for membership in the IRA. Patrick Moloney, who'd been inside his father's home, accompanied his brother to the police station.

An hour later, the police also arrested Father Moloney for weapons possession. At his initial bail hearing, Father Moloney pleaded for leniency. "I was in the wrong place at the wrong time," he said, a statement similar to claims he would make a decade later, after the Brink's heist in Rochester.

Moloney told the judge that he needed to return to the United States to continue his work at Bonitas House. The children there needed him, he said.

Told by prosecutors that the evidence against the Moloney brothers was substantial, the judge ordered both of them jailed, along with McVeigh. Father Moloney spent five days in jail before being released by the judge, who'd yet to see any of the solid proof against Moloney that the police had promised to provide. The release was not without conditions: Moloney had to appear at a police station three times a week.

Moloney complained. He had a letter directly from the papal nuncio and American labor leaders urging the judge to allow him to return to New York, he said. "No book of evidence has been produced here and I am only held by the devil's advocate on the threat of further charges," Moloney told the court.

The judge told Moloney to sit down and shut up. Another hearing was scheduled for a later date, he said, and any further bail considerations would be taken up then. "The court will not take anything like [the nuncio's letter] into account now," the judge said.

Moloney continued to rail against the court, angering the judge, who said: "The court has given you the benefit of the doubt up till now [and] would advise you strongly to sit down now."

The courtroom kerfuffle ended there, but at the next hearing the judge's ire would be redirected—toward the prosecution. More than a month after Moloney's arrest, the prosecutor informed the court that he'd decided to drop all charges against the priest. The judge asked what had happened to all of the supposed proof of Moloney's guilt.

The prosecutor said the investigation had been thorough, but fairness dictated that Moloney be removed from the list of the accused. "This court must conclude that Father Moloney is entitled to a bit more than having the charges dropped," the judge said.

Still, the prosecutor offered nothing more about why the charges needed to be dismissed. Moloney returned home and tried to rally support for his brother through the media and friends. The legal proceeding was a sham, he contended, and his brother was being denied the legal rights he should have as an American citizen.

"John is a United States citizen and his constitutional rights have been violated because he had no power of subpoena—witnesses, I may add, who could prove his innocence," Moloney told one reporter.

Moloney said he was appalled by the police who had arrested him and asked whether he was really a priest, a question he had also heard from a reporter for a Dublin newspaper who asked about the legitimacy of his priesthood. "To them, the fact that I am not a Roman priest means I am not a priest at all," he said.

John Moloney ultimately pleaded guilty to possession of the AR180 semiautomatic rifle and the 672 rounds of ammunition that had been hidden beneath the roller skates in the container. He was imprisoned in Ireland and returned to New York City after his release.

Two years after Moloney's conviction, McVeigh was also found guilty in a case that, for the first time, included FBI agents and federal prosecutors from the US Attorney's Office testifying in a Northern Ireland courtroom.

The convictions of Moloney and McVeigh were a small part of an investigation that, according to the FBI, when coupled with the American arrests, had kept an arsenal out of the hands of the IRA. "It was better than sex," FBI Special Agent Stephens told the PBS news show *Frontline*, in a show about the IRA. "Three times better. We really saved a lot of lives."

A decade after his conviction, John Moloney was interviewed by the British edition of *Esquire*. Asked about the criminal case and his earlier claims of innocence, he answered: "Me, well, I'll say this: I didn't know exactly what was in the container, but you could say I knew generally. I did my time. I'm not ashamed of what I did.

"I'd do it again."

But Moloney said his brother, the Melkite priest, was completely innocent: "Pat had nothing to do with it at all. Nothing whatsoever."

Despite his brother's insistence on his innocence, despite the lack of evidence, and despite the dismissal of the criminal charges against him, Patrick Moloney would never escape the taint of the allegations that he had run guns for the IRA. Years later, when FBI agents saw him hanging out with Millar—a man for whom he'd apparently purchased a costly Ford Explorer—Moloney's past criminal allegations fit neatly with the FBI's suspicions of an IRA-orchestrated theft of millions of dollars.

Moloney would do little to free himself of those suspicions.

CHAPTER 14

— — —

Sam Millar was loading bags into the back of his Explorer—good-size black duffel bags bulging with whatever was crammed inside. Maybe it was wishful thinking on the part of the surveillance team, but the sharp rectangular edges pressed against the nylon fabric looked a lot like stacks of cash.

Counting the February surveillance, the team had now spent about two months watching Millar. How he hadn't spotted his new friends was anybody's guess, but many of the agents were itching for something to happen soon.

There had been a few moments that at least kept the investigators' curiosity piqued. In late July, Millar had left the store and gone to a nearby post office, where he picked up a money order for $700, paying in cash. A New York City Transit detective, part of the surveillance team, had walked in behind Millar and occupied himself at a nearby counter as Millar pulled a thick, precounted wad of cash for the purchase. Millar then left, went to another post office in the area, and paid cash for a second money order.

Now it was the morning of August 3, and the heat was moving from tolerably muggy to oppressive. The temperatures were inching upward daily, the humidity thickening into soup. A cool spell was predicted for later in the week, but for the next few days, the forecasts called for steamy temperatures in the mid-90s, the type of weather that brought some parts of the city to odiferous life.

Millar was working up a mild sweat, loading the weighty bags into his suv. He then drove to the comic store and unloaded a box, packed with comic books, into it. Later in the afternoon, he drove home for a brief spell and then returned to the shop. Around 5:00 p.m., he shut down the store and headed back to the apartment.

This was shaping up as another typical day in the life of Millar and more doldrums for the cops—except for those mysterious bags in the Explorer and the mounds of money that might be inside. Years later an FBI agent would still be amazed at how Millar did nothing to hide the fact that the bags were packed with money, the outline of the cash so obvious. "You think he would have used a box," the agent said.

Then, after a brief stop at his apartment, Millar returned to the Explorer. New York City Transit Police Detective Michael Mandzik and officers in two other cars picked up the tail.

Millar rarely traveled beyond his Queens neighborhoods, except for occasional trips to the John F. Kennedy International or LaGuardia Airports. Now Millar was heading south through Queens, dealing with the stop-and-go rush-hour traffic. The SUV's distinctive color—there weren't many others like it on the road—helped the cops keep the vehicle in sight.

Millar drove into Manhattan across the 59th Street Bridge—the span made famous by Paul Simon and Art Garfunkel's "feelin' groovy" refrain—and passed through the Bowery and into the commercial Stuyvesant Town neighborhood.

Millar parked in front of 330 First Avenue, a high-rise apartment building. He pulled the two duffel bags from the rear of the Explorer and headed into the building, unlocking a front security door for access. Then he returned empty-handed to the Explorer, unloaded two more bags from the vehicle, and carried them into the apartment building.

Mandzik left his car and walked to a shoe store near the apartment building. Millar came out again and pulled another smaller duffel bag and a gray backpack from the Explorer. He tossed the backpack over his shoulder, as Mandzik, apparently eyeing the shoes in the shop's window, watched Millar's reflection in the glass.

When Millar went to unlock the door to the apartment building's main lobby again, Mandzik followed him. Millar walked through the door, and Mandzik caught it before it could close and the lock snap shut. Standing beside Millar, Mandzik played the part of a resident waiting for an elevator. Millar said nothing.

An elevator arrived. Mandzik opened the door and motioned for Millar to go in ahead of him. Millar declined the polite gesture with a shake of his head.

Mandzik stepped inside the elevator, got off on the first floor, and took the stairs back down to the lobby. He peeked out from the stairwell door and saw that Millar was no longer in the lobby.

Mandzik left the building, radioing his colleagues about Millar's location. Dinnertime activity was picking up on the street—home to a combination of shops, restaurants, and apartment buildings—when Millar came out, again carrying nothing.

He got into the Explorer and pulled out into First Avenue traffic. Mandzik directed his colleagues to follow Millar. He planned to stay at 330 First Avenue a little longer. He'd decided the place might merit some more attention.

— — —

Millar's visit to the apartment building infused the surveillance team—and, for that matter, the investigation—with a new energy. There had been plenty to raise suspicions about Millar—the comics store that somehow survived with little in the way of clientele, his family vacations, the wads of cash he and Bernadette Fennell always seemed to have at hand—but nothing to justify an arrest. Thus far, the money that had been inspected from the travel agency and Margaret Booth was not a match with cash from the Brink's robbery. That didn't prove that the money hadn't been stolen from Brink's; the company had the serial numbers of only a small percentage of the $7.4 million. But to make a criminal case, some money that could be tied to the robbery had to be found.

The surveillance team decided to set up a rotating squad at 330 First Avenue, just in case Millar returned. If nothing suspicious happened in coming days, or if Millar didn't come back, the decision could be reexamined and new investigative steps mapped out. But there were more than three hundred apartments in the building, and little could be done unless Millar returned. There were no surveillance cameras inside the building's hallways, so any attempts to determine where Millar had left the duffel bags and backpack would likely be futile.

On the afternoon of August 8, Millar did return to the apartment building. He was inside when New York City Police Detective Gary Beekman arrived at 330 First Avenue for his afternoon shift. Beekman decided he'd take a chance and see if he could narrow down just where in the building Millar was going. Figuring out which of the thirteen floors he visited would be a start.

As a resident stepped out of the apartment building, Beekman stepped in. He went to the elevators and found neither at the lobby level. Lighted floor numbers above the elevators told him just where they were now stopped.

Beekman pushed buttons, summoning the elevators to the lobby. Both came down empty. He waited and watched as the doors closed and the elevators again started upward. He noted the floor where the elevators came to a halt.

Several times the elevators returned to the ground floor, either empty or with someone stepping out whom Beekman did not recognize. Beekman waited patiently, the work of a surveillance cop now shifting from biding one's time in a car to biding one's time in an apartment building lobby. Luckily, no one else was in the lobby who might grow curious about his loitering there.

One elevator ascended, stopping at the tenth floor before returning to the lobby.

Out stepped Millar. He wasn't alone: with him was the priest, Patrick Moloney, who it seemed was becoming increasingly attached to Millar.

Beekman had now added some information to the investigation: Millar was apparently going to the tenth floor. Just where on that floor was the next question to answer. Then investigators could try to find out what he'd been carrying in those mysterious bags.

— — —

The cops didn't have to wait long before Millar and Moloney returned to the Manhattan apartment.

Over the next few days, they visited the building several times. Once they left it and went to a nearby cafe, downing Budweisers, according to police surveillance reports. They then took Millar's (or Moloney's, since he had bought it) Explorer back to Queens and stopped at a popular Irish pub. The drinking continued, and the two walked out, staggering slightly according to police logs of the day. (By all accounts, Moloney has been a teetotaler his entire life; he later claimed that the FBI mistook a relative of Millar for him.)

On another August day, as the investigators wandered along First Avenue, mixing with regular pedestrians, one agent noticed Moloney leaving a black Ford Taurus nearby. Three men—none of them Millar—were with him.

The men stepped out of the Taurus and locked the doors. Unfortunately, none of them had turned off the ignition, and the engine was still running.

Realizing their faux pas, one of the men went into a nearby shop and returned with a coat hanger. He slipped the hanger through the driver's side window and manipulated it for fifteen minutes before he was finally able to grasp the pop-up lock and open the door.

This time, they locked the car with the engine turned off. Members of the surveillance team shook their heads, realizing that these guys—if they were criminals at all—were not criminals of the brightest variety.

With the comedy routine of the foursome complete, FBI Special Agent Julian Clark Jr. followed them into the apartment building. He stepped into the elevator with Moloney and the others. Clark waited as Moloney pushed the button for the tenth floor, confirming the earlier suspicions. Clark then pushed the button for the eleventh floor.

At the tenth floor, Clark was able to hold the elevator door ajar and watch Moloney and the others enter apartment 10D. Clark could only wonder whether there might be millions of dollars in the apartment. Once he reported the news to the rest of the surveillance team and his superiors, they wondered the same thing.

— — —

Despite its rigorous attentiveness, the surveillance squad did not have Millar and Moloney under watch at all times. And during August and September, much happened that they did not observe that would have elevated suspicions even more.

In early August, Moloney visited Tampa, Florida, where he had plans to open a new home similar to Bonitas House. One afternoon, Emilio Penalver, a security guard at the Bank of Tampa, was strolling through the bank's parking lot. There had been a rash of purse snatchings there and nearby, and the bank security guards were trying to keep a more vigilant eye out for would-be criminals.

In the lot, Penalver spotted two men hunched over inside a parked car. As he walked closer, he could see what they were doing. "They were counting money," he later said.

The white-haired man on the driver's side wore a priest's collar and noticed Penalver approaching. The priest appeared unbothered. The two men were holding stacks of money, each an inch or two high. A briefcase filled with cash lay open between them. The amount of cash was "considerable," Penalver said.

Penalver walked to the car's open window and warned Moloney of the recent crimes in the area. He encouraged Moloney to "go inside the bank" if he needed to count money.

"We are going to open an account in a few minutes," Moloney answered.

"I know, sir, but this is not a safe place to do it."

"Okay," Moloney said.

Penalver returned to the bank and, moments later, saw the priest enter. Penalver was pleased that the priest was now inside, with his money secure. Penalver, with an ulterior motive, approached Moloney and stopped him. Moloney recognized the guard and smiled at him.

Penalver, a devout Catholic, asked for a blessing, and Moloney accommodated him in the bank lobby, placing his hand on Penalver's head and assuring him of his single importance in the eyes of God.

"Well, I'm Catholic," Penalver later said, when asked why he had made the request. "I thought he was Catholic, too, so I asked him. . . . 'I want to be blessed.'"

His godly work complete, Moloney went to a counter. He pulled a wad of cash from his pocket and told the teller that he wanted to open an account. He had $21,000 to start the account, Moloney said.

The teller, Rebecca Melton, informed him that, along with the basic forms for opening an account, she would need to fill out a Currency Transaction Reporting Form (CTR). The federal government required the form—which had been created to alert authorities to possible money laundering—for individual deposits of more than $10,000.

Moloney assured Melton that his motives were not nefarious. He planned to open a home for troubled children in Tampa, he said, similar to one he operated in New York City.

Neither Moloney's charm nor his religious collar could sway Melton. The law was the law; she had to complete a CTR. Also, she said, the CTR would be forwarded to the Internal Revenue Service (IRS).

Moloney's typically unvarying smile disappeared. He again questioned the need for the CTR. Melton told him that she was complying with the law, and that the form was used to alert the IRS to any suspicious movement of money.

Perhaps, Moloney said, he could open the account with $9,000. He would return on other days and deposit the rest in increments of less than $10,000.

Melton told Moloney that she could lose her job if she allowed the money to be deposited over several days.

By now, Melton had had enough. Whatever the priest's intent, however solid and devout his connection with God, he was not acting like someone who simply wanted to open a bank account. She said that she would need to fill out the CTR and report the transaction regardless. Melton believed that Moloney wanted to circumvent the CTR requirements.

Moloney suggested another option: he'd write a check to open the account. Melton would not budge; she'd still fill out the CTR, she said.

Moloney finally opened an account with $1,000, an amount that he apparently assumed would not trigger a CTR. But his repeated attempts to sidestep the law had proved too much for Melton. The bank sent a CTR as an alert to the IRS, highlighting a box on the form denoting "suspicious activity."

Weeks later, Moloney visited the Empire Safe Company in Manhattan, which sold safes of all sizes and protective strengths.

Moloney was looking for two safes, a small one that would fit in his car and a larger one to keep at his home, he told the salesman. In the larger safe, he planned to secure important papers and upward of $20,000 in cash. Attired in his priestly garb, Moloney wandered the store, looking at different safes, and told the salesman he'd likely return later.

Business had been particularly slow for the salesman. Over the next few days he called Moloney repeatedly at a number the priest had given him. Moloney never answered, and the prospect of the sale dimmed.

But weeks later, after the salesman had given up on him, Moloney returned. He first chose a small safe that would provide several hours of protection from fire for whatever was stashed inside.

As Moloney had indicated, he also wanted a larger safe. He settled on a model with an electronic push code for entry and multiple protections against burglars. Moloney had earlier told the salesman he'd pay in cash, and he did just as he had promised. The total cost was just under $1,500, and Moloney paid mostly in $100 bills.

The cash payment was good news for the salesman, and part of the reason he had kept after Moloney with phone calls. The salesman was having monetary problems at home. He did not record the sale to Moloney. Instead, he pocketed the cash.

On another day, in the early weeks of a brilliant fall, a Westchester County real estate broker thought she had a certain sale. A priest, Father Patrick Moloney, had contacted her about a family that wanted to escape the hurly-burly of life in Queens and settle into a sylvan suburb with good schools. Westchester County seemed the perfect fit.

Home sales had been flat, and few new homes were coming on the market. In addition, many of the homes for sale in Westchester County—million-dollar estates—were out of the range of most prospective buyers. But there were some homes in the $300,000 range that the broker felt comfortable showing the family. Moloney had said that the church intended to help finance the purchase if necessary.

One morning the broker met the family—Andre Singleton, who owned a comics store; his wife, Bernadette; and their three young children. Moloney rode with the broker in her car, and the family followed in their Explorer.

The broker was not bothered by Singleton's occupation. She recognized just how much money could be made in the comics and collectibles business. One former buyer had been in the same business and had bought a home much costlier than what Singleton was considering.

They visited two homes, including a charming four-bedroom contemporary house on a quiet cul-de-sac in Ossining. Only a half-mile away, at the end of the cul-de-sac and within easy walking distance, was an elementary school for the kids. The family seemed especially taken with this house.

In late afternoon, the broker and Moloney and the Singleton family went their separate ways, agreeing to talk again later. She did not hear from them again and figured they were taking their time making a decision. A new school year had started, and perhaps they did not want to disrupt the schedule of the children. The market was starting to percolate a little more, and homes would likely be available when the Singleton family and their benefactor priest wanted to make a purchase, if they ever did.

— — —

Throughout October, the surveillance team watched as Moloney and Millar visited 330 First Avenue. Apartment 10D was rented in the name of Charles McCormick, and agents had looked into his background. He'd had various jobs, including teaching parolees, but nothing that counted as a steady career. Agents kept a photograph handy should McCormick ever show up. Balding, trim, and professorial in appearance, McCormick was a bit of an enigma. His connection to Moloney or Millar was unclear, though his last job—records showed that he was now unemployed—had been in the same Lower East Side neighborhood as Bonitas House.

McCormick had been seen stopping in at the apartment, but only rarely. And unlike Moloney and Millar, he was not entering or leaving the apartment with anything that seemed suspicious. However, Moloney and Millar had been in the apartment enough times to convince the squad that apartment 10D could well be a stash house for money.

In early November, FBI Special Agent Louis Stith, the lead agent on the Brink's case in New York City, got permission from his bosses to ramp up the surveillance even more by adding an electronic eye to the team—a camera planted on the tenth floor so all comings and goings there could be observed.

The building owner gave the FBI access to the tenth floor, and agents affixed a pinhead-size video camera on an exit sign at a stairway. The camera pointed directly at apartment 10D. Agents secured a transmitter on the roof of the apartment building, and the transmitter served as a conduit, transferring video from the camera to the FBI headquarters in Manhattan.

At headquarters, three shifts of agents monitored the video, which was captured on cassettes, around the clock. Once Millar paused and stared directly at the exit sign, as if something had caught his attention. But again he remained oblivious to the continued scrutiny of his activities.

On November 7 Moloney returned to the apartment building alone, driving a white Plymouth Reliant with rental tags. He carried a white plastic bag close to his chest, struggling to hold the bag securely.

Mandzik thought at first that Moloney was carrying a small appliance. He noticed a beige device poking from the opened top of the bag. Then he recognized what the device was—a money counter.

After Moloney entered 330 First Avenue, Mandzik returned to his van, only to spot Millar walking toward the apartment building. The video camera filmed Moloney and Millar entering apartment 10D together. They stayed inside for an hour, and then Moloney exited and returned to the street and the Reliant.

Mandzik maneuvered his van out of its parking spot and followed Moloney. Only blocks away, Moloney came to a stop at an Avenue C stoplight. Mandzik pulled alongside, stopping at the Reliant's passenger side.

Moloney's attention was no longer on the traffic signal. He had in his hand what Mandzik thought was an inch-thick stack of cash, and Moloney was leafing through the bills, counting the money.

He counted intently for thirty seconds. Then he noticed that the light was now green and drove off. Mandzik did not follow, abiding by one of the key surveillance rules—don't be obvious.

FBI Agent Deborah Flor had also followed Moloney, stopping behind him and noticing him tallying money. She, too, reversed course and returned to the apartment as Moloney drove away. (Moloney insists that this never happened.)

Flor and Mandzik decided to take a chance and approach apartment 10D, if only for a few seconds. As a tenant left the building, they walked in, took the elevator to the tenth floor, and paused there to ensure that the hallway was clear.

With no one nearby, they went to the door of apartment 10D, certain that Millar was still inside. From inside, they heard a noise, what Flor would later describe as a "whirring" sound that occasionally paused and then resumed. "I heard this three times and I didn't need to hear any more," she said.

Flor had previously worked in an FBI forfeiture unit and knew the distinctive sound of a money counter at work. She'd heard it many times as agents fed bills into a counter and watched as the machine then spat the bills out, all the while tabulating the total.

Flor even recognized an occasional slight rapping sound from inside the apartment, a noise she heard during the breaks in the machine's counting. That sound, she knew, was Millar tapping cash on a table—or something similar—and neatening the stack before slipping it into the counter. She'd heard the same sound as agents counted cash in the forfeiture unit.

After thirty seconds, she and Mandzik left. Father Moloney had clearly left a money counter behind for Millar, and Millar was now using it.

The two agents sent news back to headquarters. For the cops, this was enough. It was time to go inside apartment 10D.

"We decided we had to shut it down," said FBI Special Agent Paul Hawkins. "We said, 'If they're counting it, they're getting ready to move it, so we've got to take it down.'"

— — —

In Rochester, Assistant US Attorney Charles Pilato had already been preparing for agents to enter the Manhattan apartment. In fact, he'd been trying since late October to get a court's permission to have them go in.

In late October he'd put together the history of the robbery and the surveillance and forwarded the information to a federal prosecutor in New York City to include in a request for a "sneak and peek" warrant. The official legal term—a more sterile name—was Delayed Notice Warrant, but the cops had always called them "sneak and peeks" because, in essence, that's what cops did when they secured such a warrant. Unlike a standard search warrant, which allows specific items to be seized as part of an investigation, the "sneak and peeks" allow police to look and touch but rarely take.

In mid-October Pilato determined that the surveillance team had accumulated enough proof at Apartment 10D to justify a visit inside. He was finding himself in an unusual spot, and it was growing uncomfortable. He'd been friends with Tom O'Connor and some of the local people connected with NORAID who'd been interviewed about the Brink's robbery. He'd even participated in one of the Vikings Revenge boat trips to Canada with O'Connor and others.

The connections ran deeper than that. Pilato had grown up in the same neighborhood as Liam and Cahal Magee, two brothers who were especially tight with Millar and O'Connor. He and Cahal, who'd been the protector of any childhood buddies who came up against bullies, had remained friends.

Handed the case after the robbery, Pilato did not refuse it. Asked years later why he had not stepped aside from the case because of possible conflicts of interest, Pilato said that he did not envision the case mushrooming as it did. And as months passed and the investigation deepened, he did not feel that he could hand the case off to someone else.

But in mid-October of 1993, he was knee-deep in the case and pursuing it, he believed, as would any other prosecutor. That's why he was insistent that a sneak-and-peek warrant was needed, and why he grew so irritated when his colleagues in the US Attorney's Office in New York City did not share his urgency.

Pilato later said that for two weeks he tried to get the request for a warrant in the hands of someone at the Manhattan US Attorney's Office who would ask a federal magistrate for a warrant. Several times, Pilato said, prosecutors in Manhattan asked for changes in the paperwork, and Pilato tweaked the language.

Once, Pilato said, he told someone, "There's $7 million stolen. We're right on the verge of cracking this case. All you need to do is walk this over to a magistrate. If the magistrate says, 'This is not enough,' then, fine, let me know."

After two weeks of altering the paperwork and complaining, Pilato said, "finally someone walks it down [to a magistrate] and they get authorization."

With the warrant in hand in early November, the FBI was ready for the next step. Agents secured keys to the apartment building and the apartment itself from the building's management. The apartment had two locks, and the agents' first attempt to go inside the apartment failed. For some reason, the key would not open the second lock.

They duplicated the key and went back the next morning—November 8—with some agents attired as workmen to blend in with a construction crew and electricians working at the apartment. Again, the lock could not be breached. "We attempted to defeat the lock," FBI Special Agent Leonard Hatton later said. "Again we were unsuccessful."

Around 4:00 a.m. on November 11 the agents tried again. This time the lock finally gave, and they entered a largely empty apartment—unsurprising given that its tenant, Charles McCormick, had vacated it for a few months. As agents would later learn, he'd sublet the apartment to Moloney.

Once inside the apartment, the five people on the investigative team ensured that they were safe. A bomb squad swept the single-bedroom apartment for explosives and then gave the okay for a search.

Investigators had a "bait list" from the Brink's Co.—the list that armored car companies keep with some of the serial numbers of the money they're transporting. This list showed the serial numbers of the $100 bills that had been minted in 1990 and were part of the millions stolen from the Brink's depot in Rochester.

Inside the bedroom investigators found two locked closets. This time, the agents quickly breached the locks and opened the doors.

In one closet, Hatton later said, were suitcases and duffel bags. Agents opened them, knowing that under the "sneak and peak" warrant they could not leave the apartment with anything.

Inside the bags, the agents found cash—lots of cash. Hatton pulled out some of the stacks of fresh $100 bills and compared serial numbers with the bait list. The numbers matched.

Investigators knew they did not have enough time to tally just how much money was there. There were far too many items of luggage to go through, Hatton later said. The agents couldn't risk someone walking in on them.

The next step was clear. The surveillance phase of the Brink's investigation was about to come to an end.

Now it was time for arrests.

CHAPTER 15

— — —

Planning the takedown of the Brink's suspects was no small chore.

First, the FBI brought another team into the mix—its bank robbery squad. The antiterrorism surveillance unit of FBI agents and New York cops had done its job; now it made sense to enlist agents who regularly arrested men and women who'd tried to make away with hundreds of thousands or—as in cases like the Brink's robbery—millions of dollars. There was a protocol for the seizure and handling of cash, and members of the bank robbery squad, especially the unit in New York City, were as well-versed in it as anyone.

"They do this kind of stuff all the time," one agent said of the bank robbery specialists.

There would be raids of apartments, houses, the comics store, and vehicles and arrests of Sam Millar, Father Patrick Moloney, and Tom O'Connor. There would be coordination between two cities, New York and Rochester.

On November 11 FBI Special Agent Louis Stith, assisted by federal prosecutors in Manhattan, wrote out a request to serve as the foundation of the different search and arrest warrants.

The history of the Brink's case—from the January 5 heist to the discovery of the cash during the "sneak and peek" visit—was encapsulated in the affidavit's dozen pages of allegations:

- With no forced entry at the depot, the Brink's robbery looked like an inside job. There was a bevy of other clues of inside help with the heist, and O'Connor, based on his actions, was "the prime suspect" from the start of the investigation.
- O'Connor's statements to police—when he wasn't evading the FBI—included ample inconsistencies with the crime. The Stith affidavit even claimed a minor point in O'Connor's statement was incongruous: he had said that

"the perpetrators put a knit hat over his face," but "during the investigation it was determined that a knit hat is not an effective blindfold when placed over someone's face."

- Millar, who'd been smuggled into the country by O'Connor, was found living in Queens. Tires he discarded had "similar characteristics" to tire tread impressions at the depot.
- Bernadette Fennell used $20 bills to pay for a family trip to Hawaii; a fellow traveler, Margaret Booth, was carrying $4,000 in $20 bills; and Millar had purchased multiple money orders with $20 bills.
- Between July and October "agents observed Millar associating with Father Patrick Moloney." Moloney purchased a new Ford Explorer for Millar with $26,000 in cash—this turned out to be untrue, since cash was only a small part of payment—and Moloney was once seen by the surveillance team thumbing through an inch-thick mound of cash at a traffic light.
- Most significantly, some of the Brink's money was found in the apartment visited multiple times by Millar and Moloney.

Throughout the affidavit, there were mentions of the suspects' alleged connections to NORAID and the IRA. The affidavit did not claim that the IRA had been involved in the robbery but provided plenty of fodder for suspicions of that involvement.

"Information was received from a source that O'Connor has been active in NORAID, a fund-raising group for Provisional Irish Republican Army activities," Stith wrote. "Information was also received that O'Connor toured Northern Ireland . . . , when he was introduced to Samuel Ignatius Millar, who had just been released from prison."

Millar had "a criminal record in Ireland for explosives and firearms violations," the affidavit said. And as for the Melkite priest, "Moloney was arrested in 1980 with his brother, John, when they attempted to smuggle weapons into Ireland from the United States. John Moloney was tried and convicted of weapon charges." (The affidavit ignored the fact that the charges against Patrick Moloney were dismissed because of a lack of evidence.)

Fearful that the suspects would soon be moving the money—otherwise, why were they counting it?—the FBI didn't want to waste any time. Stith prepared an affidavit for each location to be searched.

"It was definitely a scramble," said Hawkins, the Rochester-based agent. "A lot of paper had to be written."

First would be the arrests, then the searches. If no one was at the Manhattan stash house, then searching the apartment could wait. In fact, it would be the last location searched. And agents suspected that searching it would also take the longest. As well as seizing all of the money at the apartment, they would also need a complete forensics sweep of the premises—a hunt for fingerprints or hairs that, when coupled with the surveillance, would provide unimpeachable evidence about just who had been there with the stolen money.

Throughout the morning of Friday, November 12, the planning continued. Late that afternoon, as New York's workers headed out of the city for the weekend, phase 1 began.

— — —

The young men at the Bonitas House had just finished their dinner. As at each meal, they'd thanked the Lord beforehand for the food in front of them and particularly for the roof over their heads. Patrick Moloney, "Father Pat" to all who were present, tried to ensure that they would not be left on the streets, where they would either fall prey to the addicts and hustlers or tumble into their ranks.

Moloney worked hard to get the young men to the communal dinner table during the late afternoon. Occasionally there was friction in Bonitas House, which had fourteen bedrooms. The occupants, after all, were men in their teens and early twenties who had lived on society's margins for so long that they tended to look at everyone who approached them, even those offering kindness, with a jaundiced eye. Some had stolen, some had shot up drugs, some had prostituted themselves. But here, Moloney tried to meld them into a family—yes, a family that would sometimes bicker and battle, even physically, but a family nonetheless.

The evening dinner, around the large dining-room table, was a reminder that Bonitas House could be both a lifeline and an oasis—a lifeline for those who used the normalcy it provided and Father Pat's guidance to work toward getting a job and even having a career, and a temporary oasis for those who would return to the streets and its hard life.

On this day, the normalcy would end.

Moloney and a young African American man who had sought his guidance were going out the front door of the brownstone when they were confronted by a dozen members of a Special Weapons and Tactics (SWAT) team, their semiautomatic rifles raised. The men wore black flak jackets labeled with an assortment of law enforcement agency acronyms. Some of them in FBI jackets separated Moloney and the young man and placed Moloney under arrest.

The cops then burst through the front door with such urgency that some young men dove to the floor while others—some who had still been chatting at the dinner table—sat frozen by the ruckus as agents stormed up the narrow stairway that linked the five floors of the building.

For some of the young men, the raid was straight out of the action-adventure movies they'd seen, with cops shouting out commands and wearing bulletproof vests and helmets as if prepared for a violent response—instead of the tranquil answers one might expect from teenagers at a not-for-profit sanctuary.

Inside, the cops found proof of Moloney's ascetic life, one dedicated to charity. His bedroom was no more than nine by six feet—the size of a large walk-in closet—and his bed consisted of a worn mattress only two inches thick laid on a sheet of plywood, which in turn rested on filing cabinets.

Agents rifled through drawers and filing cabinets and appointment books. They located paperwork for the 1993 Ford Explorer purchased for Millar, as well as multiple files about Moloney's work to resolve immigration problems for people in the neighborhood. His datebooks included baptisms and meetings with Immigration and Naturalization Service officials.

A briefcase contained something quite different—$7,800 in cash. And inside a small closet off Moloney's Lilliputian bedroom, the investigators discovered one of the safes that the priest had purchased months earlier. They tried to break the lock on the safe but failed. They flipped the safe over and pried off its metal bottom. Inside they found mounds of cash—mostly $20 bills separated into piles of $4,000 each. When agents later totaled all of the money found at Bonitas House, the amount was almost $178,000.

Moloney's lifestyle surely seemed austere, and Bonitas House—with its hodge-podge of donated furniture and electronic devices—did not seem the beneficiary of home improvement expenditures. Nonetheless, Moloney had somehow managed to amass a lot of cash.

There was only one answer, the cops figured: the Brink's robbery.

Moloney did nothing to dispel the suspicions of his IRA connections. FBI agents later claimed that Moloney, when told that he was accused of a role in the Brink's robbery, said he was "relieved." "When Moloney was asked why he was relieved, he stated that he thought his arrest had something to do with the Irish Republican movement," an FBI report states. "Moloney denied any involvement in the robbery of the Brink's [depot] in Rochester NY."

After his denial, Moloney made a statement that the agents found intriguing: "I am not going to lie about anything but you are going to find a lot of things that are circumstantial."

On Moloney's person, the agents found $80.23, a toothbrush holder, an AARP membership card, and—oddly—a sheet of paper torn into twenty-one pieces. Agents pieced the paper together again, hoping that Moloney had shredded it because it was proof of his culpability. Instead, the paper, once made whole, consisted of a number of sexually explicit lines. The agents weren't quite sure what to think of a priest with written pornography in his pocket.

Moloney later explained that he'd seized the paper from one of the youths at Bonitas House and destroyed it.

— — —

Millar's arrest was far less eventful than the law enforcement assault on Bonitas House. Agents found Millar at his Explorer near his home and took him into custody. He and Moloney were charged with conspiring to possess the stolen cash, since the police had no firm evidence that the two were involved in the actual robbery.

As Millar recounted the arrest in his memoir, "no sooner had I reached for the keys than I went flying, hard, against the truck. It felt like being hit by a rhino and the first thought in my head was that I was being mugged."

Once cuffed and placed in an unmarked car, Millar seemed unfazed by the arrest. As FBI agents drove him to their Manhattan office, they read him his Miranda rights.

Millar declined to answer questions and claimed his name was Andre Singleton.

At the FBI office, agents searched Millar, finding $1,900 in $100 bills, $400 in $50 bills, one $20 bill, and another $105.25 in smaller bills and change. They removed his silver Pulsar Quartz watch and his leather belt. The large silver belt buckle proclaimed, "American by birth, Irish by the Grace of God."

Millar's leather wallet contained a social security card and driver's license in the name of Andre Singleton. The license listed his home address as that of a residence in Greece, New York—one owned by his friend Cahal Magee.

Millar had also scribbled notes to himself that were stuffed in his wallet, including comics-related reminders about purchases he'd made or planned to make. "Detective Bat Man? Did I pay for DD twice?" read one note.

The wallet yielded other assorted cards, including a AAA membership card and cards from the New York Association of Chiefs of Police, the State Park Police Honorary Benevolent Association, and the state Veteran Police Association.

Apparently Millar had contributed to law enforcement causes. Maybe those could help him avoid speeding tickets, but they could not help him now.

— — —

Millar's family was home when the cops arrived there, almost simultaneously with the raid on Bonitas House and Millar's arrest.

According to Millar's memoir, the police smashed "in the door of our home with a battering ram, pointing their guns at the head of my 9-year-old daughter, screaming at her, 'Where is all your father's money? If you don't tell us we will take you away and you will never see your mother and father again.'" (FBI and other law enforcement officials claim that Millar's memoir is occasionally more dramatic fiction than fact.)

Little was found at the Jackson Heights apartment. Nearby, another team of police officers pushed into KAC Comics, shocking the two young employees who worked there.

The police found several dozen boxes as they moved down the hallway that connected the store's front area with its larger display section in the rear. The boxes were, unsurprisingly, packed with comics. "The boxes were pretty much full," an FBI agent later said. "There was a lot of comics books in each box."

But there was also cash at KAC. A red duffel bag in a bathroom at the end of the hallway contained stacks of $1 bills. In the display room the agents broke a padlock on a cabinet and found a white plastic bag bulging with $10, $20, $50, and $100 bills—all told, nearly $13,200.

— — —

An FBI surveillance squad had been watching O'Connor from a distance since early afternoon, wanting to make the arrest once they got word that both Millar and Moloney were in custody in New York City. The agents feared that if O'Connor were arrested first, the network of friends he shared with Millar would try to get word downstate. Millar had once before managed a Houdini-like vanishing act, and the cops didn't want to give him an opportunity to do it again.

O'Connor left his house for part of the day, unaware he was being watched, and returned around dinner time. Shortly thereafter, the cops in New York City pulled in Moloney and Millar. They relayed the news to their Rochester colleagues, and a heavily enforced team rolled up to O'Connor's home in the Rochester suburb of Irondequoit.

The plan was simple: knock on the door and take O'Connor into custody when he answers. There wasn't much in the way of a contingency plan, since no one expected O'Connor to resist.

Nor did they expect him to refuse to answer the door.

The agents knocked several times, and lights inside the house went out. The agents knocked again; again, there was no response. This was January all over again, with O'Connor secured in his home and ignoring the agents who wanted to talk to him. But this time the agents had an arrest warrant.

More knocks, more silence from inside the house.

Some FBI agents grew tense. O'Connor was a suspect in two homicides, and his reputation was that of a man whose cheerful exterior masked a scheming interior. One agent worried aloud that O'Connor might take a life—either his own or an agent's.

As the federal prosecutor on the case, Charles Pilato was there for the arrest. He was regretting that he hadn't stepped aside from the Brink's case months before. He had not foreseen a problem with his past friendship with O'Connor. He had treated the investigation like any other, and now he realized that for him, it was like no other.

"At that point I wanted to run and disappear from the world," Pilato said later. "I wanted to sell shoes in Cincinnati."

In the weeks to come, some of his superiors questioned whether Pilato had been upfront with them. Why, they asked, had he not been clear with them at the outset that he was close to O'Connor and some of the NORAID members—especially Cahal Magee—who'd harbored Millar and Fennell? (Pilato has maintained that he had never heard of Millar until the Brink's robbery, and there has been no proof to contradict that claim.)

After the raids and arrests of November 12, Pilato's career as a US attorney would begin a downward descent, as he was unable to squelch suspicions that he had impeded the investigation—even though there was no evidence that he had.

But that was in the future. The FBI saw Pilato's presence at O'Connor's home on the day of the arrest as an asset. Here was a man who might be able to talk some sense into the retired cop. An agent turned to Pilato and said, "Can you call him for us?"

Pilato agreed, took the phone from the agent, and dialed O'Connor's number.

O'Connor answered, slightly surprised to hear Pilato's voice. Pilato told him he was outside the house.

"How are you?" Pilato asked.

"Charlie, things aren't good."

"Don't do anything stupid."

"Charlie, they're all over the place. They're all over the outside. I turned out the lights."

"I know, Tom. Don't do anything stupid to them or to yourself. Just come to the door."

O'Connor agreed that he would turn himself in, but he had one request for Pilato. "Call Felix for me," he said.

Pilato agreed to call O'Connor's attorney, Felix Lapine, immediately. O'Connor hung up, and seconds later he appeared at the door. An agent handcuffed him and took him to a car for the drive to the Public Safety Building and the jail's holding center.

As Pilato watched the car pull away, he again used the agent's telephone and called Lapine, whom he'd known for years and whose home number he had handy.

"Your buddy, Tom O'Connor, needs your help," Pilato told him.

"For what?"

"The Brink's robbery. He's been arrested for that."

"What? They've got no evidence on him."

"Felix, trust me. Go downtown."

O'Connor would soon be booked at the federal courthouse in downtown Rochester, Pilato said. He would be charged with the robbery, the only of the suspects to be accused of the actual heist.

— — —

From the moment of the initial planning earlier in the day, the cops knew they would arrest Millar, Moloney, and O'Connor. But what about Charles McCormick, the tenant of the rent-controlled apartment at 330 First Avenue? He'd rarely been seen there, but he did hold the lease. Could he not know that the Brink's money was stashed there?

There had been talk of charging McCormick, but no firm decision had been made. That could be decided later. If necessary they'd find McCormick another day; whether involved or not, he was not likely to go into hiding.

But there was one surprise for the agents. Moloney, the teenagers, and staff members at Bonitas House were not the only ones there at the time of the raid. McCormick was also there, visiting his friend, Father Pat.

The FBI agents called their bosses for instructions about what to do with McCormick. "There were some questions about whether to arrest Mr. McCormick, whether to detain him, and we went back and forth several times," Special Agent Leonard Hatton later said.

With more than a dozen agents searching Bonitas House and Moloney already under arrest, Hatton took McCormick aside.

Hatton started with small talk, asking about the New Jersey high school McCormick had attended. (Hatton had enough information about McCormick to know that they both had gone to school in New Jersey.) After the chat—a breaking of the ice, Hatton later said—the agent moved on to the issue at hand: Hatton and the FBI were curious about McCormick's tenancy of the First Avenue apartment where Moloney and Millar had been hiding money from the Brink's robbery.

Long distrustful of police, McCormick provided little clarity with his answers. Hatton then learned from his colleagues that the decision had been made not to arrest McCormick. Hatton let him go, only to find out moments later that FBI officials had changed their minds.

"A couple of minutes after he was released, we were told to arrest him," Hatton said. But by then, McCormick had left.

Hatton ran to the front door of Bonitas House, asking agents whether they'd seen where McCormick had gone. The agents were unsure. Hatton summoned surveillance units, whose members circled the neighborhood in their cars. Hatton sprinted to a nearby park.

"I ran around the park and I went through the park looking for Mr. McCormick and I was unable to locate him," Hatton said. "Nor were the surveillance units able to locate him."

After twenty minutes, Hatton returned to Bonitas House. A short while later, an agent yelled to him from the front: "Are you still looking for McCormick?"

"Yeah, where is he?" Hatton answered.

"He's walking up the street . . . carrying pizza."

While the FBI was running about in search of McCormick, he was at a nearby pizza joint buying food with some Bonitas House workers and neighbors. "We went and had a couple of beers and we were talking and trying to find out what the hell is going on, and we got the pizza and headed back to the block," McCormick later recalled.

The uncertainty about whether to arrest McCormick on November 12 continued into the next day. As McCormick later said, the FBI spent some time that evening deciding whether or not to charge him as an accomplice to the crime.

"They arrested me," he later said. "I was taken to the [Manhattan] Federal Building where the FBI has their headquarters. You know, I obviously wasn't happy, so they basically just processed me, and then they took me over to central booking, because there was no room in MCC [the city's Metropolitan Correctional Center]."

With the one telephone call he was permitted to make, McCormick—still not quite sure what crime he was accused of committing—telephoned his father. "I called him and he told me that it was on the news that this was a Brink's robbery, something to that effect," McCormick said later.

The next morning McCormick was released, minutes before he was scheduled to make his initial appearance before a judge in federal court. The FBI had decided not to charge McCormick with a crime after all. He was free to leave.

Months later that would change again.

— — —

As McCormick was bounced about, uncertain if his immediate fate included a jail cell, his apartment at 330 First Avenue was invaded by law enforcement officials. FBI agents entered the apartment around 9:30 p.m., hours after the first arrest.

The agents had multiple tasks to accomplish. They had to remove the money from the apartment, find connections between the money and Millar and Moloney—and anyone else, if proof was available, and try to determine if McCormick had played a part in the crime.

McCormick's leftist politics were evident to the cops, with the portraits of Che Guevara and Malcolm X on his walls. But that did not constitute a crime.

Clearly no one lived at the apartment. The food cupboards were bare, except for a can of Campbell's soup and a small container of garlic salt. The apartment was largely devoid of furniture.

The agents photographed and gathered the evidence they'd seen during their earlier visit, proof of the money-counting operation. There were two card tables, on top of which were yellow Playtex gloves, a calculator, rubber bands, and pieces of paper with dollar figures scribbled on them. The agents also located the money counter and, of course, the true target—the cash.

The agents returned to the closets where they'd earlier found the suitcases and duffel bags filled with money. One tweed suitcase, with Moloney's name and address on an Aer Lingus airline tag inside, held more than $330,000. Another suitcase held nearly $850,000, and one small duffel bag nearly overflowed with more than $55,500.

In all, the FBI seized 350 pounds of cash totaling more than $2 million—though it would not be counted for days—with most of the cash consisting of older bills but more than $100,000 of it being crisp new currency matching that stolen from Brink's. The forensics team also helped collect proof of Moloney's participation—just in case his frequent presence at the apartment, his purchase of a money counter, and the nearly $178,000 at Bonitas House wasn't enough. Hair samples pulled from one of the bags holding cash later were determined to be a match for Moloney's hair. They also lifted his fingerprint from a glass in the apartment.

The warrant also gave the cops the right to grab any information about who lived in or used the apartment. McCormick had left there papers stuffed into a box, including credit card receipts and bank statements. He also had an assortment of old college papers and letters, including some to former girlfriends, that he'd never trashed. Inside one college composition book was a bevy of figures, including the numbers 7.1 million and 2 million. Prosecutors would later determine these numbers were too close a match for the amount stolen from the depot and the cash found in the apartment. This could not be coincidence; instead, it was proof of McCormick's guilt. Authorities ignored the multitude of other numbers in the book, which McCormick had used in an accounting class.

The FBI also took away a decade-old satirical letter McCormick had written to his college newspaper at Fairfield University, in Connecticut. Typical of much college parody, the letter was heavy-handed, an attempt to mock people who relentlessly sought money with McCormick, as the writer, pretending to be in those ranks himself. The letter was headlined "For the Love of Money"—more proof for the authorities of McCormick's longing for cash.

By itself, this proof would likely be insufficient for an indictment. But there was one bit of more damning evidence: a fingerprint found on a piece of cardboard used to separate the cash in one suitcase later was matched to McCormick.

That would be tougher for McCormick to explain, given that he had been seen entering 330 First Avenue during the FBI's surveillance.

— — —

The New York City bust, with its hints of IRA involvement, quickly became international news. Publicly, the FBI maintained that it did not have evidence of IRA help in the robbery, but privately, some agents advanced the theory of involvement from overseas.

Even without the IRA, the cast of characters was so eclectic that the crime seemed right out of a Hollywood script. The *Los Angeles Times* wrote: "A priest once implicated in gun-running, a retired police officer and an illegal immigrant who was imprisoned for explosives violations—all charged in a $7.4 million armored car company theft—may have committed the crime to help finance the Irish Republican Army, FBI officials said."

Moloney was an especially enigmatic figure, as reporters sought to reconcile the criminal allegations with his past. "One day I asked him to pray for me because I was hungry," a homeless man told the *New York Times*. "So he put his hand on my hand, bowed his head and prayed for me. Then he gave me $10 to buy something to eat. As far as I'm concerned, Father Moloney is beautiful people."

The *Times*, which had written about Moloney in the past, also reported: "For nearly 40 years, the Rev. Patrick Moloney has cultivated the reputation of a humble defender of the poor and helpless in the East Village of Manhattan. But yesterday, as he stood accused of complicity in helping to steal $7.4 million from a Brink's armored car service in Rochester, a more complex question of identity arose: is he a saint, a robber, or even both?"

Moloney's distaste for British control of Northern Ireland was intense, some of his supporters and friends conceded. "He's a very anti-British priest," Long Island Rep. Peter King, who shared Moloney's views, told the *Times*.

Within days, Moloney would be back at Bonitas House, free on bail and wearing an electronic monitoring bracelet on his ankle. A judge also granted O'Connor bail in Rochester, after Lapine noted that O'Connor had been a suspect since January and had made no efforts to leave Rochester. Meanwhile, Millar stayed jailed. He would not get a chance to disappear again.

Back in the Lower East Side, Moloney would tell anyone who would listen—and media from around the world were willing to listen—that he was completely innocent. "I see this as an FBI conspiracy," Moloney told the Glasgow, Scotland, *Herald*.

NORAID officials in the United States, as well as leaders of Sinn Fein, the Irish republican political party, denied that the money had been stolen to support fighters in Northern Ireland. But some British media remained skeptical, regardless how much the FBI downplayed the possible IRA connection.

"FBI spokesmen say they have found probably less than half the money," the *Economist* wrote before the FBI had completely tallied the recovered cash. "The rest is either hidden somewhere or in someone else's hands. It would seem odd, given the circumstances, if at least some of it had not ended up on the street of Belfast."

Entryway to the vault room at the Brink's depot in Rochester, New York, at time of January 5, 1993, depot robbery. Prosecution evidence from 1994 Brink's heist trial.

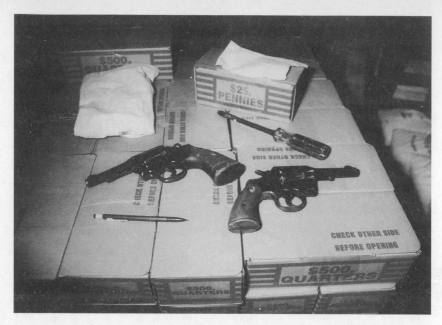

Guns taken from the guards during the 1993 robbery of the Brink's depot and left at the scene. Prosecution evidence from 1994 trial.

Father Patrick Moloney enters the Kenneth B. Keating Federal Building in Rochester during the 1994 trial. Photo by Burr Lewis, courtesy of the *Democrat and Chronicle*.

Father Patrick Moloney and his attorney, Bill Clauss, outside the
Kenneth B. Keating Federal Building during the 1994 trial.
Photo by Burr Lewis, courtesy of the *Democrat and Chronicle*.

Sam Millar enters the
Kenneth B. Keating Federal
Building in handcuffs
during the 1994 trial.
Photo by Karen Schiely,
courtesy of the *Democrat
and Chronicle*.

Sam Millar and Father Patrick Moloney are transported together
from court to the Monroe County Jail in Rochester during the 1994 trial.
Photo by Karen Schiely, courtesy of the *Democrat and Chronicle*.

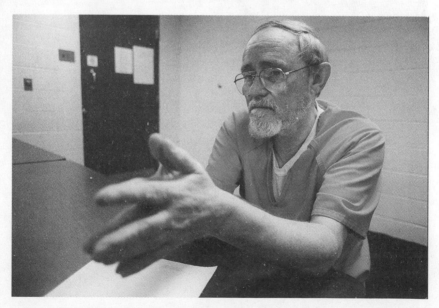

Father Patrick Moloney interviewed in the Wayne County, New York, jail after the
1994 trial. Photo by Annette Lein, courtesy of the *Democrat and Chronicle*.

Sam Millar's wife, Bernadette Fennell, enters the Monroe County, New York, jail to visit Millar as he awaits trial in 1994. Photo by Darcy Chang, courtesy of the *Democrat and Chronicle*.

Charles McCormick (left) and his attorney, John Speranza, during the 1994 trial. Photo by Annette Lein, courtesy of the *Democrat and Chronicle*.

Tom O'Connor (right) and his attorney, Felix Lapine,
during the 1994 trial. Photo by Jamie Germano,
courtesy of the *Democrat and Chronicle*.

Tom O'Connor speaks to the media following the
verdict in the 1994 trial. Photo by Karen Schiely,
courtesy of *Democrat and Chronicle*.

Ronnie Gibbons, in an undated photo.
Photo courtesy of family of Ronnie Gibbons.

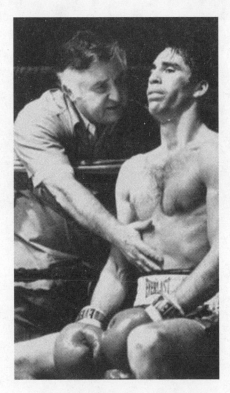

Ronnie Gibbons and his cornerman
during a fight, in an undated photo.
Copyright Abbot Genser

Ronnie Gibbons and his mother, Rita, in New York City, in an undated photo. Photo courtesy of family of Ronnie Gibbons.

Gerald O'Connor's 2004 mug shot. Courtesy New York
Department of Correctional Services.

Ronnie Gibbons with world heavyweight champion Joe Frazier, New York City,
in an undated photo. Photo courtesy of family of Ronnie Gibbons.

The August 2011 exhumation of Ronnie Gibbons's remains at Cape Vincent, New York. Photo by Max Schulte, courtesy of the *Democrat and Chronicle*.

CHAPTER 16

— — —

For a month after the Brink's arrests, Charles McCormick thought he was home free. There had been the shock of his arrest on November 12, but hours afterward the FBI agents realized their error, dropped the charges, and released him. His name had been briefly mentioned in news reports, noting his arrest as the mistake that it had been. He wasn't worried about criminal charges; if anything, he was worried about his safety.

"I really had no concerns after my initial release," McCormick later said. "I didn't think I was going to be arrested, though I was not sure whether or not someone would have benefited from seeing me dead. From an objective view it makes it a lot easier to spin a defense if the guy whose apartment was housing all the money is not around to defend himself."

McCormick knew he'd made one mistake—he'd agreed earlier in the year to let Father Patrick Moloney sublet the apartment when McCormick traveled to Jamaica, where his brother lived.

McCormick had met Moloney the previous year. McCormick taught general educational development (GED) classes to high-school dropouts in Manhattan and was so popular with the students that they once gave him a trophy and plaque. In late 1992, the students worried about whether some of their tuition was being used improperly. Like Moloney, McCormick could also be a bit of a rabble-rouser. He wanted to help the students protest, and a lawyer whom McCormick knew was also familiar with the priest from the Lower East Side. If the students wanted to protest, they and McCormick should work with Moloney, the lawyer suggested. Moloney had been protesting everything from British control of Northern Ireland to Lower East Side gentrification for years.

McCormick contacted Moloney and was impressed with the priest's work at Bonitas House. They became friends. Sometimes McCormick would take adult students from another school where he worked to clean and do home repairs at Bonitas.

In the summer of 1993 McCormick wanted to sublet his apartment. Out of work, he planned to travel to Jamaica to visit his brother and spend time with his parents in New Jersey. He told Moloney of his plans, and Moloney offered to be responsible for the apartment for the months McCormick was away. McCormick knew that Moloney sometimes sheltered illegal immigrants, and the priest was likely to use the apartment as a haven. That didn't bother McCormick; in fact, he found it admirable.

Now, late in 1993, McCormick regretted that decision. Moloney continually claimed he was innocent, but to McCormick the proof against Moloney was overwhelming. McCormick hoped that the FBI had fabricated some of its case—he believed law enforcement officials fully capable of such duplicitous injustices—but until he saw evidence of FBI misdeeds, he had to assume that Moloney had intended to use his apartment as a stash house for the Brink's millions.

Then, in December, McCormick received a subpoena, asking for a handwriting sample and a hair sample. He met with FBI agents and was surprised at the handwriting request. In fact, they wanted something to match against words he'd written in some of the papers they'd seized from his apartment and never returned.

Still, McCormick saw no reason to fret. He was so light-hearted about the meeting that he made his own request of the agents who took his hair sample: His hairline, he said, was "deeply receding," so he asked if he could have the hairs back.

McCormick went back to his life, which largely consisted of looking for work and occasionally evading questions from friends and acquaintances about all the money found in his apartment. Shortly after the November arrests, a federal grand jury in Rochester indicted Moloney, Millar, and O'Connor on charges connected to the robbery and stolen cash. They would be tried in Rochester, and McCormick would watch from afar.

In the following months, a grand jury investigating the Brink's robbery continued to subpoena witnesses. Some NORAID members in Rochester complained of harassment, alleging that the federal government was on a witch hunt to draw NORAID and the IRA into the crime when no proof existed, other than the political leanings of the accused.

In May 1994, another shoe dropped: the grand jury returned a new indictment—a superseding indictment—that included a few new tidbits. The allegations included spending by some of the accused that had not been revealed before.

Defense attorneys downplayed the significance of the indictment; superseding indictments were common in federal court. "The government's obviously stalling," said Rochester-based defense lawyer Anthony Leonardo Jr., whom Millar had hired. And Felix Lapine, Tom O'Connor's attorney, called the indictment a "non-event," a rehashing of past allegations.

For Charles McCormick, however, the indictment was a very big event. He also now was accused of possession of cash from the Brink's robbery.

— — —

Father Moloney wanted a trial on his home turf.

A Manhattan jury, he thought, would be more receptive to an altruistic priest whose life had been spent among the last, the least, and the lost. His attorney, Stanley Cohen, was a battler, a left-leaning throwback to the 1960s who relished the chance to fight for the likes of Moloney, and who would later defend Osama bin Laden's son-in-law. For Cohen, whose office was also in the Lower East Side, a trial in Manhattan would be practical, involving only a simple subway trip to the courthouse.

In the months after the Brink's indictments, Moloney and Cohen encouraged federal judges to hold the trial in New York City instead of Rochester. Since the money had been discovered in a Manhattan apartment, there was a New York City nexus to the crime that was just as substantial as the Rochester connection, they contended in court papers.

In addition, they argued, a Rochester jury would be tainted by media that had been spoon-fed lies and managed by federal authorities. These wild stories about IRA connections were a prime example.

Federal prosecutors in Rochester got a good chuckle out of the claims of media manipulation, as did members of the Rochester media. As prosecutors noted in a court filing, the reporting of the Rochester media had largely hewn to the facts of the case, while Moloney's assertions that a run-away FBI was targeting a liberal priest anchored some of the New York City coverage. "It is not unfair to conclude that defendant Moloney seeks a trial in those [New York City] districts . . . in which he has attempted to manipulate media accounts in his favor," a federal prosecutor wrote in a court filing.

A federal magistrate in Manhattan, Edgar Maxwell, dispensed with the argument that the breadth of news coverage in Rochester ensured that Moloney could not receive a fair trial there. Maxwell ruled that the discovery of the Brink's cash and the arrests were also the focus of intensive news coverage in New York City.

The New York media had published and aired multiple stories about Moloney and his work at the Bonitas House even before his arrest, Maxwell wrote, stating that in New York City Moloney "has some newsworthy interest because of his vocation and professional interests." Moloney could be tried in Rochester, Maxwell ruled—a decision that, ironically, would later be beneficial for Moloney's defense. With the venue decided, a trial was scheduled for the fall of 1994. Only Millar remained jailed, awaiting trial.

US District Judge David Larimer, a 1987 federal court nominee of President Ronald Reagan, would be the trial judge. Even-tempered with a wry and quiet sense of humor, Larimer was a brand of judge that would become less prevalent on the bench in ensuing years: a moderate Republican. He abhorred the mandatory sentencing laws that Congress had passed, statutes designed to bring more nationwide uniformity to sentences but had instead, in Larimer's mind, created sometimes Draconian punishment that eliminated the discretionary power of the bench.

Larimer was also a thoughtful analyst of legal arguments, and the Brink's trial—as it would be labeled in the media shorthand—would provide plenty of them.

Larimer, in short, was likely the perfect judge for the case—not only because of his rigid adherence to and appreciation of the law but also because of his ability to keep attorneys focused, even those whose personalities could sometimes dominate a court proceeding. And the attorneys in the Brink's case were not short on personality.

Millar's attorney, Leonardo, was six feet three inches tall, trim and fit, a broad-shouldered former college basketball player who could overwhelm even the grandest courtroom, shrinking it as he controlled it like a stage. His opening and closing statements brimmed with bravado, sometimes fiery and passionate, other times solemn and sober—whatever the case called for. He enthralled jurors, especially female jurors, and especially when he would recall their names or small details of their lives—their children, livelihoods, and neighborhoods—that they'd mentioned in pretrial voir dire questioning.

This was Leonardo's secret: he had a photographic memory, and he knew how to use it in court. He was not the most astute legal scholar in Rochester, and he might not even have been in the upper tier of attorneys who knew how to apply the arcane nuances of state and federal statutes to the specifics of a criminal case. But there was little that he forgot, whether the approaching birthday of a juror or the slight variance between a witness's testimony and the deposition the witness had given to police months before, a variance that could be used to erode and ultimately destroy the witness's credibility.

This ability had served Leonardo so well that he once had five straight acquittals in homicide cases—an absolutely unheard-of string of successes for a defense lawyer. That run of trial victories in the late 1980s brought him to the attention of the mob boss John Gotti. Leonardo interviewed for Gotti's defense team when Gotti was preparing to go on trial in New York City for ordering a string of murders.

Leonardo did not end up on the Gotti team, but the simple fact that he had been considered for it only added to his luster in Rochester. For the fifteen years before the Brink's trial, Leonardo had been one of the go-to attorneys for mobsters, drug dealers with money, and well-heeled white-collar criminals. He once defended David Bowie after the rock star had been arrested for partying with fans and a half-pound of marijuana at a Rochester hotel after a concert. Irked that he'd been criminally charged for pot possession, Bowie never returned to Rochester for another show, though his police booking photo circulated for years to come and resurfaced prominently online after his death in 2016.

Leonardo was also a good fit for Millar's defense. Both were warriors—Leonardo louder and profane, and Millar stolid but equally passionate. Millar liked fighters, and that's just what Leonardo was.

Leonardo also recognized Millar's strength. After Long Kesh, life in the county jail—with its regular meals, its beds much cozier than a concrete floor, and its daily recreational times—was a cakewalk for Millar. Once, returning to his cramped and barred home after a meal, Millar walked past another inmate inside a cell, standing on a chair and preparing to hang himself with a noose manufactured from a bedsheet. Millar did not see the need to alert deputies; a man so weak that he could not survive a jail as comfortable as this did not deserve to live.

"Take it like a man," Millar told the prisoner—who, perhaps swayed by Millar's admonition, decided against killing himself.

O'Connor continued to be represented by Lapine, another Rochester lawyer with an oversized personality. Wiry and bespectacled, with an angular face, he was no less a fighter in court than Leonardo.

Lapine's approach was different, to be sure. He did not need bombast. Instead, he used barbed humor that endeared him to jurors just as much as Leonardo's good looks and keen recall of detail. Whereas many lawyers took copious notes during the testimony of witnesses, Lapine could appear unconcerned, especially with witnesses whom the prosecution considered the centerpiece of its cases.

He would toil away at crossword puzzles during some testimony, a tactic that sent subtle signals to juries that the witness was not worth his—or their—time.

McCormick's family, sure of his innocence but fearful that he could still be convicted, initially hired a New York City attorney for him. In the months after the indictment, with the trial slated for a Rochester courtroom in the fall of 1994, they turned to a Rochester lawyer who came highly recommended—John Speranza.

Speranza had a singular courtroom approach: he was the gentleman barrister. Judges loved him; prosecutors liked him; and he was courteous in court to an uncommon degree. That did not mean that Speranza was not as passionate about his role as a defense lawyer as Leonardo or Lapine. When necessary, Speranza could verbally eviscerate a witness, but he did so with aplomb and dignity.

The lawyers Speranza, Lapine, and Leonardo were known commodities to Larimer. He knew what to expect of them in his court, and they also knew what to expect of him.

Cohen was another matter. Larimer knew him only by reputation but knew that he would bring additional fireworks to the courtroom. There was also the concern that Cohen would try to paint the prosecution of Moloney as political, a tactic that could distract jurors from what the evidence showed. Try as he might to maintain that the FBI targeted him because of his support for an independent Northern Ireland, Moloney could not escape the simple fact that extensive police surveillance had watched Millar and Moloney go in and out of the apartment where the Brink's loot was stashed.

Furthermore, Moloney seemed to have stumbled on newfound wealth in the months after the heist. He'd carried a money counter into the Manhattan apartment. And he'd subleased that apartment from McCormick.

This was the evidence and the landscape on which the prosecution and defense would fight the case. Larimer intended to keep the trial on this turf. He recognized that Leonardo could be a loose cannon and might have to be reined in occasionally. Cohen might require the same approach.

In the weeks before trial, however, Cohen confronted two problems: a severe asthma attack, and a severe lack of payment from Moloney.

While politically sympathetic to Moloney, Cohen also expected that part of his costs would be paid. And with the trial's move to Rochester from Manhattan, those costs were sure to balloon. A group of Moloney's supporters had vowed that they would host numerous fundraisers to cover much of the priest's legal costs. But the few fundraisers that had been held had been only mildly successful.

Cohen wrote Larimer, saying that he'd done about $74,000 worth of legal work and had been paid only about 10 percent of his costs. His sickness, coupled with the costly and time-consuming burden of representation for Moloney, made him unable to continue with the priest's defense, Cohen wrote.

Larimer was not pleased. The trial was weeks away, and he did not want to derail the proceedings with a lengthy delay. At a pretrial hearing, Cohen suggested that co-counsel from New York City be appointed to help him.

At the hearing, Larimer asked Moloney whether he had resources to pay lawyers. If Moloney couldn't afford one lawyer, how could he afford two? Moloney answered with a plea for the return of records seized from Bonitas House when he was arrested. The documents, Moloney said, had the names of friends and others who might help him pay legal fees.

Larimer admitted he was puzzled. How could Moloney, free on bail, not know how to contact individuals with whom he was so close that he expected they would help defray his legal costs? Eight months had passed since his arrest—surely Moloney could have figured out during that time just how to connect with these people.

"You forgot the names of the people you want to contact?" Larimer asked, his incredulity growing. "I find it a little hard to believe that you don't know any of these peoples' names or where they are."

Moloney conceded that he could not afford a lawyer. Cohen suggested that a lawyer from New York City be appointed as co-counsel. Moloney could declare himself indigent, and Cohen and the co-counsel would be paid by the government as court-appointed attorneys.

Perhaps, Cohen said, Larimer and the judge's staff could also help reduce the costs by helping with "telephones, faxes, typing." This was, to say the least, an unusual request to be made of a federal judge. "You want me to do that, do the typing for you?" Larimer said.

That was enough for Larimer. He jettisoned Cohen as Moloney's defense attorney.

The judge had prepared for this likelihood. He'd called a friend, Federal Public Defender Jonathan Feldman, and asked whether he could be in court for the hearing. With Cohen gone, Larimer chose Feldman and his office to represent Moloney.

Feldman promised that he, his investigators, and his assistant federal public defender, Bill Clauss, would quickly acquaint themselves with the case. They would be ready by the trial date—only a month away—he said.

Larimer let Moloney know he should consider himself lucky, given how shaky his representation had appeared only minutes before. "One of the best groups of criminal lawyers in this town [is] ready to step in immediately and take over," Larimer said.

Larimer knew the Federal Public Defender's Office well. Its attorneys represented indigent defendants in federal court, and there were many of them to represent.

The Rochester office was relatively new, having opened in 1992 with Feldman at its helm. Feldman was younger than the other defense lawyers in the Brink's case, as was his assistant, Clauss. But the two lawyers were well known in defense circles for their keen legal minds. Feldman had worked in private practice and as a federal prosecutor. Clauss, who had been a high-school English teacher before he decided to be a lawyer, had previously worked in the county's Public Defender's Office, where his prowess as a defense attorney became evident to all who saw him in court.

— — —

The Rochester-based prosecution team—Christopher Buscaglia and Christopher Taffe—had been assembled in the months immediately before the trial. Prosecutor Charles Pilato, facing questions about his friendship with O'Connor and some of the NORAID crowd, had stepped aside because of the belief that he knew too many of the players.

While the defense lawyers had a difficult task ahead of them, given the amount of evidence against the defendants, the job of the prosecutors was no less onerous. They had to take the wealth of proof—the hours of surveillance, the possibility of more than a hundred witnesses, the necessary testimony about the chain of custody that would trace the money from a Federal Reserve plant to the Manhattan apartment—and package it into a narrative that a jury could grasp.

Buscaglia decided that the best way to shape the narrative was chronologically, starting with the heist, continuing with the surveillance, and leading to the coup de grâce—the seizures of the $2 million in McCormick's apartment and the $178,000 at Bonitas House.

The prosecutors opted to have members of the FBI and New York City police surveillance team testify multiple times, detailing various points of significance along the investigative trajectory. That way, the saga would unfold day by day, with jurors following along and unraveling each investigative thread just as the police had done.

"Really, it was just a robbery case that involved a whole lot of money," Buscaglia later said. "It just so happened some of the evidence of the crime ended up in a different city.

"That's really . . . the best way to approach it, as a robbery case with a scattering of people all over the place—and some media attention."

Not every robbery case, however, has the rumors of IRA involvement, with suspicions that a paramilitary operation across the ocean had played puppeteer, directing the thieves and later transforming the millions into weapons purchases.

Those allegations were sexy and the focus of the international media attention on the robbery. But investigators had found no more evidence of an IRA link in the months after the November 1993 arrests—though not for lack of trying. British authorities were on the lookout for the Brink's money and had asked sources in the IRA community about the Rochester crime. No one had found proof—just the occasional innuendo—of an IRA role.

Yes, Millar and Moloney likely would be willing to direct the stolen cash to IRA coffers, and O'Connor, despite his goofy good-cheer demeanor, seemed capable of doing the same. The FBI had also found proof that McCormick's politics included support for a unified Ireland, but he did not seem as fervent about it as the others.

But the sympathies of the defendants, regardless of their level of intensity, could not cross the legal threshold for evidence. For prosecutors, IRA involvement would increase their motivation to convince jurors of the defendants' guilt. But Larimer recognized that the proof did not exist, at least not substantively. In the fall of 1994 he ruled that no testimony about the IRA would be allowed.

To bring the IRA into the trial, with insufficient proof, would unfairly sully the reputations of the defendants and could cause jurors to stray from the evidence in their decision making, Larimer ruled in advance of the trial. The IRA might be in the headlines, but it would not be in the courtroom.

Then there was NORAID. Testimony about NORAID was crucial, prosecutors believed, because it provided a connection between some of the defendants.

In a pretrial motion made weeks before the trial, Buscaglia noted that O'Connor had attended many of the fundraising events held by the Rochester chapter of NORAID and that Moloney had been the keynote speaker at a November 1990 NORAID dinner and dance in Rochester.

"There is nothing nefarious about association with Irish Northern Aid," Buscaglia wrote. In an odd twist, he was now painting NORAID as a nonviolent charitable organization, a stance that ran counter to what federal prosecutors and law enforcement had contended for years.

"It is a humanitarian organization which just happened to bring O'Connor and Moloney together," Buscaglia wrote. (In fact, while the two may have been in the same room in Rochester when Moloney came to give a talk, there is no proof that they had met or even remembered one another.)

Defense lawyers saw testimony about NORAID as a thinly veiled way to sneak in discussions of the IRA and to provide a back-door opportunity to mention the nationalistic motives that Larimer had precluded from trial.

Here, Larimer sided with the prosecution. Some of the defendants faced conspiracy charges, he said. (Only O'Connor was accused of the robbery itself.) Prosecutors should not be hamstrung as they built the case alleging an illegal pact among the accused.

"This is a conspiracy theory," Larimer said. "The government is entitled to show that they associated together. Motive is a more difficult problem."

Prosecutors also wanted some motive to connect Moloney to the Brink's cash. They knew that Moloney would appear in court each day in his priestly garb, the white collar possibly symbolizing purity for the jury. Although Moloney was tiny in stature, he could ignite his own supersized charm even when silent. With a contagious smile and an irrepressible gleam in his eyes, Moloney was as much pixie as priest.

"We were always worried about the jury's reaction to Father Pat and his motivation," Buscaglia said. "We were obviously concerned that the jurors were maybe naturally going to sympathize with the good father. We tried as hard as we could to establish some sort of motive on his part: why would this guy want to get involved with this in the first place?

"Father Pat was kind of a wild card."

CHAPTER 17

— — —

In September 1994, jury summons went out to more than a hundred people. The jury pool needed to be large, David Larimer decided, because of the ample publicity that the Brink's robbery and subsequent arrests had generated.

The week before the trial, lawyers crafted the questions they wanted Larimer to ask the prospective jurors. Defense lawyers tried to ensure that the questions weeded out candidates overly familiar with the case, and especially those who'd heard talk of the IRA.

In early October, Larimer's courtroom was packed with the jury prospects. For three days, Larimer tossed questions at members of the jury pool, and the attorneys spent hours during breaks deciding which ones to keep and which ones to weed out.

Some prospects clearly had followed the media coverage. One man knew of Sam Millar as a blanketman and recalled—because of the distastefulness of the image—the story of the inmates spreading their own dung on the prison walls.

Another man remembered reading an article that noted that Tom O'Connor had been a suspect in a homicide, the killing of Damien McClinton. And another remembered from news stories that the robbers had released O'Connor near a restaurant that O'Connor knew—a surprising bit of happenstance, the jury prospect decided.

These men were all eliminated from the jury pool, as was the man who heard that the money had been "funneled" to the IRA.

Then there was the man whom all the defense attorneys other than Anthony Leonardo wanted on the jury. But Millar adamantly insisted that the man not be chosen. The man wore an earring, and Millar did not like the bit of jewelry. Leonardo gave in to his wishes of his client.

Midway through the third day, a jury had been chosen, but the prosecution was not pleased. All of the jury members were women, while two of the three alternates were men.

Prosecutors argued that the defense had purposefully set out to create a female jury panel, which might be more sympathetic to the defendants, but Larimer's review of the selection proceedings found no evidence of manipulation of the selection. So on October 7, 1994, the Brink's trial—with media attention from across the country—began. The all-female jury would be the arbiter of the innocence or guilt of this unusual assortment of defendants: a sprightly priest, an IRA guerrilla who'd snuck into the United States, a retired cop who'd smuggled the guerrilla into the country, and a former teacher and counselor who was now unemployed.

— — —

In his opening statement, Christopher Buscaglia detailed the connections between O'Connor—the "inside man" in the robbery, he said—and Millar. He highlighted how cops had watched Millar and Father Patrick Moloney carry money into the Manhattan apartment. He claimed that Charles McCormick had been untruthful in interviews with FBI agents, and that physical evidence connected him to the Brink's cash.

The defense attorneys fired back. Brink's was ripe for robbery, Felix Lapine said, and the focus on O'Connor as a suspect had been wrongheaded from the start. The evidence against McCormick was flimsy at best, and the FBI had been so unsure about what to do with him that they had arrested him only months after the others, John Speranza argued. Leonardo, who was facing strong evidence against his client, tried to convince the jury that the proof would not be as solid as prosecutors claimed. And Jonathan Feldman portrayed Moloney as a giving and loving priest who sold old church pews and stained glass at flea markets to raise money for his home for troubled teens. That could well explain the cash at Bonitas House, said Feldman, who believed his emotional presentation of Moloney as a heart-of-gold priest scored with some jurors. As he sat down after his opening remarks, one juror wiped away tears.

The surveillance, prosecutors knew, would provide an ironclad link between Millar, Moloney, and the Brink's money. But that investigative legwork, as extensive as it was, did not show how the money had made its way from the Rochester depot to an apartment in Manhattan.

Constructing the connection between O'Connor and Millar was crucial for prosecutors, and they opened the trial with evidence of how the friendship between the two started and about the alleged criminal conspiracy it evolved into. The prosecutors immediately described the activities of members of Rochester's NORAID chapter, presenting testimony that O'Connor had been an active member of the organization.

Colleen Dunham testified about traveling to Europe with O'Connor in 1984 and heading to England as he traveled to Belfast. When she rejoined O'Connor in Belfast, he introduced her to his new friend, Millar, and Millar's girlfriend, Bernadette Fennell.

O'Connor's former girlfriend, Jean Arena, provided additional proof of the friendship between O'Connor and Millar, revealing that she and O'Connor had driven to the Toronto airport in August 1984 to meet Millar. Arena drove back to Rochester alone; O'Connor brought Millar back separately, she said.

Prosecutors then produced a string of witnesses to testify that Millar and Fennell had lived in Rochester and that O'Connor had remained chummy with them.

The superintendent of an apartment complex in Greece, New York, pointed to Fennell as the woman who called herself Mary O'Connor and lived with Millar at the complex.

Testimony also showed that Fennell had taken out automobile insurance in 1987 for a 1978 Mercury Cougar. She changed the insurance in March 1992, removing the Cougar and adding a 1984 Plymouth van. The insurance policy was canceled in October 1993, nine months after the robbery.

Much of one day in the trial's opening week was devoted to the testimony of Dick Popowych and Milton Diehl, the Brink's security guards.

Popowych told how Tuesday nights—the robbery had taken place on a Tuesday—were the nights when the depot tended to have the most money inside. He recalled how he, Diehl, and O'Connor had been counting the millions—much to be shipped to banks the next day—when the masked robbers quietly made their way into the depot.

"I heard a noise over my left shoulder and there was someone standing there in coveralls and a ski mask with a revolver, and [he] grunted, and it was obvious to me I better get down on the floor," Popowych said. He and Diehl told how the robbers placed canvas sacks used for holding cash over their heads, bound their wrists, and had them lie on the floor. Popowych said he was heartened when one of the robbers stuck a hand inside the bag to make sure that he was able to breathe. Then, he said, he thought that they would not be killed: "It was comforting at that point, because normally in situations like this, people are shot for no reason."

Popowych testified about the poor security at the depot, how the front door often was not bolted, and how the door was sometimes wedged open for guards to come and go. Popowych said he had complained about security, and he had quit his part-time job at Brink's after the robbery.

Prosecutors hoped to show that someone inside the operation would know what night would be best for a robbery. However, both Popowych and Diehl testified that on occasional Wednesdays, a flow of money from Syracuse and across western New York would lead to as much as $50 million in the depot, though that would typically stay guarded and locked away overnight on a truck.

Lapine used the testimony to again highlight the depot's security shortcomings, and also to question whether Brink's was willing to cut its own costs while supposedly working as a vigilant watchdog of millions of other people's dollars.

"The guard that was babysitting the $50 million or so on Wednesday night, isn't it true that he also doubled as a janitor for the night?" Lapine asked Popowych. Popowych acknowledged that the guard did neaten up the depot on Wednesdays, but at least he was armed.

As the days passed, Buscaglia and Christopher Taffe continued rolling out the Brink's tale in chronological fashion. After uniting Millar and O'Connor in Belfast, bringing Millar and his girlfriend to Rochester, and using the Brink's guards to tell of the robbery, the prosecutors moved on to the investigation. The testimony, they believed, would show the reach of the investigation, with cops telling of surveillance and the questioning of witnesses in New York, Florida, California, and elsewhere across the country.

Intermingled with days of talk about the investigation would be testimony designed to puncture the credibility of the suspects.

Photographs from Rochester Police Officer Greg MacCracken showed the empty pallets, looted of millions of dollars, inside the depot. The photos—shot on Kodak film, MacCracken noted—also highlighted the tire tracks on the depot floor. Officer Mark Sennett told of his measurements of the tire tracks and his trip to the Civic Center garage to measure the tire width of vans parked there—information that later, as jurors would learn, became crucial to the investigation.

Prosecutors knew they had no evidence that put the money squarely in O'Connor's hands. Instead, they needed to show that O'Connor, rather than acting like a retired cop and detective, became evasive and obstructionist in the days immediately following the heist.

Roman Turenko, a Brink's investigator from Toronto, told the court how he kept trying to question O'Connor, but O'Connor would not return his calls.

During his cross-examination, Lapine asked Turenko whether he was the source of a *Democrat and Chronicle* story that had appeared within a week of the robbery and identified O'Connor as a suspect. If so, Lapine said, would he expect O'Connor to take his calls?

"Was it leaked by you?" Lapine asked Turenko about the news story.

"No," Turenko answered.

"You wouldn't do that?"

"I told you I didn't do that."

Two local contractors testified that in the months after the 1993 robbery they had performed about $26,000 worth of work at the O'Connor home in Irondequoit, including installing a new patio, windows, doors, front steps, skylights, and a bay window. O'Connor and his wife always paid in cash.

"You didn't install any secret underground garage or rooms inside where nobody could see what you were doing?" Lapine asked one of the contractors, who said that he'd built no hidden compartments or safes for O'Connor.

Trying to highlight the questions about O'Connor's cash flow, prosecutors summoned an investigator for the IRS, who testified that in 1993 O'Connor and his wife spent over $27,000 more than they took in in income. However, the investigator admitted that he did not look closely at the tax records for the years before 1993, and he would not know if O'Connor had had money stashed away at his home that he could have used for expenditures.

Moloney and Millar also appeared to have unexplained cash after the robbery, testimony showed. Manhattan car dealers told how in May 1993 Moloney had purchased the Ford Explorer, with about $7,000 in cash and the rest from bank loans. (This contradicted the original claims that Moloney had purchased the Explorer entirely with cash.) That Explorer then became Millar's vehicle. FBI agents and a travel agent also told of the Millar family trip to Hawaii.

Millar's former employer in New York City, who knew Millar as Frank Saunders, told how Millar phoned in sick around the time of the Brink's robbery. Millar then quit that job, falsely claiming that his mother had died and he had to return to Northern Ireland.

Members of the joint FBI–New York City Police Department surveillance team testified about their initial days of tracking Millar, after they located him in Queens. Testimony showed that he'd been spotted disposing of tires in a lot near his apartment. FBI agents had seized the tires, which appeared to roughly match the tread prints found at the Brink's depot on the night of the robbery.

Agents told of spotting Moloney and Millar traveling together to and from the

Manhattan apartment where the stolen $2 million was found. The investigation was suspended in February 1993, FBI agents and New York City cops said, with the bombing at the World Trade Center.

Once the surveillance resumed in the summer of 1993, the investigators quickly became certain that Millar and Moloney were the right people to tail. As they related in testimony that stretched over days, investigators watched as Millar carried into the apartment bags that appeared to be bulging with cash. They watched as Moloney toted a money counter into the apartment. And they watched as Moloney, having driven away from the apartment, started counting a wad of cash when at a stoplight.

Meanwhile, the pair continued to act as if money were of no concern—except, perhaps, where to keep it safely. Moloney's purchase of two safes was detailed, as was Millar's consideration of a $300,000 house in the leafy suburbs of Westchester County as a home for him and his family. (The FBI had gathered this and other evidence after the arrests in November 1993.) The testimony mounted—more surveillance, more examples of fresh riches for Millar and Moloney—until FBI Special Agent Leonard Hatton took the stand on October 28 in what truly was, for prosecutors, the "money day" of testimony.

In a full day of testimony, Hatton discussed the FBI's "sneak and peek" search warrant, as well as the November 12, 1993, search and seizure during which some of the Brink's money was located in the Manhattan apartment.

Using the sneak-and-peek warrant, investigators found inside a closet in the apartment duffel bags and suitcases stuffed with money, as well as the money counter, Hatton said. The agents spent under ninety minutes inside, photographing and videotaping. They used the evidence to secure a search warrant and raided the apartment the next day—the same day they made the arrests in the Brink's case and searched other locations across New York City.

The money was not counted for days, Hatton said, but agents found close to $2 million in the apartment.

Hatton continued testifying the next day, with his focus on a central bit of prosecutorial business—incriminating McCormick. Little of the testimony thus far had even acknowledged McCormick, other than mentioning the fact that he had leased the Manhattan apartment.

Papers seized from McCormick's apartment hinted at his desire to get rich, prosecutors contended. For instance, Hatton told of the college newspaper letter to the editor, titled "For the Love of Money."

McCormick's attorney, Speranza, who'd had little to do until this point, complained about the significance that the prosecution assigned to his client's collegiate writings.

Buscaglia maintained that the article showed McCormick's longing for wealth. "It's the government's position that that dissertation, that letter to the editor, whatever it is, is probative of the defendant's intent," Buscaglia said.

The fact that prosecutors had turned to something written years before the robbery was proof of the "paucity of direct evidence" against McCormick, Speranza said.

There was more evidence—and more for Speranza to scoff at. During the search, investigators had found a notebook with a bevy of numbers inside, including the numbers 7.1 million and 2 million. It wasn't coincidence, prosecutors said, that the amount of money found in McCormick's apartment was the same number that he had written into a notebook.

Yes it was, Speranza answered. The notebook, he said, was from a college class of McCormick's, and it was littered with numbers.

Hatton admitted that inside the kitchen of McCormick's apartment investigators had found nothing more than a can of Campbell's soup and a container of garlic salt—evidence, Speranza said, that showed that McCormick had temporarily abandoned the apartment and left it in Moloney's control.

Nearing the end of their case, prosecutors showed the $107,980 that matched the stolen Brink's money. And while it might have been impressive to roll 350 pounds of cash into the courtroom, prosecutors instead showed jurors photos of the remaining $2 million that had been found in Manhattan. Federal authorities were being exceptionally careful with the cash. After all, it had already been stolen once.

"Everybody wants to be very cautious, and make sure none of this stuff is lost, or something happens to it," said Assistant US Attorney Bradley Tyler, the prosecutor in charge of the Rochester US Attorney's Office.

The cash was the climax of the prosecution's case, and a month had passed by the time the government reached that point. It was November, and Larimer was concerned about Thanksgiving. Should the trial go that long, he decided, there would be a long break for the holiday weekend. Some jurors had travel plans, and Larimer did not intend to mess those up for the women and men—a male alternate had stepped in after a juror's father died—who'd already devoted five weeks to the case.

On November 8, prosecutors ended their case, taking a few final shots at the defendants. In yet another bit of circumstantial evidence that prosecutors contended showed proof of McCormick's guilt, an FBI agent revealed that the agency's forensics team had lifted the fingerprint from a piece of cardboard that separated stacks of cash found in the apartment.

Under cross-examination from Speranza, the agent acknowledged that the print could have been ten years old. Speranza had scored another point: McCormick could have easily touched the piece of cardboard years before, and someone else could have slipped it between the money piles. The case against McCormick—a college notebook, a sliver of cardboard, and a letter to the editor of a college newspaper—grew flimsier by the day.

Millar's situation was another story. In testimony that closed the final day for the prosecution, an IRS investigator told how a study of Millar's personal and business accounts, some kept under aliases, showed that in the months after the January 5, 1993, robbery he had spent $62,400 more than he had earned.

In all, nearly a hundred people testified during the six weeks of prosecutorial evidence. Prosecutors also introduced hundreds of documents and videotapes into evidence.

The prosecution narrative completed, it was now the turn of the defense. But first would come a piece of courtroom formality—a defense motion that the case be dismissed.

The law permits criminal defense to challenge the sufficiency of the evidence after the prosecution's case is done. As the prosecution wound down, the defense lawyers had huddled together one evening to discuss possible shortcomings in the government's case. As the attorneys bounced different ideas off one another, Lapine—as if still in his courtroom mien—sat quietly. But, just as in the courtroom, he was completely attuned to the conversation, even if he appeared apathetic. He knew from past cases, he said, that Larimer was particularly receptive to questions about whether a trial was being held in the proper venue.

Yes, a pretrial decision had ensured that the trial would be held in Rochester, since the initial offense—the robbery that gave rise to all that occurred afterward—happened there. But the pretrial venue decision had focused only on whether a Rochester jury had been tainted by the ample media coverage. There were other venue questions to explore.

The defense team chose Feldman and Bill Clauss, probably the best analysts of dense legal issues, to pursue venue possibilities. They crafted multiple arguments to present to Larimer the next day, using Lapine's comment as the foundation for their research.

In court the next day, as expected, each defense attorney maintained that the evidence was insufficient against his client and that charges should be dismissed. To no one's surprise, Larimer did not dismiss any charges based on substandard proof.

Feldman then took up the more nuanced legal challenges. He challenged the prosecution's decision to try the charges of illegal possession of the cash in Rochester. The money was found in New York City; no one disputed that. So the charge of stealing millions should have been tried in the New York City region, not western New York, Feldman argued. There was a reason why the other defense lawyers ceded this debate to Feldman and Clauss: while Speranza, Lapine, and Leonardo were better known for their long string of high-profile defense cases, Feldman and Clauss were, quite simply, better on the law.

Larimer asked for a night to consider. The next day, in a blow to the prosecution, Larimer sided with the defense on some of its arguments, agreeing on the issue of venue and dismissed some of the charges. "The principles at stake here are no mere technicalities, and one man's view of technicality is another man's constitutionally protected right," Larimer said.

Millar, who had said little during the bulk of the trial, looked at the defense team as if in shock. He later told some members of the defense team how he'd been imprisoned in Northern Ireland by what he considered a kangaroo court, motivated solely by politics, and he said that he'd never imagined that a criminal justice system could truly embrace justice. This America was a pretty cool place, he said.

Millar recognized that, were he to be convicted, the defense team had just shaved years off of his likely sentence. He would later remark how grateful he was that Moloney's bid to hold the trial in New York City had failed.

Even with the victory for the defense—"the meat of the government's case is gone," Feldman said on the day of Larimer's ruling—the accused still had criminal charges pending. Millar and Moloney now faced a single criminal conspiracy count, but the evidence against them would be tough to overcome.

However, during one of the rare occasions when Millar spoke to the defense team during the trial, he had given Moloney a possible defense. During a chat with attorneys, Millar had told of some illegal casinos in Manhattan where he'd worked as a security guard, and how he'd sometimes transported the money between the casinos. They were run by a Westchester County man, John McGillion, who liked to hire Irishmen.

This was news to Moloney's attorneys. And it was news that could explain why Moloney claimed he didn't know where the $2 million in the apartment came from.

Maybe Moloney thought he was helping Millar store cash from the casinos. Maybe it was time for a "Hail Mary" defense.

After all, what better way to defend a priest?

CHAPTER 18

— — —

On November 10, 1994, Tom O'Connor took the stand.

Felix Lapine had opened the day's testimony with medical witnesses who told of the respiratory and cardiac problems O'Connor suffered after the robbery—evidence countering claims that O'Connor had been unaffected by the crime. But that wasn't enough for Lapine. He wanted O'Connor to testify. Moreover, he believed that he needed O'Connor to testify.

Lapine recognized early in the case that O'Connor needed to be heard. There was no question that O'Connor had smuggled Sam Millar into the country, that O'Connor had helped Millar and Bernadette Fennell settle in the United States, and that Millar moved the Brink's cash about in New York City. Those facts, coupled with the claims of prosecutors that the evidence pointed to an inside job at Brink's, could be enough for O'Connor to be convicted. All of this needed to be confronted head-on, and O'Connor was the only one who could do that.

Late on that day, O'Connor began his testimony, fielding questions from Lapine.

O'Connor told how lax the security was at the Brink's depot. He also had cause for the cold-shoulder attitude he'd displayed toward FBI agents. Quite frankly, he didn't like them. His long-standing distaste for the FBI dated back to his twenty years as a cop.

"I've had numerous experiences with them, all bad," O'Connor said.

He admitted that he'd brought Millar into the country, claiming that he'd driven Millar back from Toronto but balked for several days each time he neared the international border.

With his testimony beginning late on a Thursday, O'Connor was able to testify for only ninety minutes. The next day would be Veterans' Day, a court holiday, and David Larimer had another hearing for Monday, November 14, that could not be rescheduled. This meant a four-day break for the jurors and O'Connor—four days before he would likely undergo a grueling cross-examination.

When the trial resumed on Tuesday, O'Connor returned to the stand, with his usual happy-go-lucky demeanor. Lapine continued his direct examination.

O'Connor returned to his experiences with the FBI. Once, he said, agents wanted him to act illegally, to arrest a local bookmaker on false charges. The FBI wanted the man brought in so they could place a tracking device on his belt buckle or another piece of clothing.

O'Connor was then working in the city vice squad, and he refused to make the bust, he said. His supervisor always told him, "If you can't [arrest] them fair and square, I don't want them." This would be an arrest without cause; honorable cops didn't do that.

Also, O'Connor said, when he worked at the Genesee Brewing Company, FBI agents use to come there for free beer. A supervisor once asked O'Connor to carry several cases to an agent's car. O'Connor said he told the agent that if "this was a city policeman or a judge, you guys would be locking them up for extortion, but you can get free beer."

Some FBI agents in the court chafed. Unsure whether O'Connor's story was true or not, they were nevertheless irked that this former cop—a man whom they considered to have been particularly dirty when he was in uniform—was adopting this angelic stance.

"To wrap up here, you have been accused here of being the 'inside' man of the robbery that occurred at Brink's in January of 1993," Lapine said. "Is that true, Tom?"

"No."

"Did you have anything whatsoever to do with the robbery?"

"No, it's ruined my life."

"You are also charged with possessing stolen money . . . apparently Brink's stolen money. Have you ever possessed Brink's money that was stolen?"

"No sir."

"That's all. Thank you."

Christopher Buscaglia wasted no time in his cross-examination, hoping to reveal O'Connor as the deceitful louse he believed him to be. Buscaglia pounced on an admission that O'Connor had made in questioning—that he suffered from a gradual hearing loss and had lied about this problem when applying for the Brink's job. He then turned to O'Connor's illegal act—bringing Millar into the country—as the prosecutor worked to pierce O'Connor's blithe attitude.

Buscaglia wanted the jury to see O'Connor's ease with dishonest conduct. He wanted the jury to believe that O'Connor's devil-may-care demeanor was more devilish than carefree.

"You also used deception when you smuggled Sam Millar into the U.S.?" Buscaglia asked O'Connor.

"Yes, I did."

"And you lied more than once in doing that, didn't you?"

"Yes, I did."

Buscaglia segued to O'Connor's 1984 trip to England and Northern Ireland and the fateful meeting with Millar. Why, Buscaglia asked, would O'Connor travel into Northern Ireland and Belfast, with its relentless strife and hazards, unless he were politically motivated? "The streets of Northern Ireland were being patrolled, weren't they? There were British police officers patrolling the streets. And they wore military-type uniforms, didn't they?"

"Yes."

"Carried automatic weapons?"

"Yes."

As the questioning intensified, O'Connor couldn't help himself. He smiled broadly at Buscaglia, the grin almost challenging.

"By the way, if there's anything funny about my questions will you let me know?" Buscaglia said. When O'Connor chuckled during questioning, Buscaglia asked whether O'Connor found amusement in the cross-examination queries.

"I have a nervous smile," O'Connor said.

For hours that day and into the next one the questions continued.

On Wednesday Buscaglia returned to Northern Ireland. During his direct examination, O'Connor had said he had helped Millar get out of Northern Ireland because he believed Millar was in danger.

Buscaglia prodded deeper: "You also developed a belief that he was in danger because he had taken a side in this civil war that was going on in Northern Ireland. . . . He was in danger because of conflict that he had engaged in that subjected him to retaliation by the other side—isn't that what happened?"

Lapine quickly objected, prompting a sidebar discussion with Larimer, who dismissed the jury for a short break. At the bench Lapine reminded the judge that issues related to the IRA were supposed to be taboo at trial.

"We are getting dangerously close to those areas which you have shut off earlier, and we respected those rulings," Lapine said. "And now Mr. Buscaglia is very very near the edge and I'm afraid of what might happen."

Larimer agreed.

"Mr. Buscaglia, as we sailed close to those shoals, I was a little concerned too," he said, reminding the attorneys that there was to be no mention of the IRA crimes that had landed Millar at Long Kesh.

Larimer also instructed O'Connor "not to volunteer anything as to the specifics, even if you know the specifics, as to why Millar was being retaliated against" in Northern Ireland.

The subject of the IRA had been avoided.

O'Connor and Buscaglia continued to joust: Buscaglia worked to show that the robbery could not and would not have been pulled off without inside help and that the evidence—from O'Connor's connections with Millar to O'Connor's unwillingness to help investigators—pointed to the retired cop as the offender. O'Connor tried to deflect the questions, highlighting the security shortcomings at the depot. The publicly broadcast identification of him as a suspect was the reason for his hesitancy to help investigators, he said.

O'Connor finally left the stand on his third day of testimony, his grin still intact.

— — —

At the start of the trial, Father Patrick Moloney would have been pegged as the defendant most likely to testify. In his multiple interviews, and even in occasional comments in court before trial, he had insisted on his innocence and said that the truth—a truth certain to lead to his exoneration—would be revealed at the trial. He would relish the chance to tell his version of events, he said.

But when the time came to take the stand, Moloney said he couldn't. His priestly vow of confidentiality prohibited him from doing so, according to him.

"If I were free to take the witness stand, I am positive I would be in a position to establish my innocence. . . . I would risk being found guilty rather than violate the secrecy," he said.

Jonathan Feldman and Bill Clauss assured Larimer that the decision had been Moloney's to make. Larimer told Moloney that he could simply decline to answer questions that might intrude on any confessional confidences, and answer what questions he could. He had discussed this with others in his church, Moloney said, and there was no middle ground. The vociferous priest—the one whose claims of innocence had been so effusive and persistent that his testimony had been eagerly awaited—would instead sit quietly.

Nonetheless, his attorneys were still prepared to mount a defense. They, like

Millar, faced the enormous hurdle of Moloney's continued presence at the apartment where the Brink's money had been found.

The priest's defense was this: He may not have known the source of the cash, and therefore he could not be convicted of possession of the stolen money.

To make a convincing case, the jurors would have to decide that Moloney believed the cash came from somewhere other than Brink's. Either that, or he was incredibly—perhaps irrationally—uninquisitive about the hundreds of thousands of dollars piling up in the apartment, including the cash found in his suitcase.

Millar had other sources of cash—specifically, the illegal Manhattan casinos he'd mentioned to lawyers during the trial. What if Father Pat suspected the money was casino cash that needed a shelter, and he was simply offering a place for the money to be stashed?

In his opening statement, Feldman had not raised this possibility. Instead he presented Moloney as a priest who bought and sold things at Manhattan flea markets, and some of his sales—distinctively designed stained-glass windows—could bring a lot of money. Moloney simply kept his money tucked away at Bonitas House, Feldman implied. (Moloney would later say the money was from the "unofficial credit union" he operated for the illegal immigrants whom he assisted.)

While Moloney's attorneys to this day will not discuss their confidential trial strategy, the witnesses called to the stand by the priest's lawyers show that the theory unveiled as the priest's defense was birthed during the weeks of trial. There had been no mention of the casinos in the opening statement, but now, perhaps grasping for any reed that might get their client an acquittal, Moloney's defense attorneys focused on the casino operations where Millar had worked while living in New York City.

Testifying for Moloney were Patrick Farrelly, a freelance reporter who'd written about the casinos, and New York City Police Sgt. Brian Murphy, who'd busted up the casinos several times. The two had been subpoenaed during the trial—more proof that Moloney's attorneys had not known of the casinos' relevance only weeks before.

For jurors, this was new information, and Moloney's lawyers had to connect Millar to the casinos and the cash. Farrelly and Murphy had no trouble doing that.

Farrelly described the casinos that operated in Manhattan apartments, the betting clientele, and the individual—Millar—who sometimes worked as a security guard at the operations. One of Millar's jobs, Farrelly explained, was to transport the money from the casinos to locations where it could be safely stashed. Murphy told of arresting Millar twice. Both times Millar used the alias of Thomas O'Connor.

Prosecutors tried to undermine the testimony, soliciting other testimony that showed that $2 million would be a major score at the casinos—far more money than typically ran through the operations.

With Moloney choosing not to testify, his defense case was complete.

Millar also would not testify. The evidence against him was likely strongest of all, and to subject him to questioning could open the door to details about his past.

Besides, Anthony Leonardo never liked to put a client on the stand. There was too much uncertainty, too much opportunity for a defense case to go haywire. And if prosecutors scored points during cross-examination, those could be branded into the minds of jurors, since their deliberations would typically begin shortly after the defense completed its case.

Leonardo did not call any witnesses to help Millar either. Frankly, there were none to call. He could perhaps find character witnesses, but they could not provide any alibis or ammunition for Millar's defense.

John Speranza approached his clients differently: He wanted them to testify. In the days before he was to put on a defense for McCormick, Speranza warred with himself, bouncing different scenarios around in his head about how Mc-Cormick's testimony might go.

Speranza thought he'd done well, providing viable explanations for the cir-cumstantial evidence that was the foundation of the case against McCormick. But jurors could be an enigma: twelve people in a room could be swayed by one personality and one piece of evidence that seemed inconsequential to a defense lawyer.

That's why, when appropriate, Speranza preferred that the defendant talk to the jury. Speranza especially wanted clients to testify if he truly believed them to be innocent—as he did McCormick. Jurors could promise, as they did at the outset of each trial, that they would not hold a defendant's silence against him. But human nature being what it is, Speranza believed that testifying was better for a defendant.

But it could be dangerous. For example, a defendant, provoked by a prosecutor, could become animated and angry on the stand, responding to questions in a way that added credibility to the criminal allegations. And there was always the chance that a defendant could, innocently but with possibly bad results, open up avenues for a whole new line of questioning.

Speranza wasn't alone; McCormick was also struggling with the decision of whether to testify. He knew that Speranza was open to the possibility, but whatever Speranza wanted, the decision was ultimately McCormick's.

During a break in defense testimony, McCormick joined his brother, who was attending the trial, for a cigarette break outside of the courthouse building. During the chat, McCormick decided he wanted to tell his story. He'd been sitting silently at the defense table for weeks now, and on some days he had not even been mentioned.

He'd watched how Father Pat had shied away from testifying, a stance at complete odds with the priest's boasts that he would be the best witness for himself when the time came. McCormick had once respected the priest, helping him out at Bonitas House. But McCormick would forever hold Moloney responsible for the criminal charges against him. It was Moloney who'd sublet McCormick's apartment, it was Moloney who'd allowed the apartment to be used to hide the looted millions, and it was Moloney whose decisions now had McCormick looking at the possibility of losing years of his life in prison.

McCormick also believed that he had something in his favor that Moloney did not: McCormick was innocent. Moloney had either been criminal—which seemed likely to McCormick—or stupid.

Speranza had already been able to nibble away at the evidence against McCormick, but McCormick could provide some answers that others could not.

The final defendant to testify, McCormick said he was not surprised that a piece of cardboard bearing his fingerprint had been found separating stacks of the money. He had once used the cardboard as backing for a print a former girlfriend had given him. He'd never liked the print and once slipped the cardboard out, replacing the print with a sketch of Che Guevara. He had never replaced the cardboard.

That explained why the fingerprint was only on one slide; he'd slid the cardboard rectangle from the print when he removed the print.

As for the composition book that prosecutors insisted showed amounts similar to the $7.4 million stolen from the depot and the $2 million found in the apartment, that was, as Speranza had earlier indicated, a decade-old college notebook from a class on the principles of accounting. The composition book revealed his increasing lack of interest in the class; it started with detailed numbers and equations and turned into little more than doodles as the semester progressed. It was no wonder that McCormick got a C minus in the class.

McCormick had other proof to show that the federal agents were wildly off base with their conclusions that it could not be coincidental that some of the numbers in the composition book were a close match with the stolen Brink's money. In the months before trial, McCormick called a friend who'd been in the same class at Fairfield University. The friend still had the accounting textbook.

In the textbook was a problem involving the number 7,186,300—the same number that prosecutors were now trying to use as evidence of McCormick's guilt.

Speranza also had a witness designed to further erode the government's case. A former head of a New York City police forensics division, Thomas Horan was an expert in document authentication and had technically analyzed the writings in McCormick's composition book. Horan said that the ink striations showed that the same ballpoint pen likely was used for entries that were clearly college-related and for the numbers prosecutors had tried to tie to the Brink's robbery.

So either McCormick had written the numbers a decade before the robbery, just as he said he had, or he'd kept the same ballpoint pen for a decade. The jury was unlikely to accept the latter premise: Who keeps a pen for ten years?

— — —

Attorneys, the judge, and certainly the jurors had hoped that the trial would be complete by Thanksgiving. It was not to be.

On the Monday before Thanksgiving attorneys revisited their cases in eight hours of closing arguments. This was their last chance with the jurors, and the lawyers did not want to go out with a fizzle.

"You heard Patrick Moloney described as a pious, holy man by his attorney," Buscaglia said. "You heard Samuel Millar described generally as a poor soul who wanted to come to America to start a new life. You heard about, according to McCormick's lawyer, an innocent bystander in all of this. And you heard, as far as O'Connor goes, about a distinguished retired police officer. That's what their lawyers said."

Buscaglia revisited his evidence, bit by bit: O'Connor's illegal spiriting of Millar into the country; the apparent involvement of an insider in the Brink's robbery and O'Connor's lack of cooperation with the subsequent investigation; the extensive surveillance linking Millar and Moloney to the money and resulting in the discovery of the cash; and McCormick's connection to Moloney and the Manhattan apartment, and his evasiveness with the police and FBI.

The defense attorneys, working with the facts and evidence at hand, tried to dismantle Buscaglia's case: There was no physical evidence tying O'Connor to the robbery or the cash; Moloney may have simply been helping a friend, Millar, store money that the priest thought was from the casinos; and the evidence against McCormick—a composition book and a letter to the editor of a college newspaper—was proof of an overzealous prosecution and not McCormick's guilt.

Leonardo had a tougher job defending Millar. There was no alternative theory to explain why Millar had toted around stolen millions. So Leonardo simply tried to find weaknesses with the criminal case and highlight them.

On Tuesday, the jurors began their deliberations but could not finish. Again on Wednesday, they could not reach a verdict. They occasionally asked about past testimony and evidence, once inquiring about Millar's telephone records, which had been introduced as evidence weeks before. One call had been from Millar's home in Queens to O'Connor's home two months before the trial. Another had been a collect call from a pay phone in Greece, New York, to Millar's home about ninety minutes after the robbery.

Prosecutors had hoped to connect the latter call to O'Connor, since the phone booth was not far from where O'Connor claimed to have been dumped by the thieves. But the well-used telephone had not yielded any fingerprints or other forensic evidence for authorities.

The jurors went home for four days for the Thanksgiving holiday and week-end. On Monday, as the hours dragged on, it looked as if another day would be necessary for them to reach verdicts. Instead, the jurors returned to court around 4:00 p.m., their decisions complete after twenty hours of evaluating the evidence.

First was O'Connor, accused of the robbery and conspiracy to possess the stolen money. The jury acquitted him, cheering his family and attorney and leaving the prosecutors fearful that more than a year of investigation and six weeks of trial would end with no one heading to prison.

Those fears were short-lived. The jury forewoman next announced that the jury had found Millar guilty of conspiring to possess the cash.

The verdict was the same for Moloney—guilty, the jury had decided. Millar had not been surprised by his verdict, but, the blank look on Moloney's face spoke volumes. Somehow, he had not imagined this moment.

That left McCormick, an innocent bystander who had made what he now considered the mistake of befriending Moloney.

His verdict: not guilty.

With the verdicts read, Larimer told O'Connor and McCormick they were free to go. Millar would remain jailed pending sentencing, while prosecutors asked Larimer to revoke bail for Moloney, who had been free before and during the trial.

Larimer agreed, noting that much of the Brink's money was still missing. "There's at least $5 million that have not been accounted for, and that can purchase a lot of freedom," he said.

Moloney pleaded for some time to get things in order at the home for troubled teens that he ran in the Lower East Side of Manhattan. Larimer refused, noting that the trial had gone for nearly two months, and Moloney had had a year of freedom after his arrest to prepare for a possible conviction.

"I have not been found guilty in this courtroom," the priest said. Instead, he called himself the victim of "the FBI who perjured themselves and a prosecutor who supported perjury."

Weeks later, Moloney's supporters, using property and cash as security, would get him out on bail, and he would return to Manhattan on electronic monitoring as he awaited sentencing.

On the night of the verdicts, O'Connor celebrated at a local bar with friends and family. McCormick headed to New Jersey, planning to look for work while wondering if the verdict was too little and too late to save his reputation. From now on, he would be the man accused of being part of one of the country's largest armored car company robberies. He'd been acquitted, but that was only one headline amid hundreds. The trial had ruined him, McCormick thought. So had Father Pat, simply because McCormick had made the well-intentioned mistake of subletting his apartment to a priest.

The verdicts stung federal prosecutors, but they praised the jury for its lengthy and thoughtful deliberations.

"I felt there was sufficient evidence to get this case before a jury," Buscaglia said. "That's my duty. I'm convinced the jury did a good job, took its job very seriously, so I have no quarrel."

In particular, prosecutors had wanted O'Connor imprisoned. So had the FBI. And so had some of O'Connor's former police colleagues.

Many people still considered O'Connor responsible for the killing of Damien McClinton. But the evidence there had been lacking—just as it had with the Brink's robbery.

"The only proof was that Tom O'Connor knew Mr. Millar," Lapine said. "Just knowing someone is not enough."

CHAPTER 19

— — —

There was a certain symmetry—one that Father Patrick Moloney hinted bordered on the divine—about the Melkite priest being shipped to Loretto, Pennsylvania, for his federal prison sentence.

Medium-security Loretto federal prison is tucked away in the sylvan splendor of Pennsylvania's Allegheny Mountains. Appropriately for a temporary home for Moloney, the prison and the nearby borough of Loretto were rich in religious history.

The prison had been constructed just a decade before on the site of a for-mer Franciscan seminary. And the borough itself was named after the Italian village of Loreto, which, according to legend, was where angels carried the home of the Virgin Mary after it was at risk of ruin while under assault—first in Nazareth during the Crusades, and later in modern-day Croatia, during a Muslim invasion.

Originally a Roman Catholic mission settlement, Pennsylvania's Loretto (it added a *t* to the Italian name) was awash with religion and spirituality. With religious shrines prominent throughout the small municipality—some of them visible to the prison inmates from their dormitories—Loretto tried, as other nearby rural localities struggled economically, to keep itself relevant as a site of pilgrimage for the devout.

Within the prison confines, the Lord's handiwork was apparent to Moloney. "I do believe that the finger of God has sent me here to tell the world about the unjust and dehumanizing conditions that prevail in our prison system," Moloney told the *New York Times* in a 1997 interview. "The seminarians who prayed here were voluntary prisoners of God, but I am here as a political prisoner."

By then, Moloney had confronted what he considered proof of the federal government's ham-handed unfairness in its supposed administration of justice.

He had not stopped claiming innocence, but prison officials had revived an allegation against him—that he was sympathetic to IRA violence—to crush his spirit, he believed.

A young man whom Moloney had once legally adopted, Jason Patino, had been found dead in a Manhattan apartment on July 8, 1996, and word reached Moloney in prison. The death, federal prison officials wrote in a report, was likely a murder.

"While the details of this death remain sketchy, it is believed Mr. Patino is a homicide victim who was shot several times," one report stated. "After receiving gunshot wounds, Mr. Patino's body was placed either or a bed or a couch, at which time his apartment was set on fire."

Moloney wanted to attend Patino's funeral, and he did not expect pushback to his request to travel to New York for the services. Such requests were not uncommon from inmates, who were often allowed to travel, under guard, when a close relative or loved one died.

Instead, the Loretto prison administrators denied Moloney's request, highlighting concerns about the IRA that had been mentioned in a presentencing report about Moloney's background.

"Mr. Moloney"—prison officials refused to call him Reverend or Father—"was found to be in possession or in control of in excess of one million dollars and is considered an accessory after the fact," a Loretto prison administrator wrote. "Mr. Moloney's Presentence Investigation Report infers that the Irish Republican Movement may have been involved in this offense."

And a pretrial interview that Moloney gave to the British edition of *Esquire* added ammunition to the suspicions of IRA involvement, the official wrote. In that interview, "inmate Moloney admits to sympathizing with the Irish Republican Movement and its causes."

Patino's services would be held in a "high-crime" area of Manhattan, amplifying safety concerns. The administrator wrote: "We believe the circumstances surrounding this request present security issues and concerns which potentially could place inmate Moloney, escorting staff, and the general public in danger if approved."

The denial angered and frustrated Moloney, who even in prison could not escape his alleged association with the IRA. For him, the bureaucratic decision was a repetition of what he'd previously confronted.

When British authorities arrested him on gun-running charges in 1982, Moloney had been portrayed as an IRA sympathizer who cleverly used his priesthood as a cover for his support of paramilitary killers. Lacking evidence, the British dropped the charges against Moloney.

When he was accused of stashing cash from the 1993 Brinks robbery, Moloney again saw his support for an independent Northern Ireland twisted into a rationale for the crimes he was alleged to have committed. But the claims of his IRA involvement were again all smoke, no fire—so lacking in substance that Judge David Larimer refused to let the allegations be aired during Moloney's trial.

Now Moloney was again victimized by the supposed IRA affiliation that he had long contended was a falsehood. "The barbarity and incivility I suffered the week of [Patino's] death, it wouldn't happen in the most uncivilized countries," Moloney said.

Within the prison walls, Moloney found some adult versions of the same struggling teenagers whom he'd mentored in Manhattan. Those young men often struggled with addictions to alcohol, pills, cocaine, and heroin. Moloney and his staff members at Bonitas House had tried to be the stalwart support mechanisms that the teens there did not have elsewhere. Sometimes Moloney had succeeded; sometimes he hadn't.

Now, three hundred miles away, deprived of his freedom, Moloney tried to counsel inmates who reminded him of the Bonitas House teens. Many of the prisoners whom he met at Loretto had backgrounds similar to those of the teens in New York City—they were addicts whose crimes were the result of an urgent need for money to feed their cravings.

Of course, there were inmates of another stripe at Loretto, men who'd made their illicit livelihoods as drug traffickers.

"I spent my whole life fighting drugs—heroin, cocaine, crack and marijuana," Moloney said. "Now I am in a cell with five other men, all of whom are convicted dealers."

Some inmates learned that Moloney, in his activist role in a struggling Manhattan neighborhood, sometimes collaborated with police to target neighborhood drug dealers. Moloney said that, while at Loretto, one major drug dealer approached him and said, "You're the kind of person who put me in here."

"Yes, and I'm the kind of guy that's going to keep you here," Moloney answered.

In prison, perhaps with the inspiration of Loretto's history, Moloney did not retreat from his religion. Instead, he later said, he found his beliefs to be even more of a foundation of faith than he realized they could be. His mantra, which he repeated often to himself, was: "It's not where I want to have to be, but I have to be where I am."

Using the prison pottery shop, Moloney crafted a palm-sized paten—a communion plate—and a tiny two-inch-tall chalice to conduct Mass for himself and other interested inmates. According to Moloney, his creations were inside a pottery kiln with pieces of work from other inmates when a small fire momentarily swelled out of control, destroying all of the prisoners' work except for his.

"Everything blew up except my pieces," he said.

The Eastern Melkite order does not favor using juice as a substitute for wine. Moloney remembered the writings of Father Walter Ciszek, a Jesuit priest who was jailed in a Soviet labor camp because of his secret ministry work in the Soviet Union. Released in 1963 after years of imprisonment, Ciszek wrote of how he kept his sanity—and his religion—while in the Siberian Gulag. Ciszek mastered a system to secretly construct a wine—a weak one, but enough of a wine to qualify for Melkite purposes—out of grapes.

"My joy at being able to celebrate Mass again cannot be described," Ciszek later said. "I heard confessions regularly and from time to time was even able to distribute Communion secretly after I'd said Mass."

Mimicking Ciszek's techniques, Moloney created his own wine.

He also met with inmates with a Catholic background, as well as others interested in speaking with an imprisoned priest. Some inmates told him of grievances they had with individual guards—corrections officers who were inclined to harass inmates whenever an opportunity arose. One guard in particular tormented inmates, writing them up for minor and sometimes questionable disciplinary transgressions.

"It was a systematic conspiracy to persecute the already persecuted," Moloney later said.

He had an answer, and it did not involve violence. "We are going to be called 'The Smilers,'" Moloney told the inmates. Each time a prisoner walked past the guard—or vice versa—the inmate was to give the guard a wide smile. After a week of this, a prison official asked Moloney whether he knew if there was trouble brewing at Loretto. The prison officials were more accustomed to expressions of fatigue and misery than they were to grins of happiness.

In 1998, Moloney was released on parole, having served forty-four of the fifty-one months he'd been sentenced to prison. (Federal inmates can be released after serving 85 percent of their sentence if their disciplinary record is relatively clean.)

He returned to Bonitas House, whose work had continued in the hands of volunteers. He was still in good standing with his church, which had accepted his claims of innocence. The backing from the church in itself showed the insufficiency of the case against him, Moloney said.

Freed from prison, Moloney conducted masses across New York City and its suburbs, serving for several years at a small church for Ukrainian immigrants. He had one restriction: he could not conduct services in jails or prisons.

"If anyone has firsthand experience about the spiritual needs of inmates, it certainly is me," he said. "'But, that's the very place the authorities won't let me enter."

— — —

By the time Moloney was released from prison, Sam Millar was already back home—his birthplace of Belfast, that is.

A year before, elected officials, at the behest of Millar's family and friends, lobbied for him to be transferred to a prison in Northern Ireland. The US Bureau of Prisons has long had an international transfer program allowing foreign inmates jailed in the United States to be moved to their home country, and the United Kingdom was one of the dozens of "treaty transfer" partners with the United States.

In September 1997 Millar was moved to a prison in Northern Ireland to complete his sentence. In some news coverage, this would later—wrongly—be portrayed as a pardon of Millar by President Bill Clinton.

A British Embassy spokesman said of the transfer: "The jails in Northern Ireland are pretty good. There is quite a relaxed regime."

Prison officials in Northern Ireland released Millar before Moloney was freed. Years later, Moloney would question what Millar had done to deserve such treatment, wondering whether Millar had provided some assistance or information to government officials.

For Millar, prison in Northern Ireland was much like his time in the Monroe County jail—nothing compared to the horrors of Long Kesh. Even the Northern Ireland prison now seemed sincerely interested in humanitarian treatment.

In keeping with his nature, Millar kept largely to himself in prison. But while there, he decided to turn to a new profession: he would no longer be a criminal; he would be a writer.

In later years, he would write hard-boiled suspense novels centered on a private investigator named Karl Kane. He would also write a play, exploring the conflict in Northern Ireland through the eyes of two brothers—an unyielding republican dissident who spent fourteen years at Long Kesh and a supporter of Sinn Fein and its quest for peace.

"All those years I spent naked, covered in shit and piss and getting the fuck kicked out of me by the screws every day," the former Long Kesh prisoner says at one point, according to a script obtained for research for this book. "I lost a kidney because of all the beatings I received from those subhuman bastards. . . . Even now when I hear keys rattling, I have flashbacks. I can still see the screws kicking me in the head and kidneys, while pissing themselves laughin'. Just the simple sound of keys rattling triggers the nightmares."

Millar would explore his memories of Long Kesh more deeply in the memoir he began to write while in prison in the United States—an autobiography appropriately titled *On the Brinks*. In the book, he would admit what most people had suspected: he had robbed the Brink's depot. He claimed his friend, Tom O'Connor, was innocent.

"I wrote the book when I was in the penitentiary in America, really to save my life," Millar said. "It was getting me away from the dreary thought of violence that was always hanging over me in the place and I wrote it never believing it would ever be printed.

"It was just to keep me sane. I must have wrote about 800 pages and I was taking them as I was getting moved from penitentiary to penitentiary, and I was always dreading losing it all but I managed to bring most of it back home with me."

As Millar and Moloney served their prison sentences, McCormick and O'Connor returned to their homes, hoping the Brink's case was in the past.

Like Millar, McCormick considered writing a book about his experience—a tell-all about the federal government's attempts to railroad an innocent man. O'Connor had no such desire. He simply wanted to put the Brink's case behind him and get on with his life.

That would not be easy. Several years after his acquittal, a neighbor of O'Connor was shot on his front lawn. Police found little reason for the shooting and suspected that O'Connor had been the intended target. Adding more mystery to the unsolved shooting—which the man survived—was the fact that the forensics testing of a recovered round indicated the handgun had most likely been manufactured in Europe.

The suspicions were inevitable: perhaps someone in Northern Ireland worried about what O'Connor might one day say.

And the police were not done with O'Connor. He would be a suspect in yet another crime: the disappearance and suspected murder of a retired boxer from New York City, a man with his own ties to the Rochester Brink's robbery.

PART 2

Finding Ronnie

CHAPTER 20

— — —

Trading blow for blow, the two fighters whaled away at each other.

Ronnie Gibbons, wiry and muscular, was a disciplined boxer whose technique and intelligence in the ring had boxing aficionados thinking he could fight his way to the top of the super welterweight ranks. Gibbons's fitness was often unrivaled, and while he was recognized mostly for his pugilistic craftsmanship, he could also serve up a powerful punch—especially a wide hook—that landed like a hammer blow.

Danny McAloon also was known for his wily ways in the ring; he was a smart and popular fighter who always seemed on the brink of competing for a championship. McAloon could take a pounding, staggered by an opponent, yet stay upright and keep swinging. Rarely was he knocked out; most of his losses came from judges' decisions.

Dark-haired, dark-eyed, and movie-idol handsome, Gibbons looked as if he'd been chiseled from stone, with his angular cheeks and his physique sculpted by hours in the gym and his refusal to indulge in alcohol, tobacco, and unhealthy foods (with the occasional lapse brought on by a sweet tooth that he could not always keep at bay). Gibbons had a youthful countenance that showed no lasting traces of previous punches to the face. Twenty-three years old, he was a decade younger than McAloon.

Broader across the shoulders and more physically intimidating, McAloon appeared more like a barroom brawler. For his early fights—he turned professional in the mid-1960s—his hair was close cropped, almost in a military-style cut, but during the 1970s he adopted the style of the era, with his hair bushier and thick sideburns going below his ears.

Perhaps their Irish roots didn't matter to the two men battling it out at the Sunnyside Garden Arena, but they did to some ringside fans. They believed that Gibbons and McAloon were fighting for an extra bit of ancestral pride, for the opportunity for one of them to revel later in life in the memory of the day he felled another Irishman who was on the rise in the boxing world. McAloon, in fact, was nicknamed "Irish Danny," a moniker he wore proudly.

Both had entourages of Irish American and Irish-born friends whom they'd brought to Sunnyside, a historic brick boxing arena in Queens, New York, that often filled most of its 2,500 seats. With $7 ringside tickets, Sunnyside had no trouble drawing boisterous and rowdy crowds, men whose love of cigars and cigarettes created a dense choking fog.

The preliminary fights before the Gibbons-McAloon bout were underwhelming—four matches between boxers with twenty-five wins among the eight of them. McAloon himself had twenty-five wins, as well as eleven losses. Gibbons's record was an impressive twenty wins and two losses. The undercard boxers had twice as many losses as McAloon and Gibbons combined.

Gibbons first entered the ring professionally in 1974, more than two years before the contest with McAloon, and proceeded to win eighteen of his first nineteen fights. The other ended in a draw.

Gibbons was on his way to bigger arenas, bigger paydays, higher-profile fights, and maybe a shot at a belt.

Then, at Madison Square Garden on December 12, 1975, a Canadian boxer named Fernand Marcotte chased and pummeled Gibbons, knocking him to the ring three times in less than a minute and a half. The referee stepped in to bring the fight to an end and declare Gibbons the victim of a technical knockout.

Gibbons suffered a fourth-round knockout in his next fight in February 1976. With back-to-back losses, his future was no longer as promising as it had been only months before.

He won two fights before entering the ring with McAloon on August 27, 1976, and for Gibbons there was more than Irish pride on the line. If he wanted to wedge his way back into the conversation about ascending boxers, he needed a victory.

In the eighth round, neither fighter seemed ready to tire or fade. There was a freshness to their punches and a bounce to their strides that masked the fact that they were only two rounds away from completion.

Paddy Malone, a boxer who trained with McAloon, was in the crowd, cheering on his sparring buddy. By the eighth round, he thought that Gibbons had the fight in hand. Sure, the scorecard would be close, but Gibbons had connected with more frequency than had McAloon.

"It was a great fight all the way," Malone later said.

Randy Gordon, who would later chair the state's boxing regulatory agency, the New York Athletic Commission, was also at Sunnyside, working as a boxing writer. He was expecting great things from Gibbons, who was such an impressive boxer that he'd gotten the legendary Gil Clancy to train him. Clancy had trained the world champion Emile Griffith and once told Gordon, "This kid Ronnie Gibbons is as close in ability to Emile Griffith as I've ever seen."

Gordon had watched Gibbons's rise and recent struggles in the ring, and he saw the McAloon fight as a chance for Gibbons to resume his pursuit for a championship. Gibbons was "a baby-faced fighter with unlimited ability," Gordon said.

But as rigorous as Gibbons's training was, the fighter seemed unable to transition to the heat and mugginess of New York City summers. And Sunnyside Gardens could be particularly hot—wretchedly so for the ill-prepared.

Wearing a T-shirt and dungarees at ringside, Gordon himself was drenched with sweat as a spectator. "It had to be 120 degrees in there," Gordon later said.

Aware of Gibbons's troubles with heat, Gordon noticed something early in the ninth round that others might have missed: the fighter seemed a step slower, his punches lethargic, and his refined technique unable to compensate for the dehydration that was setting in.

McAloon also saw a weakness in his once-feisty opponent, and an opening. "Danny unleashed a left hook and caught him on the chin," Malone recalled. "Down went Ronnie."

Gibbons could not stand up before the referee's count to ten. For this day at least, Irish Danny McAloon was king of the Irish super welterweights.

Gordon joined Gibbons's corner men and helped the downed and dazed boxer to his dressing room. There, they packed much of his body in ice to lower his temperature.

The fight seemed to sap Gibbons's resolve. Known for his buoyancy and optimism, he seemed drained of more than energy after the fight. McAloon's left hook did more than drop Gibbons to the mat; instead, it was as if McAloon had reached into Gibbons's chest and ripped out the boxer's heart, spirit, and soul.

Not long after the fight, Gibbons met with his trainer, and said, "Gil, that's it. I'm not fighting anymore."

Despite that remark to Clancy, Gibbons would have several more fights in his career, though the McAloon match —one that Gibbons likely recognized he should have won—was a turning point. He would work to get in prime shape physically for his later returns to the ring, training in gymnasiums and fitness centers across New York—including Brooklyn's legendary Gleason's gym and the

New York Athletic Club—but he'd never show the same spark. Boxing aficionados saw that, despite Gibbons's fitness, he now also had a wariness in the ring, a lack of assurance that he had never demonstrated before.

Even his father warned him in a letter from Liverpool, England, that fitness alone would not return him to the championship-level fighter he once longed to be.

"Unlike other sports, boxing entails more than physical condition," his father, Joseph Gibbons Sr., wrote a month after the McAloon fight. "A psychological peak is involved. . . . Keep your nose clean and walk easy. I know times are tough at the moment, but time passes and we'll make it. So relax."

Once a fixture in the boxing circles around New York, Gibbons also seemed to disappear from the occasional award dinners and ceremonies that brought the Big Apple's fighters together. Paddy Malone recalled thinking years later, when retired fighters would sometimes gather and remember their bouts, "I wonder what happened to Ronnie Gibbons."

It was as if he'd simply vanished, Malone said.

— — —

Joseph "Ronnie" Gibbons Jr. came to boxing almost as a matter of course. Both his father and grandfather boxed, and Gibbons, a natural athlete from his youth, followed in their footsteps. An excellent runner and soccer player, Gibbons found the boxing ring more to his liking. He started boxing when he was only eleven and, as a teenager, became an amateur fighter in the United Kingdom.

His father had a brief amateur career in Liverpool, before moving to New York City and leaving his wife and three children behind in England.

The American city beckoned to him, its opportunity supposedly endless—especially for a man like Joseph Gibbons Sr., who refused to have a boss or to be a cog in a corporate machine. He preferred to be a self-made man; he would succeed or fail on his own merits and drive, and New York City promised much more likelihood of success than Liverpool.

Once one of Europe's busiest mercantile cities, Liverpool and its port became less active during the second half of the twentieth century as businesses found far cheaper ways to transport their goods and merchandise. Longshoremen—the men who'd loaded and unloaded commercial vessels at the port since they were teenagers—found themselves without work. Manufacturers shut down, as an economic downturn grew more and more severe.

Ronnie Gibbons, who idolized his father, was thunderstruck by his dad's move to the United States. "Ronnie was in a bad state," his mother, Rita, recalled. "He worshiped his father."

His father kept in touch with letters and telephone calls, but Ronnie could not help but think that he and his siblings—his younger brother, Frank, and younger sister, who was also called Rita—had been abandoned. For Ronnie, there was an emptiness, one that could not be filled.

With a man whom he revered now gone from his life, Ronnie was adrift. He could think of only one way to regain his footing: move to New York City himself. His mother knew that this was the wisest choice for her son, though she hated the thought of rarely seeing him.

Ronnie Gibbons made the move to New York when he was nearly twenty, joining his father and embarking on a boxing career that he'd started as an amateur in Liverpool. Both lovers of athletics, the father and son shared a passion for sports. But the likeness of mind did not end there; instead, it extended to an offbeat longing to dissect life and its mysteries, a curiosity that had both men constantly questioning and challenging their world, as if they could somehow rejigger their existence through their own keen if eccentric analysis.

The son was an avid reader of great philosophers, known to have volumes of their writings and musings always at hand. He believed himself to be a poet whose perspective on life was broader than that of the average person.

Like boxing, Ronnie Gibbons had inherited this worldview from his father, who thought himself privy to secrets of science and spirituality that could disrupt much conventional wisdom. Joseph Gibbons Sr. longed to tell the world of his knowledge, so much that he authored a book titled "Relativity or Reason." In an era before widespread self-publishing, he could not find an American agent willing to send the book to publishers. One agent politely told him that "they wouldn't know how to handle it."

The book was concise—perhaps too concise, he wrote to Ronnie. There was simply too much wrapped in its pages for the world to understand—a sprawling buffet of erudition crammed into a snack-size package.

"I'm beginning to write deeper and more profound than Aristotle, plus I'm giving out too much knowledge," Ronnie's father once wrote. "Readers just can't grab it."

The book's contents are lost to the ages, since Joseph Gibbons Sr. died of cancer in 1985, at the young age of fifty-two. In one letter to Ronnie, he said he hoped to speak to the world about "matter, space, gravity" and "the formal problems of God, free will, beauty, ethics and so on."

Such high-mindedness—whether grounded in off-kilter genius or a crackpot mind-set—may not align with the other predilection shared by father and son: both liked to sell things. It could be clothes, it could be jewelry, it could be tchotchkes, but, whatever the product, the pair believed that there was always money to be made, and they could make it better than others.

Again, the father was always willing to pass his lifelong learning to his son. "In the event you don't know how the best peddlers operate in the States, allow me to enlighten you," Joseph Sr. wrote in a 1976 letter from Liverpool, where he'd returned to live for a short time.

Go to the diners and restaurants in midafternoon, he advised his son, because those were the dead hours. Chat up the waitress, tell her that you're a "travelling jewelry salesman" and then display the "shining stones." "Make a sale or two and so on. Borrow a car"—Ronnie did not own one—"and try it between the hours of two and four in the afternoon."

With boxing income sometimes reliable but sometimes meager, Ronnie supplemented his money with sales. Sometimes he sold on the streets—offering shoes, belts, ties, and jewelry—working to convince passersby that he had deals no one else did. At one point he also sold silk scarves and ties from his own rental space in Soho in Manhattan, though to call it "rental" is misleading because a friend allowed him to use the space gratis.

While some overly aggressive salespeople border on hucksterism, Gibbons was not one of them. He did love to sell, and he approached it with the same enthusiasm and zeal he'd typically demonstrated in the ring, though this sparring—the beauty of haggling and bartering over prices—was less debilitating mentally and physically.

John "Bomber" Martin—a fellow boxer and friend of Gibbons—remembered how Gibbons once wanted to purchase a bevy of dresses left over from a Manhattan fashion exhibit. On racks in a makeshift shop, the dresses had been reduced in price after having been worn by runway models during a show.

Gibbons, who planned to resell the dresses, approached the saleswoman and said, "I'll give you a deuce for the lot of them."

"What's a deuce?" she said.

"Two," Gibbons answered.

"$2,000? These dresses are $2,000 each."

"No," Gibbons said. "$200—for the lot."

To this day, Martin is unsure just how the dumbstruck saleswoman went from believing Gibbons was a madman to agreeing to let him and Martin take as many dresses as they could carry. They walked away with several dozen dresses—for $200.

Even when out on the town at a restaurant or bar (where he would drink water as others imbibed stronger beverages), Gibbons could not help trying to make a sale. Once, friends of his who were also buddies of the comedian Colin Quinn took Gibbons to a Quinn performance. Quinn's mother was in the crowd, and Gibbons tried to sell her a pair of shoes during the show.

Between his years as a boxer and his constant workouts at New York City gyms, Gibbons developed an entourage of friends with an eclectic assortment of livelihoods. There were firefighters, actors, writers, and roustabouts—all of whom found Gibbons funny, oddly endearing, and certainly unconventional. They were mostly Irish American, or Irish born. Though born in Liverpool, Gibbons was of Irish descent. He joked that he was conceived in Ireland, and his birthplace should not be held against him.

A street-corner peddler who read Aristotle, a boxer without a touch of punch-drunkenness, Gibbons often became the focus of attention when he strolled into a room—and he did so without effort or vanity. He also knew how to take advantage of his charm, using it occasionally to inveigle people to give him free meals and get him into shows.

"He was always on scholarship everywhere he went," said his friend Terry Quinn, a firefighter who owned a bar in Manhattan with the actor Matt Dillon. "I don't know if he ever even tipped."

The actor Jim McCaffrey, who starred in the FX network series *Rescue Me* (Quinn was the show's firefighting consultant), remembered being at a popular hip restaurant in Soho with Gibbons, Martin, Quinn, and others. The dinner bill ended up in McCaffrey's hands, and he asked for contributions. Gibbons said nothing; Martin refused to pay anything. McCaffrey tried again; neither Gibbons nor Martin—who would later say he had had nothing but a soda—provided any cash. The division of the bill escalated into a tussle, with McCaffrey and Martin scuffling and overturning a table. Gibbons simply looked on as glasses fell to the floor, cracking into sharp-edged slivers. Gibbons smiled at the wrestling and fisticuffs, which finally came to a peaceful if destructive resolution. When all was settled and restitution promised if sought, Gibbons had still contributed nothing to the bill.

Gibbons also knew a Melkite priest on the Lower East Side—Father Patrick

Moloney—who was known to help Irish immigrants navigate the labyrinthine immigration process. Gibbons took Irish immigrants to Father Pat, who would become their guide through immigration laws, documents, and interviews.

Once Moloney took Gibbons and a friend of Gibbons to the swank Manhattan apartment of a British gentleman who'd been a member of high society in his home country. Gibbons found the man enchanting and—though he was rarely impressed by celebrities—decided that he wanted to take him and Moloney to dinner the next night. According to Moloney, they ended up in an upper-tier Manhattan steak restaurant, and Gibbons was never given a bill.

"I'll never know who paid for it," Moloney said.

Another time, Gibbons took Moloney to the Metropolitan Opera. Again, there was no indication that he'd paid for the fine seats at the performance.

Gibbons's sister, Rita, once traveled to New York City to watch her older brother box, and, like her brother and father before her, could not leave. She too was overcome by all the city offered and decided to stay.

"I'd never seen buildings so big and highways so fast," she later said. "And the people were so funny. Watching garbage pickup was a big thing to me. You'd see women in mink coats taking in the garbage. They could afford mink coats and they're taking in the garbage. And there were the cabdrivers with the big cigars hanging out of their mouths. I was just fascinated with this place. I was like a kid in Disneyland."

Ronnie was both her guide in New York and, she said, "my protector, my defender." "You always felt safe with him," she said. "Anything you needed or wanted, Ronnie could get. . . . He knew someone who worked in the motor vehicles [department]. He knew someone in Con Edison, if your lights were turned off. He knew someone who had a truck if you needed one. He knew everybody."

This was the enigma of Ronnie Gibbons. Here was a fellow who rarely if ever picked up a tab, whose habits—the frequent quotation of philosophers and the disdain for stable employment—could be interpreted as the hallmarks of instability, and who took unusual pride in his ability to sell even the most worthless of items. Yet he had a charisma and a gentlemanliness that were both arresting and authentic. Indeed, Ronnie was nothing if not authentic. He did not possess an ounce of insincerity.

Gibbons took an intense interest in the lives of the people he met, whether they picked up his trash or drove his cab. And those whom he met could not forget him. Yes, he could occasionally diverge into ramblings that seemed in search of a center, but somewhere in the verbal thicket there were always seeds of wisdom, some perspective about how to live a fulfilling life.

"He always had something unique and interesting to add to any conversation, be it the Irish Troubles, American sport, boxing, or women," said McCaffrey. "He would draw you in with his stories, but he always seemed more interested in your stories."

Billy Devlin, another New York City–based actor, said of his friend Gibbons, "He was authentic, with an undying sense of humor. He understood the absurd that came to be passed as ordinary and pointed it out in spectacularly articulate and hilarious ways."

Even Gibbons's language was compelling. He spoke, his friends say, in an almost poetic lilt, his Irish brogue sometimes difficult for New Yorkers to grasp, but the rhythm and fluidity of his speech compelling nonetheless.

Still, he was a bit of a puzzle, even in a city that was home to nearly every nationality and type of personality one can imagine. His friends found him captivating but were sometimes unsure just what to make of his idiosyncratic ways. As McCaffrey said, "He was an intriguing and mysterious character."

Gibbons loved underdogs, including the impoverished kids living in the tough New York neighborhoods that reminded him of those he had known in Liverpool. He had a distaste for the criminal elements in the neighborhoods in which some kids lived, and this prompted him occasionally to do crazy things, dangerous things—like approach drug dealers with a video camera and ask them why they were hawking death. Somehow he came out of these encounters alive, the drug dealers scurrying from street corners like cockroaches subjected to a burst of light.

Sometimes Gibbons would take several young kids and teens from lower-income neighborhoods to an upscale Manhattan dining establishment. He would stroll in with the motley gang of youngsters, some slightly unkempt and others wide-eyed at the posh restaurant, and somehow cajole the manager into providing a free meal—hinting that otherwise the establishment would be known as uncaring about those mired in poverty in the city.

"You just fed some hungry children in the city of New York," Gibbons once told a restaurateur after the meal. "You can pay your rent in heaven."

His sister recalled the looks he'd get. "You'd have all these snobby people that were out of touch with reality and the downtrodden," she said. "He'd get a kick out of these people."

He once dressed as Santa Claus to hand out toys on a Harlem street. "But he got jumped by a gang and it must have looked funny to see Santa scrapping with a mob on 110th Street," his brother, Frank, said.

Though he often was short on cash, Gibbons was known to hand over what little he had to someone who needed it more than he did. "He was one of the most generous guys I ever met," Devlin said. "If he had five bucks, he would give you four and a half of it."

Gibbons also did not like to see people victimized. Once his sister remembers being at a New York coffee shop with him. A male and female worker behind the counter got into an argument, and the man slapped his colleague across the face.

"Ronnie jumped over the counter and slugged the guy. [Ronnie] was a combination between dandy and Braveheart," Rita said.

This was far from the only time that Gibbons fought outside of the ring. Though not quick to fight, he was known to throw a few punches for noble—and occasionally, if challenged, less-than-noble—reasons. An example was when he was excited to hear about a film set in his hometown of Liverpool.

When he learned from a friend about a Manhattan showing of the movie set in Liverpool, Gibbons was elated. He gathered some friends—Martin was among them—and went to the theater. What the individual who recommended the movie deliberately didn't tell him was that male homosexuality played a major part in the film.

Early in the film, Gibbons became perturbed about the gay themes of the story line, and he stood up in the theater, yelling: "That ain't Liverpool. Liverpool ain't like that."

Theater security people quickly appeared, asking Gibbons's friends to shut him up. Bomber Martin, who could be as eccentric as Gibbons, replied that Gibbons was simply exercising his constitutional right of freedom of speech.

The encounter went downhill from there—ending with the boxers and friends leveling the theater security people before leaving the movie well before its denouement.

Gibbons's ability to use his fists—he continued to train even as his boxing career tanked—would not go unnoticed. In fact, his punching prowess would be spotted as he worked out in a Manhattan gym and would, in the mid-1980s, land him a job that provided him with a more lucrative income than did his street-corner sales.

It was an illegal job, but a good one nonetheless.

CHAPTER 21

— — —

Tucked into apartments across New York City, illegal casinos bustled during the weekend evening hours as men and women—finding the joints either by word of mouth or through business cards handed out discreetly at nearby bars—sauntered in after dinners and drinks.

New York State outlawed casinos but could not stifle the insatiable demand for gambling. John McGillion, an Irish American who made his home in a leafy and pricy Westchester County neighborhood, knew there was money to be made with gambling. He rented apartments and lofts across the city in the names of other people and transformed the vacant spaces into compact casinos.

Unlike Las Vegas or Atlantic City, the selection of games at the casinos was severely limited—there was nothing more than makeshift blackjack tables. Still, that's all it took to attract both the degenerate and the fun-seeking gamblers.

The casinos could handle only so many gamblers. A typical casino, squeezed into a furniture-less living room, accommodated five to nine tables, with each table seating up to six people. But the casinos operated twenty-four hours a day, and often the tables were full while more gamblers waited their turn.

By the mid-1980s, McGillion's handful of casinos thrummed with activity, and he continued to add more throughout Manhattan and the other boroughs, some on the Upper East Side, some in midtown, others in Queens and the Bronx. The clientele was polyglot, including Poles, Greeks, and Korean women who often came together in small groups and were known to be particularly tough on dealers who they believed dealt the cards too slowly.

The stakes were small—a minimum bet of $5 and a maximum of $100—but the around-the-clock wagering provided McGillion with a healthy illicit return.

Nicknamed "Johnny Mack," McGillion liked to help out his fellow Irishmen with jobs at the casinos. Their immigration status did not matter to him; after all, the casinos were unlawful. And he thought the Irishmen were tough, especially those who had IRA backgrounds. He trusted the politically inclined renegades; they were men of reliable moral fiber who never ripped him off.

One of his hires was Sam Millar, who was living illegally in Queens. Millar had been in the United States only a few years, living in Rochester, New York, before moving to New York City's Jackson Heights neighborhood.

Millar had a lengthy back story. An IRA member who'd been one of the blanketmen in Long Kesh prison, he was a friend of a Rochester cop who'd smuggled him into the United States. Targeted by the FBI, Millar and his family had slipped out of Rochester in the mid-1980s and moved to New York City. They settled in Jackson Heights, and not long afterward McGillion gave Millar, seriously in need of money, a job in the casinos.

Some of the casino jobs required training; some didn't. Millar was often tasked with security, ensuring that the gamblers inside the casino behaved and keeping watch outside for the Public Morals Division of the New York Police Department. (In his memoir, Millar refers to the police division as the Public Morals Squad, allowing him to write about "the PMS" and its occasional raids on the casinos.)

Millar used multiple false identities—including Andre Singleton, Frank Saunders, and Tom O'Connor—and kept documents at hand that were aligned with the aliases. When working at the casinos, he chose to be Tom O'Connor, the name of the cop who'd brought him into the United States.

McGillion modeled the casino operations after their professional and legal brethren. Gamblers paid cash for plastic chips, which were used for wagering. McGillion employed spotters, who kept an attentive eye on the dealers to ensure that they were not ripping off the house.

The gamblers handed their cash to the blackjack dealers, who'd slip the money into a carved-out hole in the gaming table. The money dropped into a slot in a locked metal container, which held a separate box that was the ultimate destination for the currency.

The casino managers frequently visited the tables, unlocking the exterior containers and replacing the cash boxes. The apartments had secret traps—sometimes in the floor, sometimes in a wall—where they'd hide the money.

Millar occasionally worked as a manager, whose role was not only to secure the money but also to step in if a gambler was acting irrationally—an interaction that would determine whether the casino security worker might need to intervene more forcefully.

Patrick Farrelly, a reporter and filmmaker who wrote about the casinos, said of the managers: "It was important that a manager oversee things and make sure that . . . disputes didn't get out of hand [with] people claiming that they should have won money when they didn't. . . . The games go very fast. People can lose an awful lot of money very, very quickly."

A section of the New York Police Department's organized crime bureau, the Public Morals Division investigated a host of vices, with gambling, prostitution, and loan sharking among them. When the division became aware of a casino, it would send in an undercover cop to play blackjack on two or three separate nights before a raid. One casino worker recalled: "They dressed in regular clothes and would sit at the tables and play. After a period of time they would stand up and pull out their [police identification] and say, 'Nobody move.' And everyone would scatter."

At other times the raid was more forceful and disruptive, with cops wielding sledgehammers to shatter the door and crush the blackjack tables. McGillion would simply find another apartment for a new casino.

Even with the occasional destruction, the cops and gambling crews maintained a nonantagonistic relationship. Once the cops had their own betting pool, each chipping in $5 and guessing how much money they'd find during a raid. The cop with the best guess kept the pot.

McGillion's employees sometimes tried to pose as gamblers during a raid, figuring that would save them from arrest. Knowing McGillion's hiring tendencies, the cops pulled the Irishmen from the crowd and questioned them. Once an officer remarked to a casino worker, "We know what your weakness is and it's not gambling."

The police-casino relationship was so cozy, in fact, that some workers wondered whether McGillion had cops on his payroll. Mondays and Tuesdays were the quietest nights for the casinos and, oddly, often the nights when police stormed in. The casino crew called Monday and Tuesday "bust nights" because of the likelihood of a visit from the police. There was less money to be seized than on other nights—and less for McGillion to lose.

But in a city roiled by a growing crack cocaine—and homicide—epidemic, McGillion's casinos were the least of police officers' worries, especially because the casinos were so genteel, even when compared with other illegal gambling dens across New York.

McGillion maintained strict rules: no guns, no drugs, no prostitution. The bar remained well stocked, but casino security guards had the okay to immediately toss out anyone showing signs of drunken obnoxiousness, whether the person was just tipsy or staggering. One worker remembered how a cop who led the occasional raids said: "We like you guys. We can bust other places and there will be three gamblers and twenty guns."

The city's burgeoning crime wave also gave the media plenty to cover other than the casinos, which rarely attracted any public attention—except once when the workers made tabloid headlines.

On that occasion, a gang of Hispanics had raided a casino on 80th Street in Manhattan's Upper East Side, rushing in as one of them pretended to be a restaurant delivery man. While robbing the joint, they forced the crew and gamblers to remove their pants, making it less likely they'd chase the robbers after the crime.

During the armed robbery, a real delivery man showed up at the casino with some food and was shooed away by one of the gang. Worried that something was amiss, he called the police, who arrived moments later.

The robbers had escaped out a back entrance, so the police arrested the casino employees on gambling-related charges and marched them out of the apartment without their pants. Someone had alerted a city tabloid, which had a photographer on hand for the arrests. The next day the newspaper prominently featured the photograph of the pants-less casino employees.

Among McGillion's staff members was a former boxer, Ronnie Gibbons, who had been hired for security. McGillion had spotted Gibbons pounding a punching bag at the New York Athletic Club. Impressed with Gibbons's conditioning and the strength behind his whirlwind jabs—not to mention Gibbons's Irish ancestry—McGillion asked the retired pugilist if he was interested in a casino job.

The job was a perfect fit for Gibbons, a partial break from the topsy-turvy world of sales. He did love making a good sale, and he'd surely continue to peddle any wares he could flip for a profit, but McGillion promised him a more reliable income. The worst that could happen was an arrest, but any criminal charges for the casino workers would likely be a slap on the wrist —a misdemeanor at most, but more often just a lesser violation and a fine. McGillion agreed to cover any court costs.

Once on the job, Gibbons proved himself capable of much more than simply throwing out a drunk or chastening a gambler who dared challenge a dealer. Though quirky with his occasional philosophical ramblings, Gibbons had a talent for management. McGillion saw this and eventually promoted Gibbons to overseer of multiple casinos and their managers. Gibbons traveled from one casino to another, ensuring that the gamblers were treated as valued customers and the daily money was handled properly—with no employee trying to skim a cut from the wagers.

With McGillion's blessing, Gibbons hired his sister, Rita, who was five years his junior. She had been working as a housekeeper at a hotel, but the casinos paid much better, and she left the hotel job altogether.

"I learned to be a croupier, to be a dealer," she later said.

According to her, it was Gibbons who asked McGillion to hire Millar for casino work. Where Millar and Gibbons first met is unclear, but both men knew Father Patrick Moloney and they had some mutual friends who, like Millar, were Irish and living illegally in New York City.

"Sam needed a job and Sam needed money," Rita Gibbons said. With McGillion's blessing, "Ronnie gave him a [security] job. He created a job for Sam we didn't need."

In his memoir, Millar does not address the question of whether Gibbons played a part in his hiring by McGillion. He writes: "Mac's overseer was a man named Ronnie Gibbons, from Liverpool, an ex-boxer who fancied himself with his fists and his brains. A copy of Marcus Aurelius' *Meditations* was never out of his reach and he was forever quoting the stoic philosopher."

In the late 1980s, police raids on the casinos became more frequent. The employees had several theories to explain the change. Perhaps some neighbors, after years of constant pedestrian traffic into the apartments, were complaining so much that the cops could not ignore the casinos. Or maybe McGillion was no longer paying off the police, as some workers had long assumed he was.

No one was exactly sure just why the police became more vigilant, but the raids had a numbing effect on business. Regular gamblers stayed away, and McGillion had reason to worry about criminal charges. Finally, he shut the gambling sites down. Their run, successful for the latter half of the decade, was now over.

After the closure of the casinos, Millar and Gibbons stayed in touch, despite occasional tension between the two. Gibbons even lived with Millar for a brief time, Millar wrote in his memoir, "driving my wife, Bernadette, crazy with his daily recitals of Marcus Aurelius.

"I knew it was time for him to go when he borrowed the complete works of Socrates from the library. Enough was enough."

Millar's memoir often paints Gibbons as weird, erratic, and unreliable, a portrait that riled Gibbons's family and friends after the 2003 publication of *On the Brinks* (though even they acknowledge that Gibbons could be offbeat, to say the least).

Moloney was also irritated by Millar's portrayal of Gibbons in *On the Brinks*. "Ronnie Gibbons was a character and sometimes a con man, but he was the most caring, sharing, and kind individual," Moloney said.

Clearly, there was friction between Millar and Gibbons, who, Millar hints in his book, was not a reliable steward of the casino finances. But that friction did not prevent the two men from coming together several years after the casinos had shut down in a money-making scheme that could make them millions.

The plan: they would rob the Brink's depot in Rochester.

CHAPTER 22

— — —

In late 1992, Sam Millar returned to Rochester to visit his friends there. According to his memoir, he reunited with Tom O'Connor over a beer. O'Connor was then working at the Brink's depot. Millar claims in his memoir that O'Connor suggested that Millar get a job with Brink's. (This anecdote seems unlikely, given Millar's lack of US citizenship and IRA criminal history, but perhaps O'Connor said this in jest.) Millar, according to his memoir, laughed and said: "That would solve all my problems. I'd rob the fucking place and open my own casino!"

O'Connor was silent and offended, Millar wrote: "As a New York cop he was highly respected both by colleagues and the community, which he served. He was an ah-shucks-Jimmy-Stewart kind of guy who did everything by the book."

Still, O'Connor took Millar on a quick tour of the depot, and Millar saw its vulnerabilities. He also saw the potential that those vulnerabilities could be exploited. He let the idea simmer then percolate into a full-blown plot, one that might seem outlandish on its face but one that he believed could be carried out successfully.

He thought he could rob the Brink's depot, but he knew he couldn't do it by himself. He'd need some help.

"I was beginning to doubt if another person could be found [for the robbery] and in desperation I put forward the only name open to me," Millar wrote in his memoir. That individual was Ronnie Gibbons.

Millar had some hesitations about enlisting Gibbons. He wasn't sure he trusted his former casino colleague. But if anyone was crazy enough to undertake such a criminal caper, it was probably Gibbons.

"I told Ronnie as little as possible, allowing him to only whiff the potential," Millar wrote. "The less he knew, the better."

Shortly before the planned heist, the two met at a café near Washington Square in Manhattan. Millar provided some details, telling Gibbons, "You'll probably have to smack one or two of the guards with that knock-out punch you have." Gibbons stood and started "doing the Ali shuffle, followed by upper cuts and left and right jabs aimed at an invisible opponent," Millar wrote. "Everyone in the place was in stitches, except me."

Two days later, Millar wrote in his memoir, he drove up the New York State Thruway from New York City to Rochester to pull off one of the country's biggest armored car company robberies. Following Millar in the van to be used in the robbery was Gibbons. Millar could practically smell the money. It wouldn't bring him out of the shadows as an illegal immigrant, but it would surely allow him and his family to live something other than a hand-to-mouth existence. He had a job as an elevator operator at a seventy-five-unit Manhattan co-op, where his employer knew him as Frank Saunders. The job paid just over $20,000 a year, a pittance to survive on.

Millar didn't know how many millions he might find at the depot, but that didn't matter. Whatever the score, it was sure to be plenty.

Gibbons, following Millar, could not help but think about the pot of gold off the Rochester exit of the New York State Thruway. Then Millar and Gibbons hit a snowstorm.

According to Millar, "everything was going fine until halfway through the journey when I happened to glance in my mirror, just in time to see Ronnie exit the thruway. He had taken the wrong exit. Fuck! I couldn't get off the thruway until the next exit, which was 30 miles away."

Millar did not see Gibbons again until he returned to Manhattan. Convinced that Gibbons had gotten cold feet, Millar confronted him, calling him a "typical gutless fuckin' Brit." Unaffected by Millar's anger, Gibbons said he'd been blinded by the snow and thought he'd seen Millar's car leave the highway. He drove a distance, he said, then realized his mistake. By the time he reversed course, it was too late to correct his error.

"It's all academic now," Millar responded, according to *On the Brinks*. "It's finished. The opportunity will never come again. We fucked it up."

Gibbons, Millar wrote, was "the moth who simply wanted to boast of touching the flame without being burnt."

Whether this is a true version of the short-lived criminal collaboration between Millar and Gibbons is hard to say; Millar is the only individual who offers this version. In addition, Millar's memoir often lacks specifics about the planning for the robbery and is even more implausible when he writes of the robbery itself. The memoir may be self-serving or, as Millar has claimed, an accurate version of events.

Father Patrick Moloney offers a different story about the collapse of the Millar-Gibbons partnership. While on bail awaiting trial in 1994, Moloney said that Gibbons visited him at Bonitas House. Gibbons asked if he could speak to him about the robbery; Moloney said he hesitated at first, but Gibbons was persistent.

Gibbons told him "I was in on the planning," Moloney said in an interview years after his conviction and prison sentence. (Even when discussing Gibbons, Moloney insists on his own innocence in connection with the Brink's robbery and the stashing of the stolen cash.)

According to Moloney, Gibbons decided not to get involved because he heard there would be guns. Guns could lead to violence and death, no matter how intricate and sophisticated the plot. All it would take would be one security guard pulling a weapon. What choice would the robbers have then, except to use their firearms?

If there were to be violence—and no one could be sure there would not be—Gibbons wanted no part of the heist. At least that's the story Moloney says Gibbons told him.

When Millar and others robbed the Brink's depot in January 1993, Gibbons was in Manhattan, unaware that Millar had continued the planning without him. Once he heard about the heist, he knew that Millar was the likely mastermind behind the robbery. According to Millar, in the months after the robbery Gibbons occasionally approached him for a cut of the millions. Millar was annoyed; Gibbons had clearly been too scared to do the actual criminal deed, but now, through some warped and illogical thinking, he believed he deserved some of the money. Millar tried to ignore him.

Gibbons realized he wasn't likely to get any cash from Millar. But he needed money from somewhere. In fact, from anywhere.

— — —

Gibbons had confronted stretches of time before without much in the way of money, but he had never been overly worried. He'd always found ways to survive, and it didn't hurt that he was masterful at getting others to foot the bill for his meals and sometimes even his housing.

But now he needed money more than ever. Ronnie Gibbons was now a father.

In the mid-1980s, he had a girlfriend, and in 1989, she gave birth to Gibbons's daughter, Jolie. Unfortunately, the relationship between the couple was volatile and unsteady. Who was at fault is difficult to say, with their domestic disputes a tangled mess of allegations and counter-allegations, but Jolie's birth did not ease the stress.

The two separated. Since they were unmarried, they did not face the legal strains of divorce proceedings. But there were still custody issues, and Gibbons's girlfriend did not want him seeing their daughter as often as he wanted to.

Gibbons found a lawyer to help him out, and the custody fight moved into family court. The attorney did what he could to keep his fees reasonable for Gibbons—he saw the limitations of Gibbons's revenue stream—but Gibbons still struggled to come up with the necessary cash.

Those who knew Gibbons, friends and family alike, rarely saw him disconsolate. He'd been in occasional sour moods as his boxing career came to an end, but typically he was ebullient and joyful, his outlook on life—not to mention the unorthodox way he lived his life—providing a humorous lift for all whom he knew. Even the inspiration of his favorite philosopher Marcus Aurelius—the man who said, "When you arise in the morning, think of what a privilege it is to be alive, to breathe, to think, to enjoy, to love"—provided no solace for Gibbons now.

This was a different Gibbons. This was a down-in-the-dumps Gibbons—a man whose lifelong aversion to steady employment had left him, because of mounting legal fees, practically penniless.

And as the legal papers and hearings piled up, he seemed no more assured that he was getting closer to the regular custody of Jolie that he sought.

"He was at a loss, a low ebb in his life where his heart was broken," said his sister, Rita. "He couldn't see his daughter because of the system."

Gibbons decided that begging was not beneath him, though he would only do it in his typically unconventional fashion. During the holiday season of 1992, Gibbons sat at a bar owned by one of his friends, and, with his perfectly neat penmanship, wrote a note on a napkin to pass to another man at the bar—an individual Gibbons knew to be fairly well off: "Don't tell no one but could you please lend me $500 smackers until Christmas. Loads of people told me you are loaded with no responsibilities. I will be forever indebted to you, if I don't pay you back by Christmas."

Gibbons occasionally frequented the bars owned by his friends Jim McCaffrey and Terry Quinn, hoping that some of the New York City glitterati might come in and find it in their hearts to help him out financially. When that approach failed, Gibbons fell back on the profession that, once upon a time, had looked promising for him—boxing.

In 1993 he decided to return to the ring, training mercilessly and working out at Gleason's Gym in Brooklyn as well as at the Equinox Fitness Center on the Upper West Side. Hector Rocca, a boxing coach at Gleason's who would later train Hilary Swank for her Oscar-winning role in *Million Dollar Baby*, saw the intensity and seriousness in Gibbons, who exercised with ferocity.

Rocca encourages his boxers to respect the sport and their opponents, to box not with anger, but with humility, technique, and skill. He likes his fighters tough but gracious. He does not countenance bad losers or poor sportsmanship.

In Gibbons, Rocca saw a similar appreciation for the world inside the ropes. "He was very humble, friends with everybody," Rocca said. "This is a respectable sport."

Gibbons did not seem to have lost his boxing acumen during his time away from the sport. He was technically astute, knowing when to pounce, when to lay back, and when an opponent's small opening was enough to land a potent punch. Rocca was not as surprised as others who saw Gibbons train.

"When you're a talented fighter, it's easy," Rocca said.

However, Gibbons was forty years old, past the standard prime for a boxer. Randy Gordon, who'd seen Gibbons early in his career when Gordon wrote about boxing, was now the head of the New York State Athletic Commission. The commission would have to grant Gibbons a license to return to the ring professionally, but Gordon was hesitant to allow older fighters to lace up the gloves again. Some wanted to return out of pride, believing themselves superior to the latest crop of pugilists; some wanted to return out of nostalgia, in an attempt to revisit the days of glory that they missed so much; and some, like Gibbons, simply wanted to return out of necessity.

Gordon then watched Gibbons go three rounds at Gleason's with one of the best middleweights in New York. Gibbons more than held his own.

As Gordon told a reporter about Gibbons' return, "I'm not thrilled about it because you don't get better [with age]. But I feel that if he can go three rounds with the baddest middleweight in New York, he's worth a try."

His trainer and friend, the businessman Jim Sterling, said of Gibbons, "He has tremendous natural talent and hits like a mule. . . . It's a question of how much age has affected him."

Gibbons was honest—partly—about his reasons for boxing again. "I'm coming back for the money," he told the *Irish Echo*, the New York City-based newspaper that wrote of the successes of Irish Americans. "If I make great money, I'll give it dignity and put it to noble use."

That "noble use" was not so much humanitarian—contributions toward the cure of disease or antihunger initiatives—as necessary: Gibbons needed to pay his lawyer. And he wanted to see his daughter.

— — —

Gibbons was in a preliminary fight on November 12, 1993, at Madison Square Garden.

His opponent, Luis Santana, had gotten close to a world championship before but, much like Gibbons's 1976 foe, Danny McAloon, Santana had fallen just short. Both Santana and Gibbons were motivated to win the fight: Santana wanted to make a push for a belt, while a win for Gibbons would ensure him future fights and future cash.

Gibbons expected his training could overcome age. He'd managed to forget the fights he'd lost to McAloon and others and once again seemed to have a sense of invincibility. He did not see his age as an impediment to a successful return to the ring.

Santana was no kid himself, only six years younger than Gibbons at the time of the fight. But he'd been boxing regularly. He'd had twice as many fights as Gibbons and had boxed twice in the previous year, winning once and losing once.

Gibbons had not entered the ring professionally since 1981.

Jay Mwamba covered the fight for the *Irish Echo* and had written earlier of Gibbons's return to boxing. Gibbons seemed intent on resuming a career—this was not a lark for him—and in the early rounds of the fight he looked like the Ronnie of old.

"Ronnie boxed pretty well the first three rounds," Mwamba said. "He was actually the better technical fighter. You could tell he knew his way around the ring, and I was kind of surprised at his ability. He was out-boxing Santana the first three rounds."

Then the years caught up with Gibbons. Even the intensity of his training could not repel Father Time. "The rust and fatigue set in," Mwamba said.

Santana, who'd survived a bevy of Gibbons's punches in the early rounds, now was on the attack—he the pursuer and Gibbons the pursued. When young, Gibbons had known how to withstand a brief spell of fatigue; he understood how to stay standing, avoid and sidestep his opponent's offensive attack, until the physical weariness passed.

But this fatigue was not to pass. To the crowd, Gibbons now looked tired—and old.

Santana, sensing weakness, became more aggressive in the fourth round, landing punch after punch. He laid Gibbons on the mat with a knockdown. Gibbons stood, his exhaustion showing.

In the fifth round, Gibbons again went down, felled by another Santana punch. Wobbly, he mustered the strength to get to his feet, but the referee had seen enough. He stepped in and called Santana a winner by a technical knockout.

"He saw that Ronnie was gassed out, just taking too much punishment," Mwamba said. "Ronnie wasn't seriously hurt, just winded. But I was surprised by Ronnie's boxing skills. That's how smooth and competent he was."

Gibbons knew he was unlikely to get another chance at a return. He was simply too old for boxing regulators to take another shot with him. The Santana match would help defray some of his legal costs, but he needed a lot more.

The next day Gibbons heard news that shocked him: only hours before he had entered the ring with Santana, Millar and Moloney had been arrested on charges tied to the Rochester Brink's robbery, along with O'Connor, the retired Rochester cop who had smuggled Millar into the country.

The media coverage of the arrests was everywhere—in New York City's tabloids, splashed across the more staid *New York Times*, and on all of the television newscasts. Gibbons couldn't escape it.

"Priest and Ex-Policeman Arrested in $7 Million Brink's Car Hold-Up," the *New York Times*'s headline proclaimed, missing the minor detail that the depot—and not a Brink's truck—had been the heist target.

"All three suspects had connections with the Irish Republican Army, the Federal Bureau of Investigation said," the article stated. "Though the I.R.A. has been responsible for bombings and other criminal acts in Ireland, Northern Ireland and Britain, the group has largely confined itself to legal fund-raising in the United States."

The IRA mentions in the news coverage dominated the chatter, especially with Moloney's arrest. "Father Hand Grenade," some jokingly called him, believing—though the evidence did not bear the belief out—that he had been in the violent ranks of the IRA.

Though he had a certain affinity for the mission of the IRA and had known some of its members, Gibbons had little concern about the aspects of international intrigue with the crime. More interesting to him was the fact that more than $5 million was still missing.

He wanted some of the money—and why shouldn't it be his?

CHAPTER 23

— — —

In 1994, as the Brink's defendants awaited trial, Ronnie Gibbons was with his friend Terry Quinn when he launched into a meandering tale about the Brink's heist.

It was Gibbons's nature to ramble on, to weave tales of his colorful life that, hard as they might be to believe, were typically constructed of fact. Gibbons could talk, and talk, and talk. But every story, even those tinged with sorrow, was injected with Gibbons's singular humor, his ability to find fun and farce in everyday life.

Gibbons's life of late had been difficult, and weaker men might well have collapsed under the burden. But Gibbons was not a quitter. He was fighting for partial custody of his six-year-old daughter but was pretty much broke. His boxing career done, he had no career to speak of. He worked some at a youth center, teaching boys to box, but that was no route to riches. He still sold things, but only so much money could be made from hawking clothes and knickknacks.

Gibbons was in dire need of cash, and he thought he knew where a lot could be found, he told Quinn. As was his nature, Gibbons detoured, bobbing and weaving with his story. But despite his stops at peripheral way stations throughout the narrative, Quinn grasped what Gibbons was saying. It was a hell of a story.

It began during Gibbons's employment at the illegal casinos run by John McGillion. McGillion employed a number of Irish immigrants, some of them legally in the country, some of them not. One of them was a man named Sam Millar, whom Gibbons had encouraged McGillion to hire. Millar used multiple aliases, but Gibbons had known his real name when they worked together in the 1980s.

Millar had many reasons to live as someone else, Gibbons told Quinn. First, Millar and his wife, Bernadette Fennell, had been in the country illegally for years. Also Millar had been active in the IRA while living in Northern Ireland and had spent years in Long Kesh prison. When his sentence was finished, he and

Fennell decided they'd had enough of Belfast and the Royal Ulster Constabulary, so they headed to the United States.

Millar and Fennell, whose visa had expired long ago, had dodged the cops and immigration authorities for years before settling into a life in Queens. But Millar had wanted to return to Rochester, the New York city he'd once called home, because he knew there was an opportunity there that he could not overlook. Millar had a friend—Tom O'Connor, a retired Rochester cop—who worked in a Brink's security depot in Rochester, and Millar learned from him just how poor the security in the depot was.

There were millions of dollars in the tiny depot at night, millions that were ripe for the picking.

Millar had a plan to knock off the depot and get his hands on some of those millions. But he needed help, and Gibbons seemed like a perfect fit for the job.

However, Millar had gone ahead with the robbery in the winter of 1993 without Gibbons. Lo and behold, Millar had succeeded, and he and some of his buddies— not including Gibbons—had made off with more than $7 million.

Millar, unfortunately, wasn't as smart as he thought, nor was he as careful as he should have been with the cash. Before 1993 was over, the FBI had arrested Millar in Queens, where he owned a comic book store.

Bits and pieces of the story became familiar to Quinn as he listened to Gibbons. He remembered hearing about the IRA rebel and a priest and a Brink's robbery in Rochester. That had been big news in the New York City media late in 1993 after some of the Brink's money had been discovered in a Manhattan apartment.

Only $2 million had been found in that apartment, Gibbons said. Somewhere out there was another $5 million. Though he had not been a part of the robbery, Gibbons believed he should get some of that money. He'd helped Millar in the early days, emboldening him to do the crime, encouraging him that the robbery could be a success if the security was in fact as bad as he'd said.

Then Millar had gone and done the robbery without him.

Millar had been dumb enough to get caught, but not dumb enough to lose all $7 million of the take from the robbery. Millar had been arrested with what was probably his cut.

More of the money, Gibbons said, was in Rochester, in the hands of people Gibbons was sure helped Millar with the robbery.

Perhaps, Gibbons said, Quinn could give him a hand.

"We could go there and make some money," Gibbons said. "Do you want to make some money?"

"I've made money," Quinn said. And he said that making money legally was hard enough—he wasn't inclined to do it any other way.

Gibbons did not give up, even after the Brink's trial of 1994 sent Moloney and Millar to prison. Occasionally thereafter he'd mention the robbery to Quinn, and his belief that millions could be found in Rochester. He'd learned the names of some of Millar's friends who still lived in the western New York city. He was sure O'Connor and Cahal and Liam Magee, other friends of Millar, knew where the cash was. A jury had acquitted O'Connor, but Gibbons didn't believe that he was innocent. Cahal Magee and O'Connor had both been active in NORAID, and Magee had helped shelter Millar in Rochester. Millar had also known Liam Magee in Rochester; Gibbons thought he was Cahal's brother but wasn't sure.

Quinn continued to refuse to get involved. But Gibbons, persistent as he was, found someone else willing to go along—his good friend Bomber Martin. Twice in 1995, months after the end of the Brink's trial, Martin accompanied Gibbons to Rochester. One time he went to try to ensure his friend's safety; the other time he was duped into the trip.

In the latter instance, Martin and Gibbons drove—naturally in a car Gibbons had borrowed—to Gloversville, New York, near Albany. Gibbons had a simple mission: to buy gloves from the town known, as its name implies, for its glove-making history. He would then resell the gloves in New York.

After they had visited a factory outlet and purchased what Gibbons could afford, Martin took a nap in the car. When he awoke, he realized that Gibbons was driving west on the New York State Thruway, in the opposite direction from New York City. Aren't you going the wrong way, he asked Gibbons. No, Gibbons said, he was making the short drive to Rochester since he was in the area.

While many New Yorkers considered the regions beyond Westchester County to be a single uninteresting geographic region, Martin knew the state well enough to recognize that Gloversville was nowhere near Rochester. In fact, it was 200 miles away.

Martin also knew just why Gibbons was heading to Rochester. Like Quinn, Martin knew the whole story, and like Quinn, he wasn't interested in pocketing a bunch of stolen cash. He simply wanted his pal to come back alive.

On both Rochester trips, Martin later said, Gibbons had O'Connor's phone number and called him. The first time was unsuccessful, but the second time Gibbons met O'Connor near his home in a suburb north of the city and near Lake Ontario. Gibbons asked Martin to wait in the car while he and O'Connor took a walk. The two men disappeared for a while, then strolled back. Afterward

Gibbons seemed spryer, more content. On the drive back to New York City, he did not tell Martin much about his conversation with O'Connor, but Gibbons's appearance of satisfaction was evident. Martin couldn't help but assume that Gibbons finally would get some of that money he wanted so badly.

Two decades later, Martin would still remember that trip, and how relaxed Gibbons was during the return to the city. Perhaps, Martin surmised, that was why Gibbons decided to go back to Rochester again—and why he felt secure enough to go alone.

It was not a good decision.

— — —

On the night of August 8, 1995, Gibbons showed up at Quinn's Engine 76 firehouse on the Upper West Side. He'd earlier asked Quinn if he could borrow his car for a few days, and Quinn agreed.

Gibbons was heading to Rochester again, this time by himself. Quinn gave him the keys to his 1992 Toyota Tercel—Gibbons had borrowed the car for an earlier trip to Rochester with Martin—and Gibbons drove away.

Hours later, Quinn was home with his wife, the actress Patti D'Arbanville, and their young children. He found a message on his answering machine from Gibbons. Gibbons had a request: if he did not return, he wanted Quinn to call his brother, Frank, in Liverpool and tell him the whole story about the robbery and Gibbons's trip to Rochester.

Apparently Gibbons was getting more concerned.

CHAPTER 24

— — —

Gary Brown was enjoying a quiet morning at his Rochester home when, to his surprise, a childhood friend showed up at his door.

"Out of the blue sky, he knocked on the door," Brown later recalled. "He didn't tell me he was coming or anything."

Nonetheless, Brown was happy to see Ronnie Gibbons. Brown was close friends with Ronnie's younger brother, Frank, and Brown had always been slightly in awe of Ronnie and his self-assurance. "He was this real confident person," Brown said of Ronnie Gibbons.

Brown lived with his mother, Winnie, in one of Rochester's crumbling neighborhoods spotted with vacant, deteriorating homes. Brown worked odd jobs and cared for the ailing Winnie, who felt uncomfortable in her low-income neighborhood but found that other homes cost more than she could afford.

Winnie had grown up in Liverpool before marrying and moving to Rochester. When Brown was a child, he'd occasionally visited Liverpool with his mother, and there he befriended Frank. The two became so close that Frank, as a child, convinced his mother to let him spend seven months—including a school semester—in Rochester with Brown.

It was August 1995 when Ronnie Gibbons surprised Brown with a visit. The two had stayed in touch through the years. When Winnie had been healthier, Brown had visited New York City and helped Gibbons sell gloves on the streets of the city and spent a short time working with him in John McGillion's casinos. But that had been in the late 1980s. Brown had not seen Gibbons in at least five years.

It was rare for Gibbons to visit Rochester. And this was a different Gibbons than the upbeat man that Brown was accustomed to seeing. "He was really really tired and very nervous," Brown said. "He looked very weary and nervous, and that wasn't like Ronnie."

When Gibbons had borrowed Terry Quinn's car, he'd shown no fear about his trip to Rochester. But somewhere along the 330-mile drive doubt had set in, though not enough to convince him to reverse course.

There was something else about Gibbons that surprised Brown. "He did have a gun on him," Brown said.

Gibbons was vague about his reasons for dropping in, saying that he was returning from Niagara Falls. As the two men chatted throughout the morning, Gibbons obliquely mentioned the robbery at the Brink's depot, and how Sam Millar and Father Patrick Moloney—both of whom he knew—were now in prison for their crimes.

Gibbons apparently was intrigued by the robbery, and Brown drove him by the depot to show him just where the heist had occurred. Gibbons said nothing about how he'd once been part of the scheme to rob Brink's. Instead, he said he was simply curious about a facility that had been vulnerable to such a bold crime.

The rest of the day was devoted to more idle chatter, childhood recollections, talk about families, and promises to get together again. Before going to sleep in a spare bed at Brown's home, Gibbons asked his friend about a suburban Applebee's restaurant. "He said he had to meet somebody there the next day," Brown said.

Gibbons knew how to get to the highway that would take him to the restaurant in the Rochester suburb of Greece, and Brown told him which exit to take from there. Applebee's was immediately off the highway; Gibbons couldn't miss it.

The next morning, Brown said goodbye to Gibbons, who still seemed rattled. Gibbons drove away in his borrowed Toyota. Brown would never see his friend again.

"A few days later I started to get calls from the family," Brown said. "He was missing, and nobody knew where he was."

— — —

On the morning of August 10, 1995, a waitress at the Applebee's in Greece noticed a man waiting in the parking lot in an olive green Toyota Tercel. She assumed he was waiting for friends to join him for breakfast.

Once as she passed the restaurant window, she saw a man pull into the parking lot in a large white luxury vehicle. He exited the car, met up with the man outside the Toyota, and then the two drove away, leaving the Tercel in the parking lot.

Two weeks later, when the Tercel was still unmoved, Applebee's management called the Greece police. They traced the car back to Patti D'Arbanville, who was the owner on the car's title. Later the car was returned to Terry Quinn and

D'Arbanville, with the police unaware of Gibbons's trip to Rochester and the reason behind it.

Even if the police had known about the trip, they would have found little in the way of clues in the Toyota. By the time police returned the car to D'Arbanville, the Toyota had been visited by Gibbons's friends and brother, all of whom were trying to figure out just why Gibbons had vanished and where he was, if he was still alive.

— — —

Several days after Gibbons borrowed Quinn's car, he still had not returned. Quinn did as he'd been directed. Gibbons had left the telephone number for his brother, Frank, and Quinn called him and told him everything he knew.

Frank was the more stable of the brothers—a family man who had a steady job and had even been elected to the Liverpool City Council. As difficult as it was, he tried to react to Quinn's story with calm.

Frank did not want to notify the police in Rochester or the FBI. His brother could still be alive, and police intervention could bring trouble for Ronnie if he were connected—albeit loosely—to one of the largest robberies ever to have happened in the United States. Frank also knew men in Belfast with ties to the IRA. He traveled to Belfast to meet one of them, asking whether the organization might have been behind the robbery and whether he and his family should have any worries if they started prying into the disappearance of Frank's brother.

After his own research into the Brink's robbery, Frank's IRA contact assured him that he should not be concerned. "He told me to do whatever I had to do," Frank said.

Frank figured that he had only one choice: he needed to go to the United States and try to retrace his brother's steps.

He was not the only one with that thought. After learning from Quinn that Ronnie Gibbons had not returned to New York City, Bomber Martin decided that he needed to go back to Rochester. He enlisted the help of his sister, Sophie Martin-Canning, and her husband.

On the drive to western New York, Martin discussed his earlier trips to Rochester, thinking that perhaps Gibbons had revisited some of the same areas. But through a bit of good fortune, once Martin and his companions were in the Rochester area, they located Quinn's car in the Applebee's lot.

Years later, Martin would remember that Gibbons had said something before going to Rochester about a planned meeting at the Applebee's. It's also possible that Brown, who had been talking regularly to Gibbons's family since Ronnie's disappearance, had also mentioned his plan to go to the restaurant.

Whatever the case, Martin and his companions found the Toyota. The interior of the car was clean and empty. Martin was able to pry open the trunk. (How he did so is unclear; he and the others did not recall when asked years later.) Inside they found a pager, a diary, a newspaper, and other assorted papers, as well as a carrying bag with clothes.

"It wasn't thrown in haphazardly," said Martin-Canning. There was no sign that Gibbons "left in a rush or a panic." In fact, "all his belongings were left as Ronnie would have left them," she said. "He was a perfect example of OCD [obsessive compulsive disorder]."

Also inside the trunk was a Rochester map with different areas circled. The circles corresponded with the neighborhoods where Cahal Magee and Tom O'Connor lived.

One piece of paper had telephone numbers for Cahal and Liam Magee and O'Connor. Next to Liam's name was a question mark, and a note that he was Cahal's brother—a possible sign that, while Gibbons knew Liam's name, he was not completely certain of the relationship between the two Magees. The newspaper included errant jottings, among them a dollar figure of more than $100,000.

Martin-Canning went inside the restaurant and asked various employees if they'd seen a man leave the Toyota days before. Apparently the one waitress who had spotted Gibbons was not then at the Applebee's.

"I asked everyone who worked in the restaurant," Martin-Canning said. "The [managers] were dismissive, saying there's no way anyone would notice [because] it's such a busy restaurant."

Martin-Canning was sure that no one had returned to the car after Gibbons's disappearance. "If they knew his car was there, they would have got rid of the evidence," she said.

However, someone obviously had known that the Toyota was at the Applebee's; after all, someone had picked Gibbons up there. Whoever did so apparently saw no need to return to the car, unless he had already done so and left Gibbons's papers neatly organized in the trunk.

The trio decided not to approach O'Connor or the Magees. To do so seemed foolhardy. But like Frank Gibbons, they also were wary of contacting police. They returned to New York City, trying to determine what steps to take next.

Within days, Frank Gibbons was making the same journey. He traveled to Rochester, met with his friend Brown, and learned that his brother had asked for directions to the Applebee's. Again following the trail of Martin and his companions, Frank went to the restaurant, located the Toyota, and found a way to enter the trunk.

As Frank recalls, he located the same materials that Ronnie's friends had. Martin-Canning has a different recollection: she remembers that she and her companions took the items back to New York City and gave them to Frank when he returned from Rochester, days later.

What is clear is that the papers ended up in the hands of Frank Gibbons, who went to his sister's home in Queens after leaving Rochester. Before he left the western New York city, he drove by the home of Tom O'Connor. He didn't approach O'Connor; he didn't think that anything positive could come from a confrontation.

He just had a simple goal in mind: he wanted to see the house of the man who might have killed his brother.

— — —

In late August 1995, Quinn got his Toyota back—and the police still had not been alerted to Gibbons's disappearance. Gibbons's family and friends still held out some hope that he was alive—perhaps even wealthy.

But there was plenty of reason to be doubtful.

For one thing, Gibbons had made no attempt to contact anyone. As the weeks passed, he also did not try to contact the attorney handling his custody fight. This was unlike Gibbons: he so badly wanted to see his daughter, Jolie, more frequently that he constantly called the lawyer, even when there was nothing new to report.

"His daughter was everything to him," the attorney later said. "If anyone thinks he's out living the high life somewhere, that's not the case."

After several months, Gibbons's family realized that they had little choice but to alert the police. Ronnie, they assumed, was dead.

Frank contacted the FBI, which had been the lead agency in the Brink's investigation. He agreed to return to New York and bring the papers found in the Toyota. (He did not bring the pager, apparently an oversight.)

He met with FBI agents in New York City. Agents also interviewed Quinn, annoying him because of treatment that he later said made him feel like a suspect. He told them what he knew, and the agents apparently were skeptical that he had not accepted Gibbons's suggestions that they work together to collect some of the stolen Brink's cash.

Information from the interviews was sent to the Rochester FBI office and handed off to Paul Hawkins, who'd been the lead Rochester agent on the Brink's case. Hawkins contacted Bill Mackin, the lead criminal investigator with the Greece Police Department, and the two tried to re-create Gibbons's days in Rochester and Greece. They interviewed Brown about Gibbons's visit and spoke with the waitress who'd seen Gibbons in the parking lot.

They opted not to talk to O'Connor or the Magees, realizing that none of the three would likely be of any help. They approached some friends of O'Connor but made no headway.

Hawkins put together a missing person's report to be circulated to law enforcement officials. The report included Gibbons's age—forty-two—and his height, weight, and "self-employed" status. Gibbons was "last seen at [Greece] Applebee's," the report said. "Missing person was subject of an FBI investigation."

"Dental records available," the report stated, asking that any information on "unidentified deceased" remains with similar physical characteristics be forwarded to Hawkins. And it said, "Foul play suspected."

The report generated no response, and Gibbons became simply another missing person's case.

In late 1996, Quinn—believing that the FBI and police were doing nothing to find his friend—contacted the media about Gibbons. In November 1996 the *Democrat and Chronicle* in Rochester reported Gibbons's disappearance on its front page, and two months later the *Daily News* in New York City used the anniversary of the robbery to run a story about Gibbons. The *Daily News* interviewed Martin and, while not using his name, noted that Gibbons had made multiple trips to Rochester to try to see O'Connor.

"Yesterday, on the eve of the heist's third anniversary, Gibbons is still missing," said the *Daily News* article, by the columnist Michael Daly. "A man who answered O'Connor's home phone said the retired cop was away for the weekend."

Those stories, like the FBI's request for help, generated no tips about Gibbons, whom FBI agents admitted they'd never heard of before the reports of his disappearance.

Gibbons slipped from the news. His mother, Rita, accepted that he was dead, but she longed to bring his body home for a burial in Liverpool.

A spiritually strong woman, she knew the odds were long that her son would ever be found. The FBI and police had plenty to do without spending endless hours looking for Gibbons.

Were it not for a two-time killer, Gibbons might well have remained forgotten.

CHAPTER 25

— — —

Only days before his February 2004 sentencing for murder, the second life he'd taken, Gerald O'Connor had a plan. He'd spent nearly half his life in local jails and state prisons—some of them, including the notorious Attica Correctional Facility, the meanest of the mean—and he did not want to live another day locked away.

Unfortunately, in November 2002 he'd shot a man in the head. Then he'd kidnapped the man's wife and taken her to a nearby motel, where he'd forced her to perform oral sex on him.

These were not the kinds of crimes that made freedom likely, even for a first-time offender. And the sixty-six-year-old O'Connor was no newcomer to crime. His criminal history began at an early age, when his love for booze led to arrests for loitering, vagrancy, drunken driving, public intoxication, and urinating on sidewalks. Jail became a second home, as his crimes elevated into nonviolent felonies (bank robberies and con jobs to steal money) and then seriously violent felonies (beatings and murder).

After the 2002 murder, the police quickly traced O'Connor to the motel where he'd taken the abducted woman. Now, fifteen months later, after his conviction, he awaited sentencing for the murder and assorted other crimes—kidnapping, sexual abuse, and criminal possession of a weapon.

O'Connor knew that the no-nonsense district attorney, Joseph Cardone, wanted to ensure that O'Connor would never be free again. He would ask for the maximum sentence—a half-century or more—and O'Connor would die in prison.

O'Connor figured he had one way to save himself. He knew it was a long shot, but it was also his only shot.

O'Connor decided to tell the world about the disappearance and murder of Ronnie Gibbons.

— — —

By 2004, O'Connor, nicknamed "Bingo," was showing the wear and tear of his lifestyle. His face was withered and weathered from his lifetime of drinking, and his hair was as white as Santa Claus's—though almost as thick as it had been when he was a younger man, a strikingly handsome man known for his ability to charm women before he turned violent against them. And he did inevitably turn violent.

Patricia Richards was one of the unlucky ones. She met O'Connor when they were teenagers. At first they were friends; then girlfriend and boyfriend; then, when she became pregnant and had a son at age eighteen, mother and father.

As a teenager, O'Connor had been all charm and gentlemanliness with Patricia, his humor sweet and his adoration of her pure. But he would not marry her. And his jealousy could be intense, like his taste for liquor.

Richards began to see a different O'Connor also. His anger, especially when fueled by alcohol, would erupt without warning. She sometimes paid the price simply by being the closest person for him to punch. At first, she thought he was a Jekyll and Hyde character, one who could not control his darker side. Eventually she realized he was all Hyde, and the man she had first met—the man with a luminous smile and magnetic personality—was nothing more than an act, a con.

She worried about raising a child with him. Then, with her son only two years old, she met another man, Cliff Manz, a member of the Coast Guard who was visiting Rochester. There was a spark, and she continued seeing him, eventually leaving O'Connor and marrying Manz. They had two children together, but— much to the dismay of her family—she would spend time with O'Connor when she returned to Rochester. It was as if he had some Svengali hold over her, her sister would later say, and her family knew that her continued relationship with O'Connor would eventually destroy her marriage.

The marriage finally ended in divorce, and Richards, keeping her married name of Manz, returned to Rochester with her children. O'Connor was now in and out of jail. He returned to Richards during his intermittent stints of freedom. But when free, he was more hateful, petulant, and violent than ever before.

Once he broke Richards's toe in a physical altercation between the two of them, though her family was never quite sure how that happened. That paled compared with the time when he squeezed her face so hard that he fractured her jaw, and Richards, at a Thanksgiving dinner with her family, ate a meal that her mother prepared specially for her using a blender.

By 1975, three years after her divorce, Richards had enough. She would no longer see O'Connor. She had gone to school to learn how to do paralegal work and now had a job. She could support herself and the two children, Michael and Denise, who were living with her. She gave O'Connor an ultimatum: we're done.

Still he harassed her constantly, calling and turning up at her home. She took out a restraining order against him. It was no deterrent.

In November 1975, O'Connor broke into her home and stole a stereo console, tape deck, and albums while she was away. A neighbor saw O'Connor leaving the home and told Richards. Richards went to police, who issued a warrant for O'Connor's arrest.

Before the police could locate him, O'Connor showed up at Richards's home on the evening of December 1. She told him again that they were through as a couple. The argument grew heated and loud. Denise, then thirteen, retreated from the dining room, where the fireworks between her mother and O'Connor were escalating, to the living room. For an escape, she switched on the television; she remembers finding one of her favorite shows, *Little House on the Prairie*.

Her mother came and sat next to her, finding solace with her daughter. O'Connor then shot Richards in the head.

His last words to her were: "If I can't have you, nobody will."

— — —

Years later, those moments were still vivid in the memory of Denise Manz.

She remembers her mother, limp as a rag doll, falling back against her; the gaping wound to her mother's head; the blood—surprisingly not a lot—staining her clothes as she tried to soothe her mother. She remembers her mother, her voice weakening and growing more distant as if she were tumbling deep into a well, telling her how much she loved her.

"It all happened so quick, but it was like it was slow motion," Manz later said.

Her mother lay in a coma for a week before she died. The charges against O'Connor were increased from attempted murder to second-degree murder.

At his trial, O'Connor and his lawyer chose to have a judge and not a jury determine the verdict. O'Connor could not claim innocence, but perhaps he could convince the judge that he was in such an alcohol-induced haze that the killing was not premeditated and intentional.

A jury surely would not be sympathetic. Once jurors heard how the victim's teenage daughter had been inches away at the time of the killing and how she'd witnessed the eventually fatal gunshot to her mother's head, any modicum of sympathy for O'Connor's inebriation and apparent addictions would have vanished. Instead, he would be convicted of second-degree murder and would face up to life in prison.

The judge ruled that there was substance to the claim that O'Connor was not himself when he fatally shot Richards. There was testimony that he'd imbibed more than two six-packs of beer and popped seven Valium tablets before the homicide.

The judge convicted him of manslaughter, not murder, and sentenced him to 15–25 years in prison for the killing. This meant that O'Connor could one day be released from prison. And he was.

This meant that O'Connor could kill again. And he did.

— — —

As he sat in a jail cell in 2004, awaiting sentencing for his second homicide, O'Connor looked ahead at his life with a forethought and concern uncommon in a man who usually acted on his basest impulses and rarely cared what the future held. Still, O'Connor's worries were personal and selfish: how would he ever get out of prison again?

Like his first victim, who had been a former girlfriend and was the mother of his child, O'Connor's next victim had also made the mistake of befriending him.

Free on parole in 2002, O'Connor was spending an afternoon with a friend and his wife in Orleans County, a largely rural county west of Rochester. The morning had included a diet of crack cocaine, marijuana, and Budweiser. With his friend out of the living room, O'Connor offered the man's wife $1,000 for sex. She said no. He offered $1,500. She said no. He offered $2,000. She said no.

O'Connor seethed. He did not like being told no.

Later, when his friend returned to the room, unaware that O'Connor had offered his wife cash for sex, O'Connor initiated an argument over petty issues. The two men walked outside the ranch-style home, into a backyard partly littered with trash and emptied beer cans and other detritus. Only yards away from a satellite dish so large it looked like equipment from the National Aeronautics and Space Administration, O'Connor pulled out a .22-caliber pistol and shot his friend in the back of the head. The round traveled deep into the brain. Unlike the weeklong fight to survive waged by Richards, this death was quick.

O'Connor then took the man's wife to a Budget Inn twenty-five miles away, where he forced her to perform oral sex on him. Sickened, she vomited afterward.

It did not take police long to find O'Connor. They tracked him to room 115 at the Budget Inn and assembled a fifteen-man SWAT team in the parking lot.

Six cops, fortified by protective gear, burst into the motel room, shouting "Police!" One pulled the pin on a stun grenade, tossing it onto the floor. Called a flashbang, the cylindrical device produced a percussive sound, a booming thunderclap ricocheting around the walls of the dreary room. Emitting flashes of a brilliant and blinding light, the grenade stunned O'Connor and the woman, their eyes momentarily blinded and their ears pounding with temporary pain. Finding the two naked beneath the sheets, the police handcuffed both, until they were assured that the woman was a victim and not a consensual partner.

At trial, the evidence against O'Connor was overwhelming, and the jury quickly convicted him. As his sentencing approached, O'Connor knew the cold hard facts: Cardone would make sure that O'Connor would never be free again. He was sure to die in prison.

His only hope, he decided, was the story of Ronnie Gibbons. O'Connor hoped he had one more good con in him.

— — —

Michael Zwelling, a part-time reporter for the *Buffalo News*, had covered some of O'Connor's trial and conviction. O'Connor had seen some of the articles. An acquaintance of O'Connor's contacted Zwelling, offering a blockbuster story involving a major armored car company heist linked to the IRA, a subsequent murder, and the involvement of a retired Rochester police officer.

It was a story no reporter could turn down.

O'Connor had been on the periphery of some of the same Irish American circles as people who'd been questioned about the Brink's robbery. He occasionally made claims that he was part of an American faction of the IRA, a boast that many assumed was just part of O'Connor's perpetual quest for self-importance.

Days before O'Connor's sentencing, Zwelling met with the killer in the Orleans County jail.

When the two met, O'Connor told Zwelling a story that was even more startling than the reporter had expected to hear. Masterful at obscuring his malevolent side with disarming charm, O'Connor was sure he would be believed. He had to be.

The retired cop—Tom O'Connor—was the centerpiece of Gerald O'Connor's tale, along with multiple corpses.

The two O'Connors were not related, but they had met decades before the

1993 Brink's robbery. In 1964, a police officer shot Gerald O'Connor, who was trying to escape from a botched bank robbery in Rochester. O'Connor spent days recuperating in a local hospital, before his prosecution. A police guard stood vigil outside; Gerald O'Connor was not someone to be left unobserved.

One day, the officer keeping watch at the hospital was a young man new to the police force. The rookie, Tom O'Connor, shared more than a last name with the hospitalized criminal. He'd heard how much of a cretin Gerald O'Connor was, but he wanted to discuss Ireland with him. Perhaps they shared some of the same lineage, despite their different paths in life.

The chat was brief, turning into a talk about a tiny Irish village where both men might have had ancestors centuries before. But, Gerald O'Connor claimed, that short meeting was the start of a long-lasting criminal relationship.

Tom O'Connor occasionally bragged about his ability to kill and evade the law, Gerald O'Connor said. Once, he told Zwelling, the two O'Connors traveled to Genesee County to meet two men—IRA men, Gerald O'Connor said—who'd robbed a gun store in the nearby city of Batavia. Tom O'Connor planned to buy some of the guns, but he didn't like the price he was offered.

So he shot the two men. He then turned to Gerald O'Connor for help in disposing of the bodies. They went to a farm in the town of Albion, in Orleans County, and buried the bodies there.

The farm, Gerald O'Connor said, was the site of more burials, not all of victims connected to Tom O'Connor. A parolee whom Tom had known from Attica prison got into an argument with a girlfriend who was visiting from Arizona. The argument turned violent, and the parolee killed the woman. Tom again asked Gerald for help.

The woman is also buried at the farm, he told Zwelling.

Then there was the final body. Gerald O'Connor said he had gotten a phone message from Tom O'Connor, who said, "I have a piece of work that I got to get rid of." Once again, the two met to bury a body on the farm.

The dead man was Gibbons, fatally shot by Tom O'Connor.

— — —

Zwelling's subsequent story in the *Buffalo News*, appearing two days before sentencing, did not dig deep into the relationship between the O'Connors. But it gave Gerald O'Connor just what he wanted—a platform and a voice.

"Convicted murderer Gerald O'Connor said he helped bury four bodies on a Town of Albion farm over a 25-year period between 1973 and 1998," the newspaper story began. "He also said he knows who killed the four people buried there and he hopes that by speaking out he can help ease the mind [*sic*] of some family members who have searched for answers over the years."

The story continued: "One of the bodies is believed to be that of Joseph 'Ronnie' Gibbons, a 42-year-old retired boxer who disappeared from the parking lot of a Greece restaurant in 1995. O'Connor said Gibbons was killed then, and a retired Rochester police officer was involved in the death."

The article did not name Tom O'Connor, but there was no question that he was the cop Gerald O'Connor had mentioned.

Despite the claims of buried corpses and a murderous cop, the story was only twelve paragraphs long. But it succeeded just as O'Connor had hoped. The morning the story appeared, his attorney, Jeffrey Mallaber, received a call from the FBI. Two agents wanted to meet with O'Connor immediately.

For the meeting, O'Connor was taken in handcuffs from his cell to a conference room at the Orleans County Public Safety Building.

The agents asked for some details about what O'Connor knew before agreeing to talk about a deal. O'Connor told them how he knew Tom O'Connor. He said that the cop would sometimes tell him of homes and businesses—"marks," Gerald called them—vulnerable to burglaries.

When Gerald O'Connor was out of prison in the 1990s, he said that Tom O'Connor had enlisted him to kill Gibbons. Tom gave Gerald a handgun to do use. But Gerald then violated his parole terms and returned to prison.

But he'd told enough, Gerald O'Connor said to the FBI agents. Now it was time to bargain.

His demands were simple: he would provide information if he could get a deal that kept him out of prison. Unsurprisingly, the agents found the demand both ridiculous and bold. O'Connor had shown what he did when out of prison: he killed people. No bargain would change his character.

And part of O'Connor's character was an unremitting dishonesty. While the FBI had long suspected Tom O'Connor was the inside man in the Brink's robbery, the agents were skeptical of the claims that the retired cop had committed the killings that Gerald O'Connor had alleged he had.

The agents offered him something other than freedom: imprisonment at a federal prison, instead of a New York State penitentiary. His final years would at least be spent with fewer prisoners who, like O'Connor, were rapists and murderers.

O'Connor chuckled, his brazenness now coming even more to the fore. "Do you think prison scares me?" he asked. "I've spent half my life in prison."

The conversation stalled. The FBI would offer nothing else.

Cardone was uncertain whether to believe O'Connor. For one thing, O'Connor was not stupid. He likely wouldn't make such claims unless there was some semblance of truth behind them. He could not expect to get any kind of deal unless he gave police some evidence of his veracity, and that evidence had to be a body.

But O'Connor was also desperate. He was not a young sixty-six. He'd lived hard and drunk a good portion of his life, and the wear and tear on his body and health was evident. It would also be just like O'Connor to concoct a tale like this, thinking he could bamboozle the criminal justice system. He had always thought that he could finagle his way out of almost any situation with his guile, and this could be just another of his cons.

Cardone had no intention of ever letting O'Connor out of prison again. He had made this clear at O'Connor's sentencing. There, in front of a packed courtroom of victims past and present, Cardone asked the judge for the maximum sentence. "Throughout this defendant's life he's had a grave impact on a lot of individuals," Cardone said.

As County Court Judge Robert Noonan began to impose the sentence, O'Connor remained slumped in his chair, refusing to stand, looking balefully toward the judge.

"You're going to stand up while sentencing is imposed," Noonan said. O'Connor did not budge, until his attorney whispered in his ear. Then he slowly stood up, continuing to glare at Noonan.

"I don't know what makes you think you can sit there and be a god instead of a judge," O'Connor said.

"You'll meet God soon enough," Noonan answered.

Noonan imposed a sentence of twenty-five years to life for the murder, to be followed by a sentence of another twenty-five years for the rape. O'Connor was destined to serve a half-century in prison before having any chance of parole. He was sure to die in prison.

In court were Patricia Richards Manz's daughter, Kim, and sister, Christine Chirico. They applauded when Noonan sentenced O'Connor, as if Patricia was finally receiving the justice she deserved. "Hopefully he'll rot in hell," Kim Manz said. "That's where he belongs."

O'Connor headed back to prison, his gamble unsuccessful. Still, he hoped that one day the cops would care about what he had to say about Gibbons.

That day would come.

CHAPTER 26

— — —

In 2005, a New York State Police Investigator, Tom Crowley, took over some of his office's cold cases for the Rochester region, inheriting one of the most notorious unsolved murder cases—three homicides collectively labeled the Alphabet Murders.

Those three slayings, also dubbed the Double Initial killings, began with the November 1973 rape and strangulation of ten-year-old Carmen Colon, a doe-eyed dark-haired youngster who lived in Rochester and had been missing for two days before her crumpled body was found in a gully in a suburb of the city.

The killing was still unsolved when, in 1974, another city girl, eleven-year-old Wanda Walkowicz, vanished from her home. A tomboy with cropped red hair and a bevy of freckles, Wanda was known to wander the neighborhood, but she had always returned home before. She was found a day after her disappearance, raped and strangled, her body dumped off the side of a highway rest area in another Rochester suburb.

Six months later came the third killing, when eleven-year-old Michelle Maenza disappeared from her Rochester neighborhood. Her photo, like those of Colon and Walkowicz before her, was publicized by the media in the hope that she would be found. With the black-and-white image showing her rounded cheeks and slightly askew pigtails falling below her shoulders, Maenza's photo managed to reveal both her sweetness and her social awkwardness.

And as with Colon and Walcowicz, there was little time for the public to be on the lookout for Maenza. A day after her disappearance, she was found on a rural road twenty miles east of Rochester, also raped and strangled.

Like the other two victims, her first and last names began with the same letter, giving birth to the monikers for the slayings. The killer or killers must have sought out girls with alliterative "double initial" names, some law enforcement officials believed. The odds were incredibly high that the symmetry was coincidental.

By the time Crowley inherited the case, three decades after the homicides, police had pursued hundreds of leads and interviewed dozens of suspects. A DNA sample from the Walkowicz killing remained stored in a lab in Albany and provided a genetic comparison with suspects, a list that at one time included former Rochester resident and serial killer Kenneth Bianchi, half of the "Hillside Stranglers" team.

Crowley constantly culled through the massive homicide file, looking for anyone who had not been questioned but could have helpful information. Any information, no matter how inconsequential it might seem, could be a conduit to more clues, Crowley decided.

As he pored over the thousands of pages of police records, Crowley kept a running list of individuals he thought should be approached. With each name, he'd conduct basic research to see whether there was criminal or other history that could elevate the individual into the ranks of suspects or make him, in the latest faddish terminology of the police, a "person of interest."

Among the records Crowley found the name Ronald "Corky" O'Connor, who'd been friends with the Walkowicz family. With a little digging, Crowley discovered that O'Connor had a brother, Gerald, who had an unmistakable savage streak.

Then in prison for a murder and sexual assault, Gerald O'Connor was at the Clinton Correctional Facility in Dannemora, in the frigid and forested northeastern corner of New York. He'd killed twice, though neither victim had been a young person. O'Connor's modus operandi did not match that of a man who would seek out, sexually attack, and strangle young teenage girls for perverse pleasure. Nor did he seem like a man who killed with much preparation.

Nonetheless, he was a murderer and apparently conscienceless. Crowley decided that was enough cause to visit Gerald O'Connor.

What Crowley did not—could not—foresee was that his interest in O'Connor would begin as the exploration of a possible suspect in the Alphabet Murders and morph into an investigation into a missing New York City boxer and a Brink's depot looted for millions of dollars.

— — —

Rochester Police Homicide Investigator Bill Lawler had a cold case of his own, the 1987 fatal shooting of Damien McClinton at the Genesee Brewery warehouse.

The case was personal to Lawler, and he considered the leading suspect to be Tom O'Connor.

While others in law enforcement were less certain about O'Connor's culpability in the killing, Lawler felt sure of his suspicions, and he was offended—first, because O'Connor had been a cop, and second, because O'Connor was Irish American.

Lawler's own Irish ancestry was important to him. He'd long been active in the Rochester-area chapter of the Ancient Order of Hibernians of America, serving for years as its president. First formed in 1836 to counter anti-Irish bigotry and protect Catholic churches, the national Ancient Order was the oldest Irish Catholic organization in the country. The Rochester-area chapter was founded in 1896 and named itself after Patrick O'Rorke, a Union Army colonel who had been killed at Gettysburg and buried in his hometown of Rochester.

Lawler joined the Rochester police force in 1985 and was known for his impish and irrepressible sense of humor. Once assigned to horse patrol, he decided he wanted a bagel from a popular sandwich shop owned by a close friend. Lawler moseyed into the shop for his lunch, without dismounting from his mare.

Not long after transferring to the major crimes unit, Lawler inherited several unsolved cases, the fatal shooting of McClinton among them. Through interviews and a review of files, he reconstructed the work done by the investigators who had preceded him. Theories about the killing were plentiful, and none seemed significantly more likely than another, but Lawler kept returning to O'Connor as a suspect.

Lawler was deep into reviewing the homicide—he wanted to question a former cop who had provided an alibi for O'Connor—when he got a call from Crowley.

Crowley told Lawler that they might have a common interest: Gerald O'Connor. Lawler had no clue who Gerald O'Connor was, but Crowley's story was enough to pique his interest.

Crowley said he planned to go to Dannemora to talk to O'Connor about the Alphabet Murders. And Crowley said that in his research on O'Connor he'd learned about claims the killer had made in 2004 before he was sentenced for his crimes in Orleans County.

O'Connor, Crowley said, maintained that he knew the burial site of some guy connected to the 1993 Brink's robbery—a former boxer from New York City named Ronnie Gibbons. The prosecutors and police didn't believe O'Connor and refused to make any deals for the information.

As Gerald O'Connor's story went, he'd helped the man who'd killed Gibbons. That man, Crowley said, was Tom O'Connor.

Lawler didn't need to hear any more. He, too, wanted to meet Gerald O'Connor, especially if the killer could help lock away Tom O'Connor.

— — —

Years after his first meeting with Gerald O'Connor, Crowley would joke about an error he'd made when he reached out to the Rochester police. The police department in the suburban town of Greece was the one actually tasked with Gibbons's missing person case, because that was where Gibbons had last been seen. But Crowley had assumed the case to be Rochester's and instead had called the major crimes department there, connecting with Lawler.

The misstep was fortuitous—first, because of the keen interest Lawler brought to the investigation, and second, because the Greece Police Department was only a year from a major freefall that would end with the complete dismantling of much of its leadership and the criminal convictions and imprisonment of two of its officers and its chief.

Crowley met with Lawler and Lawler's partner, David Salvatore. Salvatore was as reserved as Lawler gregarious, and during interrogations the two were not the good cop and the bad cop, but instead yin and yang personalities.

Crowley debriefed the two Rochester cops on what he knew about Gerald O'Connor. Crowley's intent was to determine whether O'Connor had information about the Alphabet Murders. The odds were unlikely, but Crowley was insistent on addressing each suspect one by one, in the hope that one day the real killer would be revealed.

In February 2007 the three cops traveled to Dannemora, meeting Gerald O'Connor in a room typically used for confidential meetings between prisoners and their lawyers. O'Connor's disdain was evident, but he was smart enough to see another opening to entice police with his stories.

O'Connor was loath to reveal anything that would make him a rat, but he did talk about Tom O'Connor. He repeated the story about meeting the rookie cop Tom O'Connor at the hospital. Tom had claimed that he was with the IRA, and this resonated with Gerald, who told the cops he'd been with the "Irish mob."

Tom had bragged about killing Damien McClinton, Gerald said. That killing had cost Tom his police job, Gerald claimed.

The investigators noted the mistake in Gerald's story: in 1987 Tom was no longer a cop and was working at the brewery warehouse with McClinton. Already, the cops were doubting Gerald's veracity.

His error pointed out to him, Gerald O'Connor became less willing to talk. "I could tell you what you want to know about this and many other things but I would end up with twelve slugs in me the minute I stepped outside," he said, apparently still clinging to the belief that he would be free one day.

O'Connor told Crowley that he knew nothing of the Alphabet Murders, except from the news coverage in the early 1970s. He would never harm a child, he said. Nor, O'Connor said, would his brother ever commit an act as heinous as the rape and strangulation of young girls. If he in fact had done so, O'Connor said, he should be killed—painfully.

The investigators turned the conversation to the bodies supposedly buried on the Orleans County farm. O'Connor said he needed "incentives" to talk. The investigators told him they could do nothing to change his sentence, and District Attorney Joseph Cardone would not be party to any deals for the killer, but perhaps they could get him moved to a prison closer to home.

The three investigators left the prison with somewhat varying impressions: Lawler was unsure of Gerald O'Connor's honesty but remained hopeful that he did have information about Gibbons and Tom O'Connor; Crowley was more skeptical—he had found Gerald evasive—but was willing to continue to talk to him, in case he knew something about Gibbons or Tom; Salvatore considered Gerald a man who had no acquaintance with truthfulness.

Perhaps Gerald O'Connor had sensed Salvatore's quick distaste for him. Later, when Crowley and Lawler visited O'Connor alone, he encouraged them to continue to leave "the Italian guy" in Rochester.

— — —

Within weeks of meeting with the police, O'Connor got his move when prison officials transferred him to a medium-security facility east of Syracuse and two hours from Rochester. In fact, the police had nothing to do with the transfer. O'Connor was suffering from cancer, and his new home—Mohawk Correctional Facility—had a medical unit for inmates with serious health issues.

Nonetheless, O'Connor may have thought his willingness to continue talking to police had led to his transfer. In any case, when the investigators visited him at Mohawk in June 2007, he was now much more loquacious—if still hesitant to tell exactly where Gibbons's corpse could be found.

What was odd, however, was O'Connor's version of Gibbons's burial. In 2004, his story—what he would reveal of it—indicated that he'd taken care of Gibbons's body after Tom O'Connor killed him. But now there was a new twist: Gerald O'Connor had buried Gibbons in 1998, not 1995.

Gerald was free on parole then, he said, and Tom O'Connor had asked him to exhume Gibbons's corpse and rebury it elsewhere. Gerald was vague about the exact location where'd he found the body and even less specific about where he reburied it, except to say, just as he had in 2004, that it was in Orleans County.

If he told more, he said, someone might have to uproot a swimming pool. But he was "80 percent" certain he wanted to help, and he asked for more time.

The police, now even more doubtful of O'Connor, realized there was a good reason for a change in his story—something the media and perhaps even investigators missed when O'Connor alleged in 2004 to have been part of Gibbons's disappearance. When Gibbons vanished in August 1995, Gerald O'Connor was still in prison; he could not have helped Tom O'Connor or anyone else dispose of Gibbons then.

Now, Gerald O'Connor had cops willing to listen to him. They'd certainly figure out—if they hadn't already—that he had been incarcerated in 1995. His story was not fantastical, he thought; he could even add more details that would convince the cops of his honesty. And he did.

Lawler and Crowley returned to Mohawk in late June, and O'Connor was even more voluble. According to O'Connor, Gibbons had been buried in Rochester near Lake Ontario, close to Rochester's historic Seabreeze Amusement Park—which, with its wooden roller coasters, was one of the oldest amusement parks in the country.

Gerald O'Connor said that he had found Gibbons's rotting corpse wrapped in a blanket and then moved the body to the Orleans County farm. He still did not want to provide details; he was wrestling with the choice of whether or not to lead police to the body. Also, he worried about Tom O'Connor. Generally, he liked Tom, but he considered him a "treacherous person." With his contacts in law enforcement, and maybe even in the prisons, Tom could make Gerald's life miserable.

But don't give up hope, Gerald O'Connor told the cops. Now he was "85 percent certain" that he'd eventually tell them what they wanted to know.

The cops, meanwhile, left the prison 99.9 percent sure of one thing: O'Connor was full of shit.

CHAPTER 27

— — —

Who the hell was Marco?

If one were to believe Sam Millar and his memoir, *On the Brinks*, Marco was the lone man with him when he robbed the Brink's depot in 1993. Published a decade after the heist and six years after Millar's release from prison, *On the Brinks* provided an inside account of the robbery from the ultimate insider—the man who committed the crime.

While investigators continued to push Gerald O'Connor for information about the whereabouts of Ronnie Gibbons's corpse—and as they became more skeptical of his allegations—they navigated other investigative avenues.

Naturally, they revisited the Brink's robbery, considering the witnesses, the trial testimony, the evidence gathered by the FBI, and the history of the convicted (or, in the case of Tom O'Connor, the acquitted). They also turned to Millar's 2003 book, published in the United Kingdom, hoping it might provide something useful.

They were disappointed.

Millar's recollections of his years at Long Kesh were horrific yet captivating, but investigators found his account of the robbery laughable. According to the memoir, having jettisoned Gibbons as a criminal accomplice, Millar chose another friend—whom he identified only as Marco—to rob the depot. Marco was far more reliable and trustworthy than Gibbons, and Marco and Millar pulled off the heist in only a few minutes, escaping in Millar's van.

They then left much of the cash at the home of a Rochester-area lawyer, who was related to Marco. Marco drove away from the home in his own car, while Millar headed to New York City, holding on to more than $2 million.

This account of course ran counter to the testimony of the guards at the depot, who were sure that they had heard more than two people in the facility, one of whom was possibly a woman. Even Tom O'Connor had said that there were so many people tromping through the depot when he was held hostage there that it sounded like an "army."

And what happened to the remaining millions? The lawyer lost it, saying that "all the money . . . had been stolen, all $5 million of it, by a cocaine-addicted friend who stumbled on it 'accidentally,'" Millar wrote.

When Millar's book was first published, an FBI agent who'd been involved in the Brink's investigation said, in an understated manner, that Millar's tale was "a little far-fetched." Now, four years later, New York State and Rochester police investigators were again flipping through pages of the book, hoping to find something of value. They reached the same conclusion that the FBI agent had: to protect his true accomplices in the robbery, Millar had invented a tale about the robbery that did not incriminate anyone else. Perhaps Marco was modeled after someone real, but the details in On the Brinks didn't provide much in the way of clues.

Gibbons was featured prominently—if not favorably—in On the Brinks. The book did confirm Gibbons's claims to friends that he'd been cut out of the robbery, and that the slight was the motivation for his trip to Rochester. But there was no discussion of two of the men Gibbons apparently wanted to see—Cahal and Liam Magee—and Tom O'Connor was portrayed as a saintly humanitarian, far different from the way the police investigators thought of the ex-cop.

Millar wrote that in the months after the robbery, but before the arrests, he realized that Gibbons might become a problem because he kept asking for money. Millar turned to Father Patrick Moloney, who—according to the memoir—had no role in the robbery but had agreed to hide the money in the apartment the priest had sublet. Millar knew that Moloney still saw Gibbons occasionally, and Millar suggested that Gibbons get $100,000 of the money stored in Manhattan.

Until his November 1993 arrest, Millar believed that Moloney had given the cash to Gibbons. Instead, the money was likely part of the $178,000 found at Bonitas House during the 1993 police raid, Millar wrote.

For Investigators Tom Crowley, Bill Lawler, and David Salvatore, the hunt for Gibbons was becoming a string of dead ends. Gerald O'Connor was, if considered favorably, behaving evasively or, if considered less favorably, a flat-out liar. Millar's memoir, though often compelling, did nothing to help answer the questions about Gibbons's fate.

During several trips to New York City, the investigators connected with Terry Quinn, who again related how he'd loaned Gibbons his car. Quinn clearly was irked by his earlier dealings with law enforcement officials. The FBI had treated him like a suspect, he said, instead of a man trying to help them solve the case of a missing person.

(Quinn decided that he was fonder of the new batch of investigators. He once took them to the firehouse where *Rescue Me* was filmed, and the cops got a photo of themselves with the cast. Crowley kept the picture, even though the photographer had accidentally cropped most of him out of the photo. "I'm not in the damn thing," he later said. "It's just my hand.")

The investigators also connected with Gibbons's friends who'd traveled to Rochester to try to find him. They met his sister, Rita, and once talked to his brother, Frank, when he was visiting from Liverpool.

Frank Gibbons still had the pager found in Ronnie Gibbons' trunk, and he passed it on to the Rochester-based investigators. Unfortunately, there was little there of significance from the days when Ronnie had traveled to Rochester, just a string of calls from Sophie Martin-Canning who was trying to reach her friend after getting word that he'd not come back to New York City.

The interviews helped the investigators reconstruct much of what the FBI had learned in 1995, but not much more than that. The evidence still pointed to the Magee brothers and Tom O'Connor as the men Gibbons wanted to see, and if Bomber Martin was telling the truth about the earlier trips to Rochester, Gibbons had connected with O'Connor before his August 1995 disappearance.

However, Cahal Magee had died in 2003, and Liam Magee had been deported to Ireland in the late 1990s for drug-related crimes. The police knew that O'Connor would be no help; there was no need to try to interview him.

Investigators did have another ploy. When Damien McClinton's car was discovered after the 1987 homicide, there was a cigarette butt inside. Police decided the cigarette might not be McClinton's and hoped, with new DNA technology, that they could secure a sample of the smoker's DNA from the cigarette.

If so, then they'd need a sample of DNA from O'Connor. They were far from having enough proof to get a court order for a DNA swab, but nothing precluded police from surreptitiously getting a sample from O'Connor in a public place.

For the years after his acquittal, O'Connor and his wife—he'd married Barbara Saucke, his fiancée at the time of the trial—largely kept to themselves. But O'Connor liked to reunite with his retired police friends, who still considered him one of their group. There was a chance to do that at the annual Policeman's Ball put on by the Badge of Honor Association, a nonprofit group that raised money for the families of police officers from western New York State who'd been killed in the line of duty.

O'Connor had a ticket to the ball. The investigators saw an opportunity to walk away with some of his DNA, and to do so while he was surrounded by hundreds of retired and active cops.

— — —

State Police Investigator Mark Eifert was dressed for the job, wearing a waiter's black vest and a nametag so he would look just like any other server at the Hyatt Regency hotel in downtown Rochester. The Hyatt's management had cooperated with no trouble; if a state trooper wanted to go undercover at the Policeman's Ball, they would not get in his way.

O'Connor was seated at a table in a corner of the hotel ballroom, against the wall. Lawler discreetly entered the ballroom and pointed out O'Connor—dressed in a blue sport coat and tan khaki pants—to Eifert.

Eifert handled cleanup at the table, and it didn't take long for O'Connor to down a Labatt's Blue he'd gotten at the bar. Eifert picked up the bottle with a napkin and exited the hotel down a set of side stairs. Outside the Hyatt he met Lawler, who, wearing gloves, took the bottle. Lawler and Salvatore initialed on a piece of tape the time and date the bottle was secured, stuck the tape on the emptied bottle, and slipped it into a large envelope.

Almost half hour later, O'Connor finished another Labatt's. Eifert had watched from afar, noting that no one else touched the bottle in the ballroom other than the bartender. Eifert took the bottle from the table and carried it to Lawler and Salvatore, too.

Eifert wasn't done. Before the night was over he'd also walked away from the table with a soup spoon and a fork handled by O'Connor. Lawler and Salvatore secured all of the items, labeling them and then transporting them to the nearby Rochester police property clerk for safekeeping until a DNA test could be arranged.

— — —

Though Liam Magee was in Ireland, the cops wanted to know all they could about him.

A folk musician, Liam Magee could be found on YouTube, strumming his acoustic guitar and singing Irish standards and Bob Dylan covers. With his receding white hair and wire-rimmed glasses, he looked more grandfatherly than murderous. But the more the investigators mined his background, the more their opinion of him changed.

A recovering addict and alcoholic, Liam Magee had a criminal past that included federal counterfeiting crimes. And he had an assortment of friends that included some notorious Westies—the violent Irish American gang that had once ruled New York City's Hell's Kitchen.

"New York law enforcement officials hold the Westies responsible for more than 30 murders during the last 15 years," the *New York Times* wrote in 1987. "This is the most violent gang we've seen," Michael Cherkasky, head of the Rackets Bureau of the Manhattan District Attorney's office, told the *Times*.

One of the most violent of the violent was Joseph "Mad Dog" Sullivan, a close friend of Magee and a Mafia hit man whom police believed to be responsible for more than twenty murders. Sullivan was also the only person to have ever escaped from the Attica Correctional Facility, the maximum security prison that, months after his breakout, would be the site of the deadliest prison uprising in us history. In April 1971, Sullivan slipped out of Attica, assisted by Magee—who, with a guitar he kept in his cell, diverted the attention of corrections officers with an unplanned prison yard performance. As Magee sang, Sullivan snuck into the back of a truck that carried flour into, and empty flour bags out of, the prison. He covered himself with bags and was driven through the prison gates unnoticed. He was found weeks later in Greenwich Village.

Magee was also buddies with Tom Taylor and Tom Torpey, two men who'd been bodyguards for one of Rochester's most notorious mobsters, Salvatore "Sammy G" Gingello, a debonair Mafioso who was killed in a car bombing in 1978. Gingello lost both legs below the knees but lived for an hour after the explosion, long enough to make it to the operating table. But he died there after—according to a possibly apocryphal story—he battled with surgeons and gave them the middle finger as they tried to save him. Taylor and Torpey were also in the car when it exploded, but they survived. They later would go to prison for twenty-five years for hiring a hit man—none other than Sullivan—to kill a Rochester union leader with mob connections.

Paroled from prison in 2007 at the age of sixty-two, Torpey returned to Rochester. The police questioned him, but he had no knowledge about Gibbons—he didn't even know who he was—and had largely lost contact with Magee.

Taylor would not be paroled from prison until 2009. But the investigators found a way in which he could be helpful, even in at a state prison near Buffalo. During interviews with police, Gerald O'Connor had spoken almost proudly of his friendships with members of Rochester's organized crime factions. It was as if these links were a badge of honor for him—proof that, as a criminal, he was more than a drunken killer. In particular, he mentioned "Torpey-Taylor," the common shorthand moniker for the two strong-arm mobsters that made them sound almost like a pair of musical performers.

As loath as they were to do so, investigators kept coming back to O'Connor. As most investigative pathways failed, they held onto a thin reed of hope that he could help.

Told that O'Connor had mentioned him as a friend, the imprisoned Taylor had a very different story. In fact, he had once wanted to kill O'Connor. Taylor's daughter had been friends with Denise Manz, whose mother O'Connor had fatally shot. After the killing, Denise moved west, and Taylor's daughter lost a very close friend. She was terribly upset, and Taylor held O'Connor responsible.

When told about Gibbons and how his mother longed to have his body home for a Christian burial, Taylor agreed to help investigators. He said he would write O'Connor a letter and encourage him to reveal what he knew.

Taylor also had a warning: O'Connor was a lifelong liar who'd likely concocted the story about helping bury Gibbons, thinking he could somehow dupe authorities into a deal. "O'Connor considers himself somewhat of a short-con artist, boastful and cunning," Taylor said.

The investigators worked with prison officials to ensure that Taylor's letter reached O'Connor, because inmates could not write to one another.

"I've known you for years, and when you're not messed up on alcohol and barbiturates you're a proud Irishman," Taylor, himself an Irish American, wrote in a spring 2008 letter to O'Connor. "I'm reaching out to your Irish heritage to bring peace to an old Irish mother whose days are numbered, to be able to give her son a proper Celtic burial."

O'Connor need not reveal who'd killed Gibbons, Taylor wrote: "Nobody is asking you to be a rat."

The letter apparently had an impact on O'Connor, serving as a bona fide acknowledgment that he was more than a lowlife. There had been a certain mystique about organized crime figures in Rochester—much as there was in many cities in the 1960s and 1970s—and Taylor's letter likely convinced O'Connor that he somehow was welcome in the fold.

Taylor wrote another letter to O'Connor later in 2008, and investigators visited O'Connor afterward. Now, he said, he was sure he would give up his secret. However, there was another individual who'd helped him bury bodies—a prisoner whom he had not previously mentioned—and he needed to find a way to connect with that person before he led police to Gibbons's body. He wanted to alert the prisoner, whom he would not name, about what he was going to do.

The police were monitoring O'Connor's mail and phone calls, and he did nothing in the months after the interview that seemed like an effort to reach another prisoner. Clinging to O'Connor as their sole lead, the police interviewed his ex-girlfriends and relatives. O'Connor's estranged son even agreed to visit him in prison and urge him to help the police. However, O'Connor again found a method to reveal nothing, saying that to disclose anything to his son—or the police—would place his son in danger.

With O'Connor continuing to play coy, the police visited an Orleans County farm where O'Connor had once hidden after skipping bail on a criminal charge. While driving along the Orleans County road adjacent to the farm, they spotted a black pickup truck barreling toward them in their lane. They slowed, expecting the truck to move over, but it didn't. ·

Crowley yanked the unmarked car off the road and onto a grassy stretch, as the pickup skidded to a stop nearby. The cops jumped out, guns pulled, only to confront the farm owner—a conspiracy theorist who was certain that he was under the watchful eye of some government forces. He had grown suspicious when he saw a car apparently surveilling his farm.

He was apologetic as the police explained who they were and gave him some details about just what they were doing. They did not charge him with a crime, and for years thereafter the property owner, having researched Gibbons's disappearance, would place long-winded calls to the cops. He had new worries: he was now suspicious that there was a corpse on his farm and that the IRA might kill him. The police tried to reassure him that he was safe, but he'd call again months later as if he'd never spoken to them before.

There was an odd synergy about the remaining mysteries of the Brink's heist and Gibbons's disappearance: nobody apparently had a clue where either the missing $5 million or Gibbons were.

O'Connor continued his waltz with investigators, saying he planned to help them but never doing so. The letters from Taylor to O'Connor stopped; there was nothing more Taylor could say to O'Connor than what he'd already said. And the only person who steadfastly called the cops about Gibbons was the nervous farm owner.

The frustration escalated. For investigators, nothing they'd done seemed fruitful, and the Gibbons case seemed likely to fall into the same black hole where the remaining mysteries of the Brink's robbery resided.

Or so they thought.

— — —

In Syracuse, only ninety miles east of Rochester, a forensics medical examiner was enmeshed in his own investigation, one involving human remains that had gone unidentified for a decade. He kept on his office wall a timeline about the discovery of the remains—a torso and a foot—and the thus-far unsuccessful efforts to identify them.

The forensics expert, Ron Brunelli, had built a reputation for his indefatigable work for the dead. He did not like human remains to go unidentified. He knew with each unnamed corpse there was likely to be a grieving family somewhere, trying to navigate a purgatory of pain. For those families, the limbo of uncertainty was often worse than knowing what fate had actually befallen a loved one.

The unidentified torso and foot had been discovered separately in Cape Vincent, New York, a slightly weathered village at the juncture of Lake Ontario and the St. Lawrence Seaway. A DNA comparison showed that the remains were from the same individual.

But the DNA could do no more: no match for it could be found in databases. There was no facial reconstruction that could be drawn from the remains, since the head had not been found.

Still, advances in forensics had provided some information, such as the person's likely physique and gender. And, while limited, the remains did provide some clues. Brunelli felt one clue, in particular, was significant.

Though the torso had clearly been submerged in the water for a long time, possibly years, there was a pair of gym shorts on the remains. The shorts were in remarkably good condition, and a logo on them still visible. The logo consisted of the letters NYAC and the insignia of the New York Athletic Club, a popular gym and workout club with a location near Central Park and another in Westchester County.

From the moment he learned of the torso and the logo for the New York Athletic Club shorts, Brunelli believed that "this is going to be the information that solves this case."

It was not a lot, but it might be enough.

CHAPTER 28

— — —

The foot had floated ashore first in Cape Vincent.

On June 9, 1999, hikers, traipsing along a craggy waterfront, stumbled on the foot—a size 11 fitting snugly inside an athletic sock and a white leather New Balance, the shoe soiled and discolored a mossy green but still intact, as if part of a macabre advertisement for the sneaker brand.

With the merger of Lake Ontario and the St. Lawrence River at Cape Vincent, the river provides the connection between the Great Lakes and the Atlantic Ocean. The river meanders northeasterly, wandering through Canada before emptying into the Gulf of St. Lawrence.

At Cape Vincent, the waters can be moody, almost bipolar in personality— sometimes manic and tempestuous, sometimes tranquil and serene. Debris can travel great distances, carried by the waves of the lake and the currents of the river. Determining just where the foot had begun its journey would be a hopeless task for investigators. It might well have drifted many miles before settling on the shoreline.

While once largely impassable, the river had been transformed by engineering feats in the twentieth century into a commercial thoroughfare that helped link the Atlantic, Canada, and middle America.

Occasionally men and women would fall or, taking their own lives, jump from the international freighters moving along the St. Lawrence and the Great Lakes. After decomposition in the depths of the water, the body parts would float ashore on the mainland of the United States or Canada or sometimes onto one of the 1,300 islands—some of them smaller than a mile in length—comprising the area known as Thousand Islands. (On a single day in May 2016, Canadian authorities recovered four different bodies from the river.)

Thus, the foot found at a Cape Vincent community called Mud Bay could have been that of an American, a Canadian, or even someone from a continent other than North America.

Peter Barnett, a detective with the Jefferson County Sheriff's Department, was on call when the discovery of the foot was reported. Barnett had grown up in Watertown, fifteen miles from Cape Vincent and the largest city in Jefferson County. After completing high school and doing a stint in the Marines, he joined the Jefferson County Sheriff's Department. With only thirty-five deputies and officers, the department patrolled the roads in the 1,800-square-mile county while dealing with a drug trade that had found its way there. The deputies and officers also had to deal with the inevitable drunken drivers—and boaters—who spilled out of the bars in the wee hours of summer mornings.

Barnett patrolled the roads and sometimes the waters, warned teenagers about drug abuse through a middle school Drug Abuse Resistance Education (DARE) program, and—after ten years with the department—took on the investigation of major crimes.

Murders were uncommon in Jefferson County. Still, the county had its history with notorious and abhorrent criminals, perhaps none as ghastly as Arthur Shawcross. A lumbering troglodyte, Shawcross had been living in Watertown when he strangled a ten-year-old boy and raped and killed an eight-year-old girl.

Shawcross was allowed to plead guilty to manslaughter. When he was released from prison, Shawcross was spirited into Rochester by parole officials after other communities refused to accept him. In Rochester, his mayhem continued. There, over two years, he strangled and mutilated prostitutes. By the time he was caught, he'd murdered eleven women.

Having been exposed to Shawcross, police were particularly wary when an appendage was discovered along the many miles of county waterfront. When the foot was found, two young women from Jefferson County were missing. But the foot did not seem a match for either of them, and missing person reports from the region provided no leads.

The Onondaga County Medical Examiner's Office took possession of the foot. Located in Syracuse, the office handled autopsies and determined the cause of mysterious deaths for some central New York counties. Laid in a cardboard box, the foot was stored in the office's "skeletal room," where the thermometer was set low enough to keep remains dry and uncontaminated by mold or mildew.

There it sat—until more human remains were found.

— — —

Jefferson County is a sprawling mix of dairy farms, a few small urban centers, an Army base itself the size of a small city, and waterfront villages and towns that spring to life in the summer and fade into quiet in the exceptionally long and frigid winter.

With its location at the nexus of the St. Lawrence River and Lake Ontario, Cape Vincent is one of those villages that attracts boaters, bar hoppers, and fishermen and fisherwomen in the summer months. Modest rental cottages, some of them worn and tired, line the waterways. Mud Bay is in the southernmost section of Cape Vincent, and one of the Thousand Islands—Grenadier Island—can be seen from Mud Bay.

The largely wooded Grenadier Island is home to a handful of rental cottages and houses. Among those who spent summer months there was David Gregor, a retired surgeon who owned a small three-bedroom ranch-style house on the island. Gregor had served for years as one of the top medical professionals at the Watertown hospital. His father had been chief of the medical staff there.

Grenadier Island was a perfect retirement sanctuary for David Gregor. An avid boater, angler, and conservationist, Gregor helped establish a permanent nature conservancy on the island.

With his seasonal deep tan and sweeping white hair, Hollywood could have chosen Gregor to play the leader of a hospital. The outdoors had long been his respite from the detailed focus required of a surgeon. He had fished and hunted around the world, traveling to Russia, Scotland, and Denmark.

Grenadier Island was appealing to him because he could also enjoy fly-fishing and hunting waterfowl there. A single man, Gregor enjoyed quiet strolls along the shoreline when the morning breeze was light and fresh.

On September 3, 2000, the seventy-one-year-old Gregor walked on the beach near his summer house, striding over the rounded rocks and occasional jetsam. Something caught his eye—what at first appeared to be a pasty white chunk of driftwood.

But there was something significantly out of the ordinary: this driftwood was attired in blue Champion shorts. Protruding from the shorts were what Gregor believed to be two thighbones, their edges jagged and sharp, and a vertebra.

He found a nearby stick and pushed over the debris, though he now felt sure he knew what it was—a human torso. What he'd found "could be nothing other than human remains," Gregor later said. "I walked back up the shoreline and called the sheriff's office."

The office's investigators considered it fortuitous that Gregor had found the armless torso, which appeared to have been separated from the rest of the body just below the neck and above the knees. Others, without Gregor's keen eye, might have passed it by. The torso's bleached coloration blended with the beach's natural debris, as if it had camouflaged itself for safety. It would have been easy to ignore the shorts from a distance, believing them to be debris that had washed ashore.

The discovery was not especially grisly for Gregor, who had spent a career cutting open and navigating the insides of anesthetized patients. Gregor later told investigators that he wished he'd shown more respect for the remains; this, investigators believed, was the result of his years as a surgeon.

Barnett again got a call about a finding of remains. A new mystery began.

— — —

The Champion shorts on the torso bore the logo of the New York Athletic Club, and investigators hoped the logo would help them identify the torso. The underwear had an unusual pedigree: the briefs were Shiesser Bluebird, which were made in Germany. In addition, the police discovered the New Balance sneaker found on the foot had been manufactured only between 1993 and 1995.

Barnett and his colleagues checked in with the New York Athletic Club, but the club had heard no news that any of its 8,000-plus members were missing. The coroner in Jefferson County examined the twenty-seven-pound torso, looking for any signs of trauma that might explain the death. The coroner determined that the deceased was a woman, likely between twenty and forty years old.

With nothing more definitive than the gender, the sheriff's office figured that one starting point would be the county's two missing women. One of them had battled mental illness and vanished in September 1997, days after being discharged from a mental health clinic. Her family had not reported her disappearance to police for more than a month. The second missing woman was suspected to have been murdered. She had not returned to a hospital after leaving her premature baby there.

Weeks after Gregor's discovery, the torso was shipped to an FBI lab in Washington, D.C., for DNA and other analysis. With a backlog, the FBI could not move quickly with a forensics study of the torso, and after months of waiting, the Jefferson County Sheriff's Department asked that it be transferred to the Onondaga County Medical Examiner's office.

The office had a reputation for both its stellar forensics work and its insistence on trying to find identities for unidentified corpses and body parts. Its lead medical examiner, Mary Jumbelic, was known nationally as a specialist in mass disaster scenes. She was among the coroners who dealt with the dead when TWA flight 800 erupted into flames in 1996 and tumbled into the Atlantic near Long Island, killing 230 people; and when Korean Air Flight 801 crashed in Guam in 1997, killing 228. She would later be at the World Trade Center after 9/11, in New Orleans after Hurricane Katrina, and in Thailand after the tsunami, trying to return names to the thousands of dead so she could bring some solace—even if an anguished solace—to their loved ones.

Jumbelic's work was personal for her. "We spend all this time cataloguing death," she said. "If there's no greater end to it, then a computer could do it. The greater end is trying to find families, trying to give people comfort and peace. Even if we have bad news, we can tell them what happened."

The decomposition of the torso had been so severe that it was not a simple matter to determine the victim's gender. At the pelvis, little more than the skeletal frame remained; any remnants of genitalia had been destroyed by feeding fish, years of immersion, or both.

While the initial conclusion had been that the torso was that of a female, the Onondaga County Medical Examiner's Office started its analysis from scratch, relying on nothing from the past.

With human remains, pelvises and skulls can often help determine gender. Through X-rays, the office decided that the pelvis bone and pubic area of the torso was V-shape, common for a male. A woman's pelvic area is typically more rounded and blunter, better suited for childbirth.

Jumbelic now felt certain that the remains were those of a male, and that the Jefferson County Sheriff's Department should be looking for a missing man, not a missing woman.

She told the Syracuse-region media about the difficulty of making a solid identification. If there were a clear suspicion whose the remains were, then the task would be easier, she said: "You have to have someone you suspect it might be and work it from that end."

Still, she said, the job of her office and its staff was to work with what they had. "We try really hard to put a name to that person," she said.

Jumbelic enlisted the help of a forensic anthropologist, Anthony Falsetti, director of the University of Florida's C. A. Pound Human Identification Laboratory—one of the nation's leading forensics institutes. Jumbelic asked Falsetti to review the determination of gender and to take the analysis further, to see if he could decide the race and approximate physical dimensions and age of the victim.

Falsetti already had a reputation as a man who could work miracles with the minutest clues from the dead. A popular guest on shows on the Discovery and National Geographic television channels, Falsetti had examined the remains of hundreds of people, many of them unidentified as he labored to reclaim their names and lives for them.

After the CBS drama CSI brought forensics into the mainstream (though with occasional outlandish plot devices and incredible crime solving from the fictional team), television producers discovered that there was an audience for scientific crime analysis, no matter how arcane—or gruesome—the work of the experts. Falsetti was a real-life forensics hero. He'd conducted forensics examinations to identify mummies from Egypt and Peru. In one particularly odd case, the shriveled corpse of an infant was found bundled in a 1957 newspaper in a Florida rental storage unit. As one newspaper article described the discovery at the outset of the case, "A mummified baby boy wrapped in a newspaper, a black pair of women's pants and two suitcases are found in a musty storage bin."

The remains of the child were discovered forty years after they had been left in the storage unit. Falsetti was asked to determine an age range. Using the growth of the child's bones and the developing dental pattern, he pegged the age at ten months of life, or approximately forty months since conception. Falsetti also found no signs of trauma.

In that case, Falsetti started with a process common to his work, and he also used it with the torso from Grenadier Island. Known as maceration, the process is a gradual defleshing of the remains, with the flesh loosening and slipping from the skeletal frame as it sits in warm—but not boiling—water for days. The process is akin to the cooking technique of the same name, in which food is softened by resting in an acidic liquid.

With the maceration complete, Falsetti used wooden tools to pull and prod and pry the flesh from the remains. This ensured that there would be no accidental punctures or marks left by a metallic instrument, a mark that could be mistaken for a preexisting wound.

From head to toe, skeletal remains provide clues about age, build, and ethnicity. One just had to know where to look. Falsetti did.

The pubic area can differentiate between ages as well as between genders. The halves of the pelvis join in the pubic area, and when young, the bone there is ridged and grooved. As an individual grows older, the ridges erode and flatten slightly, providing tell-tale signs of age. The specificity has limits: typically, changes in the pelvic bone ridges can narrow an age to within ten years between the twenties and seventies.

The pelvis region of the torso revealed ridges that had been somewhat leveled—not the clear demarcations of a teenager, but also not the heavily abraded pelvic structure of an older man. Falsetti decided the torso was that of a man in his midthirties.

While there were some limits as to the details that could be deduced from the torso—for example, the cause of death was not evident—advancements in forensic anthropology let Falsetti take his scrutiny even further. In 1993, two forensic anthropologists, Stephen Ousley and Richard Jantz, released a software program called FORDISC that analyzed up to twenty-one separate cranial measurements to produce estimates of ethnicity and body size.

Later versions of the software program allowed forensic investigators to input data from other body parts that also demonstrated distinctions depending on ethnicity, height, and weight. A femur was one such bone, and the femur with the torso found at Grenadier Island was intact enough for the use of FORDISC.

FORDISC crunched the data—dimensions from the femur—and spat out these conclusions: the ancestry was European Caucasian, and the man was likely between five feet and five feet seven inches tall.

His work done, Falsetti sent the data back to the Onondaga County Medical Examiner's Office.

With the torso returned and more information available, Jumbelic decided to take a chance. The foot discovered at Mud Bay in 1999 was located only a mile or so from the torso found the next year at Grenadier Island. What if they were remains from the same person?

Utilizing a DNA lab, the office had small fleshy samples from the foot and the torso compared. The suspicions were on the mark: the DNA matched.

The revelation that the two body parts were remains of the same individual—found only about a mile apart—meant that the person likely was submerged in the waters near Cape Vincent. But there were no reports of missing men in the region that seemed a match. Investigators remained stumped.

Whoever had died in Lake Ontario or the St. Lawrence River had been wearing New Balance sneakers, Champion shorts, and European-made underwear. That didn't help investigators much. Barnett reached out to European companies that had freighters that traversed the New York State waterways but had little luck.

At the Onondaga Medical Examiner's Office, forensic examiner Ron Brunelli also took an interest in the torso and foot. Brunelli had taken an unusual route to the medical examiner's office, except for the fact that his professional career had focused on dead people.

After college, Brunelli had worked as a funeral director. With a quiet and caring nature, he was good at putting people at ease and helping them cope with their grief, but occasionally he felt that the job was like that of a salesman. He did not like trying to steer families to the more expensive caskets.

He left the business after six years and studied anthropology at Syracuse University. He took a job as a forensic examiner at Crouse Hospital in Syracuse, then joined the medical examiner's office in 1996.

After leaving the funeral business, Brunelli took a keen interest in forensic anthropology. That interest grew into a passion to identify the unidentified, to study unknown corpses and body parts and try to match them with the many missing people across New York State and elsewhere. It was natural that the case of the torso and the foot would appeal to him. There was a mystery and an opportunity to bring some closure to a family.

Brunelli learned of a Russian sailor who'd jumped from a Russian freighter on the St. Lawrence River and never been found. The international investigative legwork was burdensome, but he navigated bureaucratic channels, only to come to the clear conclusion that the sailor was not the man whom he was seeking.

He compiled all the data he could about the remains and created a case file to be circulated by a volunteer organization, the Doe Network, which highlighted the cases of missing people and unidentified corpses on its website.

The case file told the story of the remains of "an unidentified white male" that had been discovered in 1999 and 2000. "Head not recovered. Limbs not recovered. Hands not recovered," the online case file stated. "Police believe the victim jumped ship, or somehow fell from a ship passing through the Great Lakes and St. Lawrence Seaway. Autopsy results indicate no evidence of 'dismemberment attempts.'"

On his office wall in Syracuse, Brunelli kept the timeline of the discovery of the foot, the torso, and the subsequent forensics conclusions. One day, he was sure, he'd have an answer.

Meanwhile, the remains, tucked into a child-sized casket, were buried in a corner of a small municipal cemetery in Cape Vincent. A marker noted that the individual was unidentified.

— — —

During the first decade of the twenty-first century, the US Department of Justice worked to create a system that would serve as a clearinghouse of information about the nation's thousands of missing people and unidentified human remains. The effort gave birth to the National Unidentified and Missing Persons System, or NamUs. With NamUs, police agencies could plug the details about missing person cases into a computerized data base that at first was accessible to law enforcement officials only but that by 2009 could be used by members of the public.

Brunelli quickly saw how advantageous the computer program could be. With NamUs, the likelihood of identifying the previously unidentified jumped exponentially.

In 2008, Brunelli was scanning data on NamUs, looking at missing person cases across New York State when, as he said later, "up comes a Rochester case." NamUs gave details about how a New York City boxer had traveled to a Rochester suburb in 1995 and then vanished.

Gibbons was a good match for the likely height, weight, and age of the Cape Vincent remains. In addition, Rochester and Greece were both on the shores of Lake Ontario. And although they were quite a distance from Cape Vincent, there were few limits as to how far the remains could have traveled in the water before coming ashore.

If Gibbons had boxed in New York City, perhaps he'd trained at the New York Athletic Club. And Brunelli learned through more research that Gibbons was from England, which could explain the German-made underwear on the torso. Maybe it had been bought in Europe.

For years Brunelli and Barnett had explored multiple leads, from missing people in or near Jefferson County to the possibility that someone had tumbled from a freighter in the Great Lakes. Nine years after the foot was found by hikers, Brunelli and Barnett were still no closer to answers. That's what made this missing boxer all the more interesting to Brunelli: it seemed the first solid lead he'd had in years.

He compiled a package of information—extensive data about the remains and their similarities with Gibbons—and sent it to the police department in Greece, New York, where Gibbons had last been seen in public.

Then Brunelli waited. And waited. And waited some more.

CHAPTER 29

— — —

For cops, there is a distinct pleasure in solving cold cases. Getting an arrest and conviction on a street-corner homicide, a murder in which one drug dealer inserted a 9-millimeter slug into another, has its own rewards, but they are no match for the satisfaction of resolving a crime that had languished unsolved for years, if not decades.

Besides, by the early 2000s, a cottage industry of cable TV shows focusing on true crime had sprung up. The resolution of a cold case, especially with the always popular video of the "perp walk" of a killer who thought he'd escaped prosecution, was a surefire way to land an hour on cable television.

However, there was little immediacy or urgency with cold cases. Routine crimes might not be the route to brief television stardom, but they still required quick action before witnesses disappeared, memories faded, and evidence vanished. And neighborhoods that were feeling the impact of crime—burglaries, break-ins, car thefts, and vandalism—could not be ignored.

So there was a reason why cold cases stayed cold, and it wasn't because of a lack of desire to solve them from the police. Often cops tried to find spare minutes or hours to jump back into the files and clues and testimony from unsolved cases, but inevitably the latest crime would take precedence.

The Rochester suburb of Greece, with nearly 100,000 residents, was the size of a small city. Its police force stayed busy with homegrown crime and some that seeped across its border with Rochester to the east.

Unsurprisingly, the information that Ron Brunelli sent to the Greece police in 2008 did not immediately leap to the forefront of the investigators' concerns. In addition, the investigator who had been assigned the case left shortly thereafter, for a lengthy stint in the military reserves.

In a normal environment, perhaps, the information about the human remains would have attracted some attention from police within months after they received the tip that Ronnie Gibbons, last seen in an Applebee's in Greece in 1995, might have been found in Cape Vincent several years later. Or rather, that parts of him might have been found.

But beginning in the summer of 2008, the first of a series of debilitating scandals struck the Greece police.

On a June night, an off-duty Greece police sergeant was speeding along a highway after spending an evening indulging in liquor and cocaine. He rear-ended a car that had stalled on the highway and then, leaving his car, wandered away from the crash. A pregnant woman in the car struck by the cop was physically injured and gave birth to her child prematurely, and the child suffered some brain damage.

The cop was arrested, tried, and convicted.

Another Greece cop was convicted of using his badge to coerce a woman into having sex with him. The cop convinced the woman that he would violate her probation if she did not sleep with him.

He also went off to jail, as did the town's police chief—who had been convicted of trying to cover up the facts of the crash of the off-duty cop.

In mid-2010, a ramrod-straight Army veteran, Todd Baxter, was brought in to bring some order to the chaos and repair morale. And the Greece investigators had something else to focus on in 2010: a triple homicide in which three major-league marijuana dealers had traveled from their homes in Arizona to Greece and fatally shot three drug-dealing colleagues who had sold the weed across the Rochester region. Working with state police, the FBI, the Bureau of Alcohol, Tobacco, Firearms and Explosives (ATF), and other law enforcement agencies, the Greece cops built an ironclad case that would, three years later, lead to convictions in federal court.

State Police Investigator Tom Crowley was tasked with some surveillance during the triple homicide investigation. Once, during a chat with Mark Concordia, a Greece police investigator on the case, Crowley mentioned the Gibbons investigation.

Concordia recalled information the Greece police department had once received about some human remains possibly being those of the boxer who was last seen at the Applebee's. Concordia promised Crowley that he'd dig out the information and provide him with more specifics.

Perhaps it was another dead end, perhaps not. Crowley, Bill Lawler, and David Salvatore had decided to give up on Gerald O'Connor. They longed for another lead.

Concordia later sent Crowley the file from Brunelli. Crowley saw what Brunelli had: the similarities between Gibbons and the remains were striking.

Crowley and the Rochester police investigators decided to dig deeper. They reached out to Gibbons's sister, who said Ronnie had often worn New Balance sneakers. And he had had shorts from the New York Athletic Club that sounded like a match for those found on the torso.

The investigators had heard enough. Now they needed to unearth some body parts.

— — —

By late 2010, an investigative team had been organized, and a large one it was, involving police from New York State, Rochester, and Greece; the Jefferson County Sheriff's Department and District Attorney's Office; the Monroe County District Attorney's Office; and the Onondaga County Medical Examiner's Office.

The Jefferson County officials took the lead in securing court permission to exhume the human remains buried without a name in Cape Vincent.

State Police Investigator Dave Douglas, based in New York City had helped with some of the downstate interviews. He secured a DNA swab from Gibbons's sister.

Organizing the exhumation was no small task, because of the coordination involved. The state police occasionally used the services of Michael Baden, a well-known medical examiner whose career spanned decades.

Baden agreed to analyze the body parts once they had been disinterred. Maybe there would be answers to how Gibbons—if the remains were his—had been killed.

But there would be no exhumation during the winter months. Cape Vincent could be brutally cold, and there might be snow on any scheduled date.

This didn't mean that the investigation was at a standstill. Instead, it now had new life. The police investigators who'd restarted the investigation into Gibbons's disappearance, along with the unsolved Damien McClinton homicide, felt certain that the missing man had been found. And they hoped to use that information as leverage. Maybe the suspects who'd been unshakeable in the past could now be roused into making a stupid move.

Greece Police Investigator Chris Bittner joined the team and was among those collaborating with the Jefferson County Sheriff's Office and Investigator Peter Barnett to see whether any links could be made between the suspects and Cape Vincent, New York.

That didn't take long. Barnett learned of a former Rochester resident, James Merrifield, who lived in a lakefront cottage he'd built himself at Mud Bay, not far from where the foot had been discovered.

Merrifield summered at Cape Vincent while working first for Xerox and later for a health insurance company in Rochester. After his retirement in the 1990s, he decided to make Cape Vincent his home. (In a fortuitous move, Merrifield helped some stranded boaters one weekend while the cottage was under construction and then successfully enlisted their help with the project as handymen.)

A guitarist, Merrifield enjoyed relaxing with men and women who enjoyed a good singalong. When he had lived in Rochester, one of those friends had been Liam Magee. The two became so close that Magee set up a tiny one-room mobile trailer on Merrifield's property in Cape Vincent and, before his deportation, spent weekends there. Merrifield and Magee would entertain Cape Vincent neighbors and others with folk songs by a campfire.

A possible scenario was becoming clearer. Maybe Gibbons had been killed and the corpse taken to Merrifield's property, then weighted down, taken by boat into the St. Lawrence River, and unloaded.

Investigators hoped that Merrifield might be of help. Unfortunately, by the time his name arose in the investigation, he had passed away—only weeks before.

— — —

While living in Ireland and forbidden to return to the United States, Magee had found a way to reconnect with his relatives who still lived in the Rochester region. Along the Canadian shores of Lake Ontario were numerous towns and villages with active music scenes—the bars and clubs catering to fans of Irish music. Magee occasionally performed in the towns while living in Rochester, and he continued to do so after his deportation.

Twice a year, Magee flew to Canada and performed weekend sets at one of the bars. His family traveled to Canada to hear him, as did friends from Cape Vincent. Magee was so well-received that a Cobourg, Ontario, bar advertised his visits well in advance on its website. And Magee, who'd been clean of alcohol and drugs for years, enjoyed his time there so much that he called Canada "my new adopted country."

Investigators decided to take advantage of a visit by Magee in 2011 to interrogate him. The bar had promoted his two nights of performances for months in advance, letting the cops know when he would be returning. They also reviewed the border crossings of his family—trips that typically aligned with Magee's visits.

On June 3, 2011, a large contingent of members of the investigative team gathered at a Canadian immigration office, joining Canadian officials who, according to Crowley, had been "immediately interested" when told earlier why the Americans wanted to speak to Magee. The Canadians agreed to help, and as Magee prepared to go from the hotel where he was staying to the bar, he was met by members of the Royal Canadian Mounted Police.

They transported him back to the immigration office, telling him little beyond the fact that some American police officers wanted to meet him. The Americans thought they had a card to play: they could work with US immigration officials to allow Magee to return to the United States if he cooperated and told them what he knew about Gibbons's disappearance.

The Canadians sat Magee at a small table in a room so cramped that only a few of the US investigators could squeeze in. The investigators had seen Magee only on YouTube videos, which he'd filmed regularly as a way to distribute music to his American fans. He looked gentle and unassuming now, though the police also remembered a snapshot someone had given them of Magee and hit man Joseph "Mad Dog" Sullivan chatting with each other while Sullivan was between murders and out of prison.

Crowley took the lead, saying he wanted to talk to Magee about Gibbons, if he knew him. Magee reacted angrily, loudly responding, "That man ruined my life." Unsure of Magee's meaning, Crowley tried to follow up with questions, but Magee went stone-silent and glared at the cops. The amiable Irish troubadour appeared to be morphing into the friend of mobsters and hit men that the cops also knew Magee to be.

Crowley, Lawler, and Salvatore—the original trio in the investigation—tried again, telling Magee they likely could get him back to the United States if he gave them a hand. Magee said nothing. No matter what the cops said or offered, Magee simply stared back at them. Crowley handed Magee a business card; Magee shredded it into pieces and tossed it on the floor.

Within minutes the police realized the hopelessness of the cause and left Magee with the Canadians, who told them he was also not welcome in Canada. Magee would return to Ireland and never return to North America again.

Police would be left to wonder what Magee had meant with his outburst when they mentioned Gibbons's name. They would never find out.

— — —

On the morning of August 24, 2011, Brunelli, Bittner, and Barnett squeezed into a freshly dug hole in the ground, straining to pull a small casket from the soil left muddy by recent rains. The weather on this day cooperated—the day was sunny and dry—but the wind occasionally whipped wildly around the cemetery beside the St. Lawrence River in Cape Vincent. The waters of the river swirled when the winds kicked up, the waves splashing loudly against the nearby banks.

With a court order in hand for the exhumation, police had collaborated with the cemetery management to disinter the casket, buried in a distant corner of the cemetery away from the deceased who were known and named. The headstone, removed earlier, had merely noted that the buried remains were those of an unknown person.

From a distance, an observer may have thought the authorities were raising the remains of a youngster from the soil of Cape Vincent, the squat casket all that was needed for the torso and foot.

The police and Brunelli lifted the casket to a rectangular makeshift platform. Brunelli surveyed the interior of the casket, finding the body parts deep in an orange plastic bag that was surrounded by a separate external plastic covering. His hands covered by latex gloves, Brunelli reached into the orange plastic, finding the foot and torso intact, with some soft fleshy spots still remaining around the chest area.

Bittner snapped photos, ensuring that the results of the disinterment would be preserved in case investigators would ever need to visually confirm what they'd done. With Brunelli satisfied with the condition of the remains, he closed the lid on the casket, and he and the others toted it to a waiting state police sports utility vehicle for the ninety-mile drive to Syracuse and the Onondaga County Medical Examiner's Office, where Baden waited with Lawler and Crowley.

Baden had managed through a distinguished career to do something rare for a forensic pathologist—acquire a certain level of celebrity. In his sixth professional decade in 2011, Baden had written books and been the feature of an HBO series. He'd been crucial to the revelation of the truth about the 1971 Attica riot, confirming the findings of a Rochester medical examiner who'd determined that the thirty-nine prison employees and inmates killed during the violent retaking of the prison had been slain by police gunfire. Baden led a forensic team during a congressionally ordered reinvestigation of the assassination of President John F. Kennedy. In his career, he'd examined close to twenty thousand deaths—including those of John Belushi, Nicole Brown Simpson, and Tsar Nicholas II of Russia. Years after his examination of the Cape Vincent remains, he would be asked by the family of Michael Brown to conduct an autopsy on Brown, whose fatal shooting by a Ferguson, Missouri, police officer would spark days of civil unrest and ignite a conversation about the troubled relationships between the nation's black population and law enforcement.

In 2011, Baden was in private practice but under contract to the state police. He'd agreed to look at the foot and torso, expecting the latter body part to be the one to provide answers—if any were to be found.

Once he had the remains spread out on a table before him, with Lawler and Crowley watching, Baden first determined that there was enough flesh available to make it easy to take a DNA sample. DNA could be extracted in multiple ways, but the presence of some tiny meaty chunks on the mostly skeletal torso ensured that DNA testing would not be a problem.

"There was a lot of soft tissue," Baden said shortly after the examination.

He hoped he could find something that might answer how Gibbons had been killed. Like Mary Jumbelic and Anthony Falsetti a decade earlier, Baden located nothing that indicated that the body had been carved up before being dumped in the water.

"He could have come apart in the water," Baden later said. "The kind of dismemberment there was could have occurred from being struck by boats."

After two hours of examination, Baden could tell investigators little that they didn't already know. Instead, he confirmed that the remains were not enough for the cause of death to be determined. There were no bullet holes, no knife wounds, no signs of a beating. The head, still undiscovered, might have told the story.

Now the police would wait for the DNA results. But they felt certain that they'd found the remains of Ronnie Gibbons. "We were very confident that they were one and the same person," Crowley later said.

— — —

In late November 2011 the tests confirmed Crowley's belief: the DNA from the torso was a familial match with that of Gibbons's relatives.

The match also told the police something else they'd suspected: Gerald O'Connor had been lying all along. Under no scenario laid out by O'Connor would Gibbons's remains have ended up in Cape Vincent. Yet they had.

The police decided not to release their new information immediately. They wanted to map out how best they could use it.

They decided to try to spook Tom O'Connor. The earlier attempt to get his DNA had shown only that it did not match that found on the cigarette in McClinton's car. There had also been the odd incident in which a neighbor of O'Connor had been shot in his driveway and survived. The determination that the likely firearm had been made in Europe convinced investigators that O'Connor was the real target, but the investigation had gotten nowhere beyond that.

On December 2, Bittner and retired homicide investigator Bob Siersma, who now worked for the Monroe County District Attorney's Office, drove to O'Connor's home. Almost twenty years before, Siersma, then a Rochester cop, had approached O'Connor to try to talk to him about the Brink's robbery. The FBI agent with Siersma had started that conversation, ruining any possibility of a fruitful talk with O'Connor.

This time Siersma offered to chat with O'Connor first. They'd had a decent rapport while serving together on the police force, and Siersma thought he could at least ensure that O'Connor would be hospitable.

O'Connor agreed to talk with the investigators outside of his home. His wife, her arms crossed, looked on sternly before she stepped back inside. O'Connor and Siersma talked amiably, remembering old times before Siersma mentioned that they'd like to talk to O'Connor about Gibbons.

O'Connor remained pleasant, complaining that Lawler and other cops he knew were chasing this cold case while "the city's burning down" with violence. Besides, O'Connor said, "they don't even know the guy's dead."

"Yes we do," Bittner said.

"Oh, you do?" O'Connor replied.

"That's why we're here," Bittner said. Siersma then told O'Connor that Gibbons's corpse had been found.

Years later, Siersma and Bittner would still talk about O'Connor's immediate about-face in mood once he heard that Gibbons had been located. The light tenor of conversation stopped, and O'Connor's expression shifted from accommodating to stunned, his smile vanishing and his face dropping.

"Where'd you find him?" O'Connor asked.

Siersma said they couldn't answer that.

"I don't want to talk to you," O'Connor said and quickly went back inside his home.

Bittner checked the pen in his pocket, ensuring that the miniature camera inside the writing device had continued to film the exchange as he hoped it had.

A few days later the police returned, pretending to place a surveillance camera on a utility post outside O'Connor's home. They knew O'Connor was watching them, and they wanted O'Connor to think that they in turn were watching him.

There actually was no camera, but police didn't care: they wanted O'Connor to believe he was again the focus of a police investigation.

A week later police released the news: Gibbons's remains had been found, his identify confirmed by DNA.

At a news conference at the Greece Police Department, Bittner told the media about the work of the multiagency police investigative team. "For about a year and a half we've kept the investigation very close to the vest," he said. Police had interviewed numerous people in the months before the identification match, and he said, "We've received a lot of cooperation."

Investigators refused to provide much detail about the ongoing investigation, except to acknowledge that Gibbons's disappearance was not its sole focus. They also were seeking more information about the 1987 fatal shooting of McClinton and the 1993 Brink's robbery.

The IRA was not mentioned. It was now an afterthought.

— — —

Constructed of stone in 1844, the St. Francis Xavier church in Liverpool, England, is stately and grand, its spire towering upward as if reaching for the hand of the Almighty. Victorian Gothic in design, the Roman Catholic Church is on England's historical registry and once was the center of the largest Roman Catholic parish in all of England.

In February 2012 the family of Ronnie Gibbons gathered inside the church, his remains finally returned to the place of his birth. The Rev. Kevin McLoughlin knew some of the mysterious circumstances of Gibbons's demise, but they were not of importance to his role leading the memorial service.

"It was a typical kind of service," he later said. "It was traditional. It was very, very nice and dignified."

The interest in the service was far from traditional, however. The morning of the service, the *Liverpool Echo*'s front page featured a story titled "Funeral of American Brink's Heist Suspect and Boxer Ronnie Gibbons to Be Held in Liverpool."

"The funeral of Liverpool boxer Ronnie Gibbons with links to one of the biggest robberies in American history was taking place today," the story read. "Joseph 'Ronnie' Gibbons disappeared in 1995 and was only identified just before Christmas last year from body parts which washed up 12 years ago in Lake Ontario."

The story told of the 1993 Brink's robbery in Rochester, New York. "It is generally assumed Ronnie Gibbons did not participate in the robbery but was embroiled in the plans beforehand and felt he deserved a bigger cut of the loot for his troubles. . . . It is strongly believed Mr. Gibbons was killed and disposed of for confronting hardened criminals for money."

Gibbons's remains were cremated at a nearby crematorium and given to his mother, Rita.

A friend of Ronnie, who had lived for a while in New York City, handed the boxed remains to Rita. He told her of numerous times when Ronnie had given him a helping hand as he learned how to survive among the teeming masses in the American city.

"Ronnie carried me long enough and now I'm carrying him," the friend said.

The comment, loving as it was, was too much for Rita. She'd struggled to contain her emotions throughout the service and now, back at her home as the crowd of family and friends grew, she could not help herself. The torrent of tears came.

They were not tears of sorrow, such as those she'd first cried in 1995 when she learned of the disappearance of her son. Those tears—deep and painful—had visited her many nights since.

These were tears of joy.

Her son was finally home.

— — —

In the spring of 2013 Tom O'Connor was hospitalized in Rochester. He died in June, at the age of seventy-four. After the 2011 visit to his home by Siersma and Bittner, he never again discussed Gibbons with the police.

In May 2015 Magee, age sixty-eight, died suddenly of a heart attack in Ireland.

"His great love was folk music and Irish music," an obituary said. "He helped many well-known performers get into the music business. In 1999 he returned [from Rochester] and settled in the west of Ireland."

The deaths of Ronnie Gibbons and Damien McClinton are still unsolved. The location of $5 million from the 1993 Brink's robbery is unknown.

Rita Gibbons hopes one day the truth of her son's death will be known. But she does not suffer, awaiting answers.

"My son is now at peace, at rest," she said.

EPILOGUE

— — —

I always expected to find him dead.

I began looking for Ronnie Gibbons in the fall of 1996, after Terry Quinn—upset at the apparent lack of interest on the part of the police in searching for his friend—called me at the Rochester, New York, newspaper where I still work, the *Democrat and Chronicle*.

By then, Gibbons had been missing for a year. Quinn believed him to be dead, and after talking with Quinn, so did I.

Quinn told me about Gibbons's connections to Sam Millar, Gibbons's need for money, and the ex-boxer's none-too-wise trip to Rochester to try to get some of the missing loot from the Brink's heist.

I contacted Frank Gibbons and some of Ronnie's friends and learned from law enforcement sources that the hunt for Ronnie was an active investigation. My first of what would be many stories about Ronnie's disappearance appeared on November 6, 1996, the same day that Bill Clinton was reelected president.

The story opened simply enough: "The FBI is investigating the disappearance of a New York City man who might have ties to the 1993 Brink's robbery in Rochester.

"Joseph 'Ronnie' Gibbons, a retired New York City boxer, was seen in the parking lot of Applebee's in Greece in mid-August. He had driven to Rochester in a car borrowed from a friend."

As the years passed, I talked regularly with Ronnie's mom, Rita, a dear soul who wanted nothing more than to have her son's remains buried near her home. She, too, believed Ronnie was dead. I also befriended some of the police officers involved in the investigations of the Brink's robbery and Gibbons's disappearance, and they allowed me and a videographer, my colleague and friend Max Schulte, to be at the graveside when Gibbons's remains were exhumed in Cape Vincent in 2011.

There was a moment during that exhumation, when Gibbons's remains were being lifted from their muddy burial ground in Cape Vincent, when I found myself momentarily choking up. Even though I'd long sought to find his resting place, even though I was certain he'd been murdered, I'd reached a point where I doubted that the mystery would ever be solved.

Yet here he was.

But finding Gibbons did not settle much of the mystery. It did not answer who killed him. It did not answer how he ended up in Cape Vincent. It did not answer whether he died because of the Brink's robbery.

Nor did it provide any new insight into the robbery—specifically, the location of the missing $5 million.

As I have written this tale, I have again pushed to unravel those decades-old mysteries. And I have tried, as best I could, to reconstruct and understand the undeniably eccentric personality of Gibbons and just what magnetic qualities seemed to draw people to him. His friend Billy Devlin told me: "I miss him very much. I suppose one testimony to his legacy is that [Gibbons's friends] still talk about him all the time and still laugh every time."

In the years when I searched for Gibbons, I grew closer to his family, especially his mother, and that relationship perhaps colors how Gibbons is presented in this book.

For more than six years I chased the claims of Gerald O'Connor that he had helped bury Gibbons. As I've written in this book, I now know that O'Connor is a prolific liar; he is a sociopath whose killings speak for themselves. Yet for years, he seemed the only hope I had for answers, and when the police reopened their investigation in 2007, they pursued that same fruitless path.

I was the reporter who encouraged the imprisoned mobster Tom Taylor to write O'Connor in prison and see if he would cooperate. Taylor, who is now free from prison and happily married in Florida, was kind enough to prod O'Connor, though Taylor warned me—rightly—that O'Connor was likely lying.

I once went to see O'Connor in prison. He'd refused to be part of an arranged media interview with me, so I simply showed up one morning for visiting hours at the maximum-security Clinton Correctional Facility. Not long before that, I'd forwarded a letter from Rita Gibbons to him, in which she'd encouraged him to tell police what he knew about the death of her son.

"The pain and torment I and my family have endured during this time is unspeakable, that only a parent can possibly understand," she wrote. "I do not know if you have children yourself, but if you do, I hope you can understand my anguish and desperation."

He did not respond to the letter, and when he first sat down across from me in the prison visiting room, he said: "Don't try this grieving mother stuff with me. I don't care."

That told me what I needed to know about O'Connor.

There are many more stories I could tell about the rabbit holes the police and I stumbled into because of O'Connor, but I won't—especially because they add nothing to the discovery of Gibbons's remains. And O'Connor adds nothing to the unresolved mysteries.

Like the police, I did not stop investigating these mysteries after the disinterment at Cape Vincent. Am I closer to answers? Yes and no.

Let's start with the heist—the reason why Gibbons is dead.

This we know: Millar was at the Brink's depot when the crime was committed and also was the "mastermind" behind it, if that label is applicable for the robbery of such a vulnerable depot. Not only was he convicted of possession of the looted money, but he admitted to the robbery in his memoir.

Beyond that, little more can be deduced about the robbery from Millar's memoir. I have written about what Millar claims happened to the millions that were not found in Manhattan—the story of his mysterious friend "Marco." On the plausibility scale, his story falls somewhere between "far-fetched" and "absurd." I'm sure he wrote what he did for noble reasons—to protect his friends who did participate in the heist—but that makes the story no less untrue. (Millar has refused to discuss the robbery with me, despite repeated requests.)

Millar's past with the IRA, coupled with the political sympathies of Father Patrick Moloney and Tom O'Connor, gave birth to the suspicions of IRA involvement in the robbery. If the money could not be found in the United States, perhaps it landed in the hands of the IRA.

So did it?

When O'Connor, Moloney, Millar, and Charles McCormick were arrested and tried, federal law enforcement officials made much of the pasts of Millar and Moloney, mentioning Millar's IRA crimes and his Long Kesh imprisonment and Moloney's criminal charges for IRA gun running. (Again, it must be noted that those charges were dropped.) And O'Connor's spiriting of Millar into the United States was also highlighted. Naturally, the media—including those of us at the *Democrat and Chronicle*—seized on the IRA connections and questioned whether a terrorist group had been the puppet master behind the heist. Federal authorities did little to discourage that question, since they also suspected that the IRA could be involved.

NORAID officials and American supporters of the IRA scoffed at the claims that the IRA was responsible for the theft of $7.4 million on American soil. And as the months passed, no more evidence for the connection surfaced. Federal authorities spoke less of an IRA crime and more of a crime of convenience. With its lax security, the Brink's depot had practically asked to be robbed. Judge David Larimer precluded talk of the IRA at trial because of the absence of evidence of any link. And prosecutors had nothing about the IRA to raise at trial. The only purpose in mentioning the IRA would have been to taint the defendants by association, and Larimer, rightfully under the law, did not allow that to happen.

History can sometimes bring clarity, and in my research for this book, I decided to speak with the experts: men and women who have spent years studying the IRA, its activities, its crimes, and its fundraising. I've also spoken with former IRA members.

The consensus: the IRA had nothing to do with the planning of the Rochester robbery.

"The notion that they would have planned an internationally scaled robbery is the stuff of Hollywood," said one longtime IRA scholar, who asked not to be identified. "It would make no sense at all politically."

This is a common refrain from those skeptical of IRA collaboration: involvement in a major crime in the United States would dampen the political support the IRA had from some US officials. And there were other ways for it to get cash.

"If they wanted to pull off a big robbery, why not go to the traditional stamping ground for such activities—the Irish Republic?" asked the IRA scholar. "There it had sympathizers, informants, people who could be bribed, safe houses, financiers, and a means of disposing of the money. It would make no sense whatsoever to take on a huge risk for limited advantage."

Richard "Ricky" O'Rawe, one of the blanketmen I interviewed for this book, concurs. "This doesn't reek of any IRA involvement at all," he said.

Though no one died in the robbery, the criminals had no assurances that there would not be gunplay. Had one of the guards pulled a gun, the crime would have been far different—perhaps tragic and deadly. Had one of the guards been killed in an IRA-plotted crime, the public relations backlash would have been tremendous, a blow to the organization's large reservoir of support in some American circles.

The manner of the crime also does not match the more meticulous planning of the IRA, O'Rawe said.

"The hard part in these big robberies is (a) holding onto the money and (b) laundering it," he said. The IRA would have had detailed plans to quickly launder the money, he said. None of the loot would have been sitting in suitcases and duffel bags nine months later.

While IRA participation in the robbery's planning is unlikely, that does not rule out the possibility that Millar or maybe even Moloney found ways to get some of the cash to the organization. There has been no evidence of this, but there has been no evidence of the money showing up anywhere. There are ample rumors that the cash is buried somewhere in the Rochester area, and perhaps one day some of it will surface, either in a field there, in Manhattan, or in Northern Ireland.

(Some police investigators have joked that, since I spent so many hours doing research for this book, I likely learned the hiding place of the money but am keeping the secret to myself. If only that were so.)

Millar now lives in Belfast, and he has written multiple suspense novels, making a name for himself as a writer. A short story of his was included in *Belfast Noir*—one of a series of anthologies containing suspense and mystery stories from across the world, reaching from Dallas to Tehran.

Moloney still lives in Bonitas House on Manhattan's Lower East Side, its fourteen bedrooms usually vacant though occasionally the temporary home for immigrant children escaping dangers in Central and South America. He still attracts media attention and still maintains his innocence in the Brink's robbery.

The millions have never been as pressing and important a mystery to me as the questions about Gibbons's whereabouts and how he died. Thanks to the masterful sleuthing of Ron Brunelli, with the Onondaga County Medical Examiner's Office, the first question was answered, and Gibbons's remains were found in Cape Vincent. The second question is still to be resolved.

The likely suspects for Gibbons's murder are easy to pinpoint—the very men whose names he carried with him when he drove to Rochester in August 1995. They are Tom O'Connor and the brothers Cahal and Liam Magee. All of them are now deceased, with Liam the last to die.

In recent years, several people who have not wanted to speak with police (at least as I write this) have spoken to me about Gibbons's death. James Merrifield, whom I mentioned briefly in the final chapter, is a key player in their stories—not because he is a suspect in the killing but because of his friendship with Liam

Magee. And the fact that his Cape Vincent property was near the locations where Gibbons's remains were found—Mud Bay and Grenadier Island—adds to the suspicions that Merrifield's property played a part in Gibbons's demise.

Both stories I have been told point to Magee as a central figure in Gibbons's death. One person, whose information would be secondhand but from a source who would likely have knowledge of the murder, told me that Magee was supposed to steal a car to drive Gibbons to Cape Vincent. Whether Gibbons was alive or dead when driven there, the individual did not know.

I passed this information on to the police, with permission from the individual who spoke to me. (I knew that if I were to seek reports of stolen cars from 1995, I would be waiting for many months, if not years—assuming I would ever be successful.) The police found no such reports around the time of Ronnie's disappearance, which could be an indication that my source was completely wrong. But if he were the only one to mention Magee's possible participation in the killing, I would be skeptical (and would not even include the allegation here).

I've also spoken with a friend of Merrifield and Magee who did not want to be identified. This part-time Cape Vincent resident spent many months telling me that Merrifield would not be involved in something as ugly as a murder. But the person finally told me that he'd once been at a bar with Merrifield when Merrifield had one drink too many. Merrifield started talking about Magee and how Magee once told him of a man who'd wanted part of the Brink's money. The man—I can't imagine it was anyone but Gibbons—had threatened the Magee family if he did not get a cut, Magee allegedly told Merrifield. "We had to take care of him," Magee said.

Does this mean that Magee killed Gibbons? Maybe not. But I will always believe that O'Connor and the Magee brothers knew exactly how Ronnie died. I am not alone in this—it is also the supposition of police and Gibbons's friends and family.

I have written of many missing people during my more than thirty years as a reporter, but none of their stories touched me as did the case of Ronnie Gibbons. I kept a photo of him and his mom on my desk, a visual reminder to try to look for clues about his disappearance whenever I had a free moment. I spoke regularly on the phone with his mom, a woman whose tender strength was evident even in international phone calls. I never told her that her son would be found—it would have been absurd to make such a promise—but I may have been as ecstatic as Gibbons's family was when his remains were discovered. I finally met

Rita Gibbons in January 2012, when she visited her daughter in Queens. She had recently spent three months in the hospital, fighting off cancer.

Rita was dressed elegantly in a pink blouse and sweater, and she was a portrait of proper English politeness and dignity. We talked about her son and laughed at stories she and her daughter told me. We spoke of her cancer, and how she had refused morphine during the painful months in the hospital.

She would not let her pain define her, whether that of cancer or of the long uncertainty about the fate of her son.

When I covered the arrests of the Brink's defendants in November 1993, I wrote that the characters were straight out of a Hollywood plot—a priest, an IRA rebel, and a retired cop.

Were this a Hollywood production, perhaps there would be answers. We would know the fate of the missing millions, we would know the role—if any—of the IRA, and we would know who killed Ronnie Gibbons and how. I sometimes ease my own annoyance at not knowing these answers by reminding myself that I am not alone: multiple police agencies do not have much of a clue either.

I admit some frustration in not being able to provide definitive answers here. But my three decades as a reporter have made me careful about my work. The suppositions I make in this book about the IRA and Gibbons's possible killers are well-grounded in what I know, after dozens of interviews and reviews of thousands of pages of court documents and other information. I do not speculate wildly; indeed, I do so cautiously.

That does not mean the answers aren't known by others. Millar knows more about the robbery than he revealed in his book. I have heard rumors about Cape Vincent residents who might have helped dispose of Gibbons's body. And I am sure that there are people alive who know just where the Brink's money went.

All of which is to say that it would be wrong to bring this story to a conclusion with "The End."

Instead, let's simply say, "To Be Continued."

ACKNOWLEDGMENTS

— — —

This book has had a very long road to completion, and I've been assisted through the years by many people. They've come from different backgrounds, different sides of the law, and different continents. Given that, the odds are good that, as I try to thank all of them for what they've done for me and for this book, I will forget some. My apologies in advance.

Let me start with my colleague and friend Sean Lahman, who was kind enough to connect me with his agent, Robert Wilson. Thanks to Rob for having faith in this book, and for University Press of New England (UPNE) for showing the same faith. At UPNE, in particular, I'd like to thank my editor, Stephen Hull, who helped me see better ways to arrange a book that had multiple narrative threads with converging chronologies.

Also at UPNE, thanks to production editor Amanda Dupuis and copy editor Jeanne Ferris, whose eagle eye caught plenty of slips.

The court files on this case are voluminous—more than a dozen thick books of trial transcripts and thousands of other pages. Typically, they are stored by the federal government at a midwestern site. However, my friends at the US District Court Clerk's Office in Rochester, New York, have been kind enough to hold the documents there for several years, allowing me to come in and review them whenever necessary. Were it not for that kindness, this book would have been impossible for me to write.

Several friends were kind enough to read chapters along the way and to make suggestions. Thanks to them: Bill Clauss, Michael Wentzel, Janice Bullard Pieterse (whose early reporting on this case was also extremely helpful), Michael Tuohey, and Kathi Albertini.

As the text and my list of sources note, there have been individuals who did not want to be named in this project but were immensely helpful. My thanks to them.

In no particular order, I'd like to thank:

From Rochester police circles, Capt. Lynde Johnston, Investigator Nicholas Mazzola, retired Investigator David Salvatore, retired Investigator Vito D'Ambrosia, retired Investigator Bob Siersma, and two individuals who passed away in recent years, former Chief Roy Irving and former Police Major Bill Mayer. Relatives of Roy Irving were also helpful. The assistance given to me by retired Investigator Bill Lawler can't be overstated. Bill, who has been diagnosed with Huntington's disease, is a man of remarkable spirit and cheer, an individual who can show all of us how to live. Numerous Rochester police officers past and present also provided information but asked not to be identified.

Investigator Chris Bittner from the Greece, New York, police also gave me more time than I probably deserved, and I owe a special thanks to State Police Investigator Tom Crowley, whose assistance was crucial when re-creating the investigation into Ronnie Gibbons's disappearance.

From the Federal Bureau of Investigation (FBI), retired Special Agent Bill Dillon, who was vital to the Brink's arrests, has been immensely supportive and helpful. Thanks also to Paul Hawkins, Richard Vega, Dale Anderson, Lou Stephens, Maureen Moskal, and Paul Moskal. And thanks to Cornell Adams, a former New York City cop who was part of the joint surveillance team, and to others who discussed the surveillance but asked not to be identified.

When I was writing about the Irish Republican Army, Ed Moloney always had time for me and connected me with former blanketman Ricky O'Rawe, who helped guide me through the horrors of Long Kesh. As the text notes, there were others who also gave me their time but chose not to be identified. Thanks for the many insights they provided.

When writing of the Irish Northern Aid Committee (NORAID), Damien McClinton, and Tom O'Connor's journey to Belfast, I was helped by Culver Barr, Joanne McClinton, friends of McClinton who asked not to be identified, and Mark LaPiana. Thanks to all.

Thanks to US Magistrate Judge Jonathan Feldman, US District Judge David Larimer, and attorneys Bill Clauss, John Speranza, and Felix Lapine. On the prosecutorial side, thanks to Christopher Buscaglia and Charles Pilato, and—while she was not directly involved in this case—District Attorney Sandra Doorley, who is familiar with some parts of the investigation. Thanks also to Joseph Cardone and the Orleans County Court Clerk's Office. And a special thanks to investigators past and present from the Federal Public Defender's Office: George Thompson and Karen Francati.

Among the four Brink's defendants, Father Patrick Moloney has always been gracious with his time. As I have noted in the text, he says he is innocent; the jury decided otherwise. Whatever the truth, I thank him for his assistance. I attempted a number of times to speak to Sam Millar and Tom O'Connor—and also to O'Connor's wife—but had no success. Nonetheless, they were typically polite in how they responded, and I am grateful for that. Charles McCormick also shared his time and experiences with me, until we had differences over something I wrote in my newspaper coverage—but that makes me no less thankful to him. It was McCormick who informed me that FBI Special Agent Leonard Hatton died a hero on 9/11, running back into a World Trade Center tower to try to save others. While Hatton's appearance in this book is brief, his heroism should not be forgotten.

Many people helped me re-create parts of Ronnie Gibbons's boxing career: Randy Gordon, Paddy Malone, Daniel McAloon, Hector Rocca, Jay Mwamba, and Bruce Silverglade. Thanks.

Ronnie's friends were immensely helpful, especially Terry Quinn, who in 1996 first told me that Ronnie had disappeared; and Jim McCaffrey, a consummate gentleman who also gave me insights into Ronnie's character. Special thanks also to Gary Brown, John "Bomber" Martin, Sophie Martin-Canning, Billy Devlin, and others who asked not to be identified. Terry Quinn also deserves tremendous thanks for helping Ronnie's family reconnect with his daughter, Jolie. Quinn located her in New York City and brought Ronnie's mom and daughter together.

Thanks to Patrick Farrelly for his insights into the Manhattan casinos, and to others who also worked there and helped me.

Christine Richards Daly was strong enough to discuss Gerald O'Connor's killing of her sister, Patricia, as was Patricia's daughter, Denise. I cannot thank them enough for being so kind when revisiting something so tragic. And Tom Taylor deserves special thanks for trying to help find out whether O'Connor was being truthful with his claims about Ronnie Gibbons (and Tom was smart enough to suspect O'Connor wasn't).

In forensics circles, thanks to Michael Baden, Mary Jumbelic, and Anthony Falsetti. And I cannot overstate the value of the time Ron Brunelli, a true hero in this story, spent with me.

In Jefferson County, Peter Barnett was my tour guide and my primary source for reconstructing the investigation into the mysterious body parts. Thanks, Peter, and also thanks to the county Sheriff's Office for its assistance on numerous fronts. Several Cape Vincent residents familiar with the investigation asked not to be identified, but they also deserve my thanks.

I now have a special place in my heart for the family of Ronnie Gibbons. Much of this book could not have been written without their help and the willingness of Frank and Rita to talk of their brother, his disappearance, and his murder. And the depth of my fondness for Ronnie's mom, who also goes by Rita, is tremendous. It took only one telephone conversation with her for me to be struck by her kindness, strength, and longing to find her son. I had no choice after that conversation but to try to help as best I could.

I also need to thank the *Democrat and Chronicle*, where I work, for allowing me the use of photographs and for the opportunity to pursue this book. In particular, thanks to Traci Bauer, Karen Magnuson, and Dick Moss for their support of this project, and to Mark Dwyer, David Andreatta and Mark Liu, who always encouraged me to undertake it—and to complete it. Our immensely talented photographer Max Schulte and I have partnered on many projects, so it was natural that he would be with me at the exhumation and would do his typically stellar photographic work.

I have also benefited from working alongside two good friends, Michael Wentzel, who read some of this book in advance, and Steve Orr, both of whom are able to take stories of immense complexity and shape them into narratives accessible to all. Thanks to them for the lessons I have learned from their work. Similarly, another friend and former editor, Sebby Wilson Jacobson, taught me much about the value of storytelling. There are many other colleagues—past and present—who helped me with this craft, and I will always be appreciative.

My running buddies always help keep me sane. Thanks to them: the aforementioned Bill Clauss, Ray Dry, Andy White, Mark Bennett, Jason DiPonzio, Ben Jacobs, Victoria Freile, Jennifer Palumbo, and Audra Pinkerton.

A special thanks to my brother, Bob Craig, and to my brother and sister-in-law, Bill and Janice Craig. I cannot thank Bill and Janice enough for what they have meant in my life. They taught me much about parenting, as did my wonderful in-laws, Jack and Carroll Pierce.

While working on this project, I have occasionally been worthless at home, disappearing into piles of paper or spending hours at a Starbucks or library for lengthy writing sessions. But I am blessed with a kind, lovely, and understanding wife.

My world would not be so special without my wife, Charlotte, and our daughters, Brittany and Aileen. Somehow I got lucky enough to have them in my life, and no expression of gratitude here can equal how fortunate I am for that.

SOURCES

Before addressing the sources for this book, I should explain its lengthy road to publication. I began writing this book in 1995, after the federal Brink's trial. The Federal Public Defender's Office, then headed by my friend, attorney Bill Clauss, gave me access to the trial transcripts and court records, and I dove into them to re-create the night of the robbery and the start of the investigation. Over the next year I interviewed Father Patrick Moloney, then imprisoned at the Loretto Correctional Facility; Dick Popowych; Roy Irving, who has since passed away; Special Agent Dale Anderson of the Federal Bureau of Investigation and numerous others. However, for some reason (I really don't recall why), I stopped writing after a few chapters and stuffed them into a file.

In 1996 I learned of Ronnie Gibbons's disappearance. In the ensuing years I occasionally thought of the book I'd started, but I never gave serious consideration to pursuing it again. Instead I focused on finding Ronnie Gibbons.

Once Ronnie's remains were found in 2011, I remembered my chapters about the Brink's robbery sitting in a file on a basement shelf. In the next year or so, I decided to transform this tale into a nonfiction book, including the story of the disappearance and murder of Ronnie Gibbons.

With that background, let me now go deeper into some issues about the sources.

First, as noted above, the court files and trial transcripts with this case are truly voluminous—tens of thousands of pages—and provide the foundation for much of the story of the robbery, investigation, and trial. I cannot thank the US District Court Clerk's Office in Rochester, New York, enough for keeping these files there for years and allowing me to return and review them whenever I needed to do so.

I have referred to Samuel Millar's 2003 memoir, *On the Brinks*, numerous times throughout my book. My skepticism about portions of the book should be apparent, particularly about his version of the robbery. However, I have relied on his memoir for other parts of the story—namely, his childhood, his early attraction to the Irish Republican Army (IRA) and his years at Long Kesh. His stories about Long Kesh ring particularly true. I have compared them to other tales from Long Kesh inmates—some in their writings, some in interviews I conducted—and they all tell similarly horrific stories.

I was skeptical about some of Millar's story about his IRA crimes, which he does not go into in great depth in his memoir. Particularly, I questioned the claim in his memoir that he was the first person tried before the Diplock Court, created to handle the cases of suspected IRA members. But newspapers and court files I secured from Northern Ireland bore this out. This confirmation helped me feel more comfortable with other sections of Millar's memoir. (Also, as the information about sources for each chapter will note, I used interviews that others had conducted with Millar to affirm and tell some of his history. Millar has refused to talk to me.)

I have conducted interviews with people who were witnesses at the 1994 trial. In some cases I found discrepancies between my interviews and the trial testimony (the discrepancies had to do with minor details, not anything of significance), and in those instances I relied on the trial testimony. My thinking was this: When the witnesses testified, they were only a year or so removed from the events they were recalling. I decided that those versions were probably more reliable than interviews twenty years later. And, again, I am speaking of discrepancies that only had to do with minor details.

Also, my description of Rochester in 1993, I admit, is somewhat bleak. While many of the same issues remain—struggling schools, child poverty, and urban violence—the community has been transformed for the better since then. Many of the people laid off by major manufacturers have created successful start-up businesses, and even the neighborhood near the depot's location has seen a rebirth. In short, if you're thinking about a visit to the Rochester region, don't let this book scare you away. It's a wonderful part of the country.

Occasionally, I included in this book quotes from individuals in law enforcement, criminal, or journalism circles whom I do not name. In those instances, I have tried to provide as much detail as possible—for example, whether the person being quoted or paraphrased is an FBI agent, a Belfast journalist, an employee of an illegal Manhattan casino, or an IRA expert. These individuals asked for anonymity, but I am certain of the reliability of what they had to say. In every case, in fact, I sought them out because I knew they would add insightful, necessary, and accurate information to this book.

Some of the information in the book—typically of an anecdotal variety—comes from a single source. When relying on a lone source for information, I weighed the reliability of the individual, whether there was other information that I thought lent credibility to what he or she had to say, and whether his or her version of events was consistent over multiple interviews. I acknowledge that none of these measures ensure complete accuracy, and I'm sure that my re-creations of conversations are not verbatim, but I have tried my best to stay loyal to what I believe to be accurate. What the reader will not see are the many stories that I did not include (and some of them were particularly colorful) because I did not feel comfortable about the reliability of the source or the individual's memory.

My newspaper, the *Democrat and Chronicle*, and the now-defunct Rochester *Times-Union* (another newspaper where I worked) were sources for ample portions of this book. I'll pause here to thank my colleagues, past and present, for the tremendous work they did to help this book get to where it is now.

To help clarify some of these sources, what I describe as "internal records" are typically those obtained via freedom of information laws, whether in the United States or the United Kingdom. I received thousands of pages via those laws. When I refer to "trial transcripts," I am using that as shorthand for transcripts, submitted courtroom evidence, and thousands of pages of other documents from the federal court files related to the Brink's robbery. In the book, I specify the work of certain historians and authors when writing about the IRA and the history of Northern Ireland. In the source information here, I include their works and the works of others whose histories were invaluable resources. While the books are noted, specific pages are not because I would often use one to check facts in another, and in some cases I condensed lengthy sections and histories.

Finally, when I refer to "interviews," I mean interviews conducted by me unless otherwise specified. Those interviews include face-to-face, telephone, and e-mail conversations.

Also, a minor point about the Brink's Co., as I call it throughout this book. The company has used both Brink's and Brinks through the years. Its trucks and logo use Brinks. I did the same for years when writing about the heist, but I commonly found myself in the minority. Ultimately, I realized the company, other than with the exceptions mentioned above, now uses Brink's in most instances—on Wall Street, in its press releases, and in its correspondence with investors. Given that, I adopted the usage of Brink's for this book.

With all of that said, here is a chapter-by-chapter review of the sources for this book.

CHAPTER 1: Trial transcripts; Brink's Co. online history and website for investors; Northwestern University homicide data base; *American Mafia: A History of Its Rise to Power*, by Thomas Reppetto (New York: Henry Holt, 2004); the US Treasury website; Jill Cowan, "The Buck Starts Here," *Dallas Morning News*, May 11, 2016; William Diehl Jr. interviews.

CHAPTER 2: Trial transcripts; Dick Popowych interviews; William Richard Diehl interviews; Federal Reserve, "The Cash Lifecycle Video Transcript," August 2013, at http://www.frbsf.org/cash/files/Cash_Lifecycle_Video_Transcript.pdf; Jill Cowan, "The Buck Starts Here," *Dallas Morning News*, May 11, 2016.

CHAPTER 3: Trial transcripts; Dick Popowych interviews.

CHAPTER 4: Trial transcripts; Dick Popowych interviews; Police Chief Roy Irving interviews; FBI Special Agent William Dillon interviews; law enforcement sources interviews.

CHAPTER 5: Trial transcripts; FBI Special Agent William Dillon interviews; US Census; internal records of the Rochester chapter of the Irish Northern Aid Committee (NORAID); Culver Barr interviews; Irish National Caucus website, at www.irishnationalcaucus.org; George Conaty Jr., "Without IRA to Fight British Oppression, There'd Be No Ireland," *Democrat and Chronicle*, March 24, 1985; Warren Richey, "On the Trail of U.S. Funds for the IRA," *Christian Science Monitor*, January 14, 1985; law enforcement sources interviews ; Dan Collins, "NORAID Denies IRA Connection," *United Press International*, December 23, 1981; Peter Taylor, "The IRA and Sinn Fein," *PBS Frontline*, October 21, 1987.

CHAPTER 6: *On the Brinks: Extended Edition*, by Sam Millar (Galway, Ireland: Wynkin deWorde, 2010); Sam Millar 2013 interview with the *Belfast Telegraph*; Gerry Moriarty, "Millar's Crossing," *Irish Times*, September 24, 2003; *The IRA*, by Tim Pat Coogan, rev. ed. (London: Palgrave Macmillan, 2002); *Before the Dawn: An Autobiography*, by Gerry Adams (Dublin: Brandon Books, 2001); *Armed Struggle: The History of the IRA*, by Richard English (Oxford: Oxford University Press, 2003); *On the Blanket: The Inside Story of the IRA Prisoners' "Dirty" Protest*, by Tim Pat Coogan (Boulder, CO: Roberts Rinehart Publishers, 1997); Northern Ireland criminal and court records related to Sam Millar; *Ten Men Dead: The Story of the 1981 Irish Hunger Strike*, by David Beresford (Grafton,

UK: HarperCollins Publishers, 1987); "Acquittal in First Case Heard under North's Trial without Jury System," *Irish Times*, October 16, 1973.

CHAPTER 7: *On the Brinks: Extended Edition*, by Sam Millar (Galway, Ireland: Wynkin deWorde, 2010); *Bobby Sands: Writings from Prison*, by Bobby Sands (Boulder, CO: Roberts Rinehart Publishers, 1997); *Armed Struggle: The History of the* IRA, by Richard English (Oxford: Oxford University Press, 2003; *Ten Men Dead: The Story of the 1981 Irish Hunger Strike*, by David Beresford Grafton, UK: HarperCollins Publishers, 1987); Patrick Bishop and Eamonn Mallie, *The Provisional IRA* (London: Corgi Books, 1987); Richard O'Rawe interviews; Sam Millar 2013 interview with the *Belfast Telegraph*; Gerry Moriarty, "Millar's Crossing," *Irish Times*, September 24, 2003; David Hennessey, "Sam Millar: Back from the Brinks," *Irish World*, October 8, 2014; *Rebel Hearts: Journeys within the* IRA's *Soul*, by Kevin Toolis (New York: St. Martin's Press, 1995); *Before The Dawn: An Autobiography by Gerry Adams* (Dublin: Brandon Books, 2001); *On the Blanket: The Inside Story of the* IRA *Prisoners' "Dirty" Protest*, by Tim Pat Coogan (Boulder, CO: Roberts Rinehart Publishers, 1997); Northern Ireland criminal and court records related to Sam Millar; *Blanketmen: An Untold Story of the H-Block Hunger Strike*, by Richard O'Rawe (Dublin: New Island Books, 2005); Frank Shouldice, "The Not So Great Escape," *Irish America*, August–September 2004.

CHAPTER 8: Trial transcripts; Rochester police interviews; Investigator Bob Siersma interviews; Investigator Vito D'Ambrosia interviews; Culver Barr interviews; C. P. Maloney interviews; participants in Vikings Revenge trips interviews; former Assistant US Attorney Charles Pilato interviews; FBI Special Agent Paul Hawkins interviews; Steve Mills, "Robbery Probed as Inside Job," *Democrat and Chronicle*, January 7, 1993; Valerie Smith, "Abducted Worker Came in 'Pale, Sort of Sweaty,'" *Democrat and Chronicle*, January 7, 1993; Michael Wentzel, "Investigators Say Retired City Detective Is Not a Suspect in Brink's Inc. Robbery," *Democrat and Chronicle*, January 7, 1993.

CHAPTER 9: Interview with Belfast journalist who lived in the city in the early 1980s; trial transcripts; Jean Arena interview; Joanne McClinton interviews; investigative records on Damien McClinton homicide; Damien McClinton immigration records; Investigator Bill Lawler interviews.

CHAPTER 10: Mark LaPiana interviews; Rochester police interviews; investigative records on Damien McClinton homicide; Investigator Bill Lawler interviews;

Police Major William Mayer interviews; internal records of the Rochester chapter of NORAID; Culver Barr interviews; internal FBI records.

CHAPTER 11: FBI Special Agent Richard Vega interviews; FBI Special Agent Paul Hawkins interviews; internal FBI records; trial transcripts; law enforcement sources interviews; "World Trade Center Bombing of 1993," by Laura Lambert, at https://www.britannica.com/event/World-Trade-Center-bombing-of-1993; "1993 World Trade Center Bombing Fast Facts," at http://www.cnn.com/2013/11/05 /us/1993-world-trade-center-bombing-fast-facts/.

CHAPTER 12: FBI Special Agent Paul Hawkins interviews; FBI Special Agent Dale Anderson interviews; internal FBI records; Robert D. McFadden, "The Twin Towers: The Overview," *New York Times*, March 5, 1993; "World Trade Center Bombing of 1993," by Laura Lambert, at https://www.britannica.com/event /World-Trade-Center-bombing-of-1993; "1993 World Trade Center Bombing Fast Facts," at http://www.cnn.com/2013/11/05/us/1993-world-trade-center-bombing-fast-facts/; Rochester police interviews; Gaetano De Agostino interviews; 1993 interviews with neighbors of Millar; Mary B.W. Tabor, "Officials Detail Two Lives of Brink's Robbery Suspect," *New York Times*, November 15, 1993; Father Patrick Moloney interviews.

CHAPTER 13: Ed Moloney, "Why Did the Provos Hide Liam Adams in America," October 8, 2013, at https://thebrokenelbow.com/2013/10/08/why-did-the -provos-hide-liam-adams-in-america/; Ed Moloney interviews; "Liam Adams to Be Extradited on Sexual Assault Charges," *BBC News*, October 3, 2011, at http://www.bbc.com/news/uk-northern-ireland-15151865; "Liam Adams Has Been Found Guilty," *Belfast Telegraph*, October 1, 2013; Father Moloney interviews; video interview with Father Patrick Moloney, at https://www.youtube.com /watch?v=3OeFdMZrtd8; Corey Kilgannon, "A Priest Unafraid of Trouble," *New York Times*, April 13, 2012; FBI Special Agent Lou Stephens interviews; James C. McKinley Jr., "Police Credit New Tactics with Cooling Park Protests," *New York Times*, July 29, 1989; Peter Taylor, "The IRA and Sinn Fein," *PBS Frontline*, October 21, 1987; "Shipment of Arms Seized by FBI," *Irish Press*, January 21, 1983; "Priest Told by Judge to Sit Down," *Irish Press*, July 27, 1982; "Court Told of Panic During Garda Raid," *Irish Press*, January 27, 1983; John Strausbaugh, "Father Hood?" *New York Press*, July 20, 1984; Cecile Cassidy, "Compassion Brought Down to Earth at Lower East Side's Bonitas House," *New York City Tribune*, April 19, 1985; "Bail

Refused for Man on Arms Charge," *Irish Press*, July 3, 1982; William Sherman, "Blood Money," *Esquire* (British edition), July-August, 1994, 132–37; "Bail Bid by Three Men in Arms Case," *Irish Press*, June 21, 1982; "Priest Freed After DPP Drops Charges," *Irish Press*, July 30, 1982; "The Father Walter Ciszek Prayer League," 2008, at http://www.ciszek.org/About_Ciszek.html; Selwyn Raab, "Out of Prison, Priest Reopens Homeless Shelter," *New York Times*, October 8, 1998.

CHAPTER 14: Trial transcripts; FBI interviews; New York Transit Investigator Cornell Adams interviews; Father Patrick Moloney interviews; real estate agent interview; FBI Special Agent Paul Hawkins interviews; law enforcement sources interviews; former Assistant U.S. Attorney Charles Pilato interviews.

CHAPTER 15: Trial transcripts; former Assistant US Attorney Charles Pilato interviews; Father Patrick Moloney interviews; *On the Brinks: Extended Edition*, by Sam Millar (Galway, Ireland: Wynkin deWorde, 2010); Charles McCormick interviews; Ian Fisher, "A Priest, a Big Robbery, and Even Bigger Questions," *New York Times*, November 14, 1993; Jeanne King, "Irish Priest Charged in Brink's Car Raid Released on $1m Bail," *Glasgow Herald*, November 20, 1993; "America and Northern Ireland; Cash and Sympathy," *Economist*, November 20, 1993.

CHAPTER 16: Charles McCormick interviews; trial transcripts; Father Patrick Moloney interviews; Jonathan Feldman interviews; Bill Clauss interviews; John Speranza interviews; Christopher Buscaglia interviews.

CHAPTER 17: Trial transcripts; Charles McCormick interviews; Father Patrick Moloney interviews; Jonathan Feldman interviews; Bill Clauss interviews; John Speranza interviews; Christopher Buscaglia interviews.

CHAPTER 18: Trial transcripts; Charles McCormick interviews; Father Patrick Moloney interviews; Jonathan Feldman interviews; Bill Clauss interviews; John Speranza interviews; Christopher Buscaglia interviews.

CHAPTER 19: Father Patrick Moloney interviews; Selwyn Raab, "A Convicted Priest Practices His Ministry behind Bars," *New York Times*, August 17, 1997; internal US Bureau of Prisons records; Rinker Buck, "Loretto: Not Just A Prison Town," *Hartford Courant*, March 31, 2005; information on Federal Correctional Institution Loretto from US Bureau of Prisons; video interview with Father

Patrick Moloney, at https://www.youtube.com/watch?v=3OeFdMZrtd8; Selwyn Raab, "Out of Prison, Priest Reopens Homeless Shelter," *New York Times*, October 8, 1998; Charles McCormick interviews; Gary Craig, "Brink's Heist Prisoner Is Transferred," *Democrat and Chronicle*, October 19, 1997; *On the Brinks: Extended Edition*, by Sam Millar (Galway, Ireland: Wynkin deWorde, 2010); David Hennessey, "Sam Millar: Back from the Brinks," *Irish World*, October 8, 2014; *Brother in Arms*, by Sam Millar.

CHAPTER 20: Randy Gordon interviews; Paddy Malone interviews; Daniel Kyle McAloon interviews; Daniel Kyle McAloon, "It Was Always Crazy," 2013, at http://www.iknowcrazy.net/subjects.html; "Ronnie Gibbons," at http://boxrec. com/boxer/23085; Michelle Ingrassia, "Inside the Ring or Out, There's Always Action at Sunnyside," *New York Times*, April 16, 1972; Ronnie Gibbons's personal records; Rita (Ronnie's sister) and Frank Gibbons interviews; Rita Gibbons (Ronnie's mother) interviews; Terry Quinn interviews; John "Bomber" Martin interviews; Jim McCaffrey interviews; Billy Devlin interviews; Father Patrick Moloney interviews.

CHAPTER 21: Trial transcripts; *On the Brinks: Extended Edition*, by Sam Millar (Galway, Ireland: Wynkin deWorde, 2010); Patrick Farrelly interviews; Father Patrick Moloney interviews; casino personnel interviews; Rita (Ronnie's sister) and Frank Gibbons interviews; Rita Gibbons (Ronnie's mother) interviews.

CHAPTER 22: *On the Brinks: Extended Edition*, by Sam Millar (Galway, Ireland: Wynkin deWorde, 2010); Father Patrick Moloney interviews; Gary Craig, "Man Tied to Brink's Convict Missing," *Democrat and Chronicle*, November 6, 1996; Randy Gordon interviews; Jay Mwamba, "At 40, Gibbons Laces 'Em Up," *Irish Echo*, July 14, 1993; Hector Rocca interviews; Gibbons's personal records; Jay Mwamba interviews; Ian Fisher, "Priest and Ex-Policeman Arrested in $7 Million Brink's Car Hold-Up," *New York Times*, November 13, 1993.

CHAPTER 23: Terry Quinn interviews; *On the Brinks: Extended Edition*, by Sam Millar (Galway, Ireland: Wynkin deWorde, 2010); John "Bomber" Martin interviews; Frank Gibbons interviews.

CHAPTER 24: Gary Brown interviews; Terry Quinn interviews; Sophie Martin-Canning interviews; Frank Gibbons interviews; FBI Special Agent Paul Hawkins interviews; Gary Craig, "Man Tied to Brink's Convict Missing," *Democrat and Chronicle*, November 6, 1996; Michael Daly, "Going Down for the Count; Ex-Boxer Vanishes," *Daily News*, January 5, 1997.

CHAPTER 25: Gerald O'Connor court records, Monroe County and Orleans County, New York; Joseph Cardone interviews; George Thompson interview; Denise Giarla interviews; Christine Richards Daly interviews; FBI interviews; Michael Zwelling, "Killer Gives Information on Decades-Old Murders," *Buffalo News*, February 16, 2004.

CHAPTER 26: Investigator Tom Crowley interviews; Investigator Bill Lawler interviews; O'Rorke Memorial Society histories; Investigator David Salvatore interviews; Gerald O'Connor interviews.

CHAPTER 27: *On the Brinks: Extended Edition*, by Sam Millar (Galway, Ireland: Wynkin deWorde, 2010); Investigator Tom Crowley interviews; Investigator Bill Lawler interviews; Investigator David Salvatore interviews; Gerald O'Connor interviews; interviews with FBI agents; Terry Quinn interviews; investigative files on Damien McClinton homicide; Frank Gibbons interviews; Sophie Martin-Canning interviews; Investigator Chris Bittner interviews; Investigator Bob Siersma interviews; James Traub, "The Lords of Hell's Kitchen," *New York Times*, April 5, 1987; Tom Taylor interviews; Ron Brunelli interviews.

CHAPTER 28: Investigator Peter Barnett interviews; David C. Shampine, "Torso Found on Shore of Grenadier," *Watertown Daily Times*, September 5, 2000; "Torso Found on Grenadier Taken to FBI Lab in Washington," *Watertown Daily Times*, September 12, 2000; David C. Shampine, "DNA Study of Foot, Torso, Find They're from One Man," *Watertown Daily Times*, July 13, 2002; Juliana Gittler, "Body of Evidence Washes Ashore," *Syracuse Post-Standard*, July 19, 2002; Ron Brunelli interviews; Mary Jumbelic interviews; David Gregor obituary, Hart and Bruce Funeral Home; Lisa McCombs, "Stories of the Dead," *Gainesville Sun*, July 9, 2007; Anthony Falsetti interviews; US Department of Justice, "National Missing and Unidentified Persons System," at NamUs.gov; "Jefferson County Facts and Trivia," at http://co.jefferson.ny.us/Modules/ShowDocument.aspx?documentid=1675.

CHAPTER 29: Investigator Chris Bittner interviews; Investigator Mark Concordia interviews; Investigator Tom Crowley interviews; Investigator Peter Barnett interviews; Investigator Bill Lawler interviews; Tom Taylor interviews; Michael

Baden interviews; Tony Dokoupil, "Who Is Dr. Michael Baden, the Coroner That Examined Michael Brown?" *NBC News*, August 18, 2014, at http://www.nbcnews .com/storyline/michael-brown-shooting/who-dr-michael-baden-coroner-exam ined-michael-brown-n183516; Liam Magee, "Farewell to Nova Scotia," at https:// www.youtube.com/watch?v=vosCHc-i9mE&list=PLgSf3knUozYHRvZ3WUa _NeHIMNmk7KSek; "Funeral of American Brink's Heist Suspect and Boxer Ronnie Gibbons to Be Held in Liverpool," *Liverpool Echo*, February 29, 2012; Frank Gibbons interviews; Rev. Kevin McLoughlin interview; Rita Gibbons (Ronnie's mother) interviews; "Death Notice: Magee, Liam," May 19, 2015, at https://rip .ie/showdn.php?dn=256875.

EPILOGUE: *On the Brinks: Extended Edition*, by Sam Millar (Galway, Ireland: Wynkin deWorde, 2010); Frank Gibbons interviews; Gerald O'Connor interviews; Richard O'Rawe interviews; "Out of Time," by Sam Millar, in *Belfast Noir*, edited by Adrian McKinty and Stuart Neville (Brooklyn, NY: Akashic Books, 2014), 174-95; IRA expert interviews; New York and federal law enforcement officials interviews; Billy Devlin interviews; Cape Vincent residents interviews.

INDEX

— — —